Copyright © 2016 by Lani Sharp
All rights reserved. This book or any portion thereof
may not be reproduced or used in any manner whatsoever
without the express written permission of the publisher
except for the use of brief quotations in a book review.

Printed in Australia

First Printing, 2016

ISBN 978-0-9945051-4-9

White Light Publishing House
6 Lincoln Way
Melton West, VIC, Australia 3337

www.whitelightpublishingau.com

❧ DEDICATION ☙

Dedicated to my older brother Luke, the most passionate, loyal and intense Scorpio in my Universe. Thank you for your love, lessons in 'keeping the faith', friendship, passion, and for being such a wonderful part of my journey. You have taught me much more than you know - but being a Scorpio, you probably would. Much appreciation.

ABOUT THE AUTHOR

☾ ★ ☽

Lani Sharp is a Natural Born Rebel who just also happens to be an Aquarian, who shunned 'conventional' astrology courses to pursue her own path in the wondrous, inspiring and ever-evolving field of cosmic forces and stellar influences. After failing to find a course or tutor that suited her needs, Lani set out on her own starry Magic Carpet adventure across the skies, partly to discover her own 'truths' about this ancient system, but mostly to prove that one can achieve absolutely anything, including and above all, their dream careers (or lifestyle), if they put their hearts and souls into it. A self-taught astrologer who takes the esoteric and spiritual approach to this much-loved popular art, she has been studying and effectively practising astrology since she was eight years old. When she is not writing about, channelling, practising or teaching astrology, she can be found living her dream life alternating somewhere between her home in Australia's stunning Tropical North or her second home in Victoria's beautiful Dandenong Ranges, enjoying tea parties with her highly imaginative Cancerian daughter, Allira, and their gnome and fairy friends, crystal-wishing, day-dreaming, believing in gnomes, pixies, angels, fairies, magic and miracles, honing her magickal * witchcraft skills, Moon-gazing, Sun-worshipping, Venus-channelling, Jupiter-drawing, assisting others to discover, unravel and follow their true spiritual paths ... or of course walking across rainbows!

* *Not a mistake. Magick is a Wiccan variation of the word 'magic'.*

★

ACKNOWLEDGEMENTS, CREDITS & GRATITUDE BLESSINGS

★

I would love to thank the following people and entities for their amazing contributions, interest, support and faith in me as I wrote the manuscripts for each of the twelve astrological Sun signs. Firstly, the biggest thank you goes to my Mum, Sandra, and my stepdad, Barry, for their unending support, love, advice, daily Skype conversations, acceptance of our geographical distance, and above all, their inner knowing that everything always comes together in the end. Your support of me and my dreams is appreciated beyond words. Secondly, gratitude to my wonderful partner, Travis, for his patience (no mean feat for a Gemini!), for supporting me every step of the way, and for his acceptance of my 'mad scientist' Aquarian mindset by never trying to break down the invisible 'laboratory' walls I built around myself while writing the books. I would also like to extend my enormous gratitude to the following: Allira, my little Cancerian 'crab' daughter, a soul in a billion, who also had to tolerate and operate within the bounds of her nutty professor mother's antics and focus throughout the writing of the books. Thank you to Nicola, my wonderful Facebook friend, for recommending White Light Publishing House, and of course to White Light Publishing House themselves, for pouring their faith and passion into my project from the very beginning - and an even bigger thank you to the wonderful people behind the company for publishing my work, Christie and Jess! Gratitude also goes out to my dear friends, both near and far, who have inspired in me so many ideas through simply being themselves - especially Amanda and Carlie. Amanda, you have always been my 'astrology buddy' and I have always enjoyed - and learned so much through - our discussions on all things astrology and star signs: the good, the bad and the ugly! Having someone like you off which to bounce thoughts and share ideas with, has always been immensely helpful and appreciated. I have saved my final thank you for The Universe, who always delivers to me exactly what I have asked for, without exception. The Universe is my ultimate *higher power*, my guiding light, my powerful driving force, my spiritual helper, my guardian angel, my eternal friend, my inner motivator, my sympathetic listener, my inspirational teacher, and the fulfiller of all my dreams, including this one, having my very first book(s) published, a long-held dream that stretches way back through the years to my days of being a mini dreamer, inquisitor and stargazer. The Universe has always believed in me, but perhaps more importantly, I have always believed in *IT*.

So to all of the above, I wish to say:

Thank you, thank you, thank you!

"There was a star danced,
and under that I was born"

William Shakespeare

"We were born at a given moment, in a given place, and like vintage years of wine, we have the qualities of the year and of the season in which we are born"

Carl G. Jung

INSPIRED BY ALL THE SIGNS

Aries imparted courage and boldness
And helped me dance away the pain
Taurus gave me hugs and comfort
And shelter from the rain
Gemini provided me with laughter
And taught me again how to have fun
Cancer nurtured and sustained me
By reflecting back my Sun
Leo reminded me there was joy
From within myself and above
Virgo awakened my healthy glow
By teaching me how to love
Libra gave me gentle hugs
And judged me not for a thing
Scorpio lent me some of his power
And took away the sting
Sagittarius showered me with gifts
Of words so wise and true
As Capricorn led the way up the mountain
My resolve and strength grew
Aquarius gave me the gift of friendship
And carried me as his brother
And Pisces swam with me to the depths
With a compassion like no other.

Special Note

Throughout the text of this book, and indeed the whole Lucky Astrology book series, I have capitalised the first letter of the word 'Universe'. This is because, quite simply, I feel it is a very special title for the higher power that I personally choose to be guided by, and have accordingly highlighted it as such.

You may also notice that I use the words 'he' or 'she', and 'his' or 'her', when referring to your own Sun sign and other zodiac signs, and never 'he or she' or 'his or her' together. The reason for this is for simplicity, for I don't wish the sentences to be too wordy and therefore the messages within them to be lost. As a general rule, I refer to all six 'masculine' zodiac signs as 'he', and all six 'feminine' signs as 'she', and this remains a consistent rule throughout this book and the whole series.

Your Sun sign, Scorpio, is a feminine sign and will thus be referred to accordingly.

CONTENTS

	Page
ASTROLOGY	15
THE ZODIAC & YOUR PLACE IN THE SUN	24
SCORPIO THE SCORPION	31
QUOTES BY SCORPIONS	38
THE SCORPIO CONSTELLATION	43
THE SCORPIO SYMBOL	46
THE RUNDOWN & LESSONS ★	
THE ESSENCE OF SCORPIO	50
THE THREE DECANS OF SCORPIO	64
YOUR ELEMENT ★ WATER	68
YOUR MODE ★ FIXED	92
YOUR RULING PLANET ★ PLUTO	95
YOUR HOUSE IN THE HOROSCOPE ★	
THE EIGHTH HOUSE	109
YOUR OPPOSITE SIGN ★ TAURUS	115
MAGIC, DRAWING, ATTRACTION, SPELLS,	
RITUALS, WISHING & POWER	122
ASTROLOGY & MAGIC	127
PLANETS ★ DAYS OF THE WEEK	
& THEIR POWERS	133
YOUR NATAL MOON PHASE	137
SPELLS, MAGIC & WISHING WITH MOON PHASES	140
THE MOON IN THE HUMAN PSYCHE	
& NATAL CHART	147
YOUR MOON SIGN	150
YOUR BODY & HEALTH	159
THE CELL SALTS ★ ASTROLOGICAL TONICS	165

	Page
WATER SIGN SCORPIO & THE PHLEGMATIC HUMOR	168
MONEY ATTRIBUTES	171
COLOURS ★ YOUR LUCKY COLOURS	174
LUCKY CAREER TIPS	186
LUCKY PLACES	190
GEMS & CRYSTALS	192
SCORPION POWER CRYSTALS	205
YOUR LUCKY NUMBERS	217
YOUR LUCKY MAGIC HOURS OR TIME UNITS	227
YOUR LUCKY DAY ★ TUESDAY	232
YOUR LUCKY CHARM / TALISMANS	236
YOUR LUCKY ANIMALS & BIRDS	239
YOUR METALS	256
PLANTS, HERBS, SPICES, TREES, SHRUBS, FLOWERS, SCENTS & INCENSE	261
YOUR FOODS	266
YOUR LUCKY WOOD & CELTIC TREE ★ MAHOGANY & IVY OR REED	269
THE POWER OF LOVE	276
LUCKY IN LOVE? SCORPIO COMPATIBILITY	288
YOUR TAROT CARDS	306
LUCKY 13 TIPS	332
HAVE YOU PACKED YOUR MAGICAL BAG FOR THE JOURNEY?	335
A FINAL WORD ★ TAPPING INTO THE MAGIC OF SCORPIO	336

LUCKY ASTROLOGY

By Lani Sharp

SCORPIO

*Tapping into the Powers of Your Sun Sign for Greater
Luck, Happiness, Health, Abundance & Love*

"That which is above is like to that which is below, and that which is below is like to that which is above, to accomplish the miracles of one thing ... the Father thereof is the Sun, the mother the Moon."

The Emerald Tablet, Hermes Trismegistus, (circa 3000 BC)

★ ASTROLOGY ★

Astrology: "Divination through the correlation of earthly events with celestial patterns"
'Real Magic', I. Bonewits, 1971

A BRIEF HISTORY

Astrology can be defined as the calculation and meaningful interpretation of the positions and motions of the heavenly bodies, and their correlation with human experiences. Its central concept is based upon this interconnectedness or correspondence between the stars and ourselves.

The word astrology is derived from the Greek word astron, meaning 'star' and logos which means 'word'. Astrology, therefore, literally means language of the stars. It is based on the ancient law known as 'As Above, So Below', otherwise known as the Law of the Macrocosm and Microcosm. The Macrocosm is the Universe, symbolised by the sky, the starry dome that we can see from the Earth; the Microcosm is us - humans, and all other life on Earth. 'As Above, So Below' is a well-known and deeply impressing maxim of Hermetic origin, inscribed upon the famed Emerald Tablet among cryptic wording by enigmatic figure, Hermes Trismegistus, around 5,000 years ago. These four powerful words are adopted by astrologers and believers in magic to explain, in very succinct wording, the meaning behind the art and science of celestial influences upon our Earthly affairs.

Astrology and many other magical and occult studies, propose that we are not separate from the Universe, we are part of it. The Sun, Moon and planets all follow exact patterns of movement and their motions can be measured precisely by astronomers. The basic idea of astrology is that all individual parts of the Universe, from plants to animals, cooperate with each other and work together in harmony.

Anyone can apply astrological knowledge in their daily lives, but it hasn't always been like that. At one time, astrology was reserved only for Kings and nations, and only the court astrologer/astronomer could cast and interpret horoscopes. Ancient astrology and astronomy used to be one and the same. To be an astrologer, you first had to be able to interpret the stars in some systematic way, and then track the movement of the Moon and the planets against the background of the constellations.

Astrology, the knowledge and language of the cosmos, goes back to the ancient kingdom of Babylonia and was adapted by the Mesopotamians, Greeks, Egyptians and Romans to incorporate their own deities (as indicated in mythology). It is upon a combination of Greek and Egyptian interpretations of astrology that our present knowledge is based.

In the ancient Mesopotamian world, as far back as 800 BC, people lived precariously beneath the open skies. The skies and the stars which filled them, were the real founders of astrology. Today we are aware that the Sun and Moon exert a profound influence upon our Earthly affairs, but for our primitive ancestors, the heavens, the stars and the planets must have been a matter of great and mysterious significance. Early humankind, its senses influenced by natural processes of ebbs, flows, growth, decay and cycles, tended naturally towards a physical explanation of the Universe. At first, the movements of the planets - and all celestial occurrences - were observed as omens affecting the Ruler and his nation; it was only in Egypt in the fifth century AD that the casting of horoscopes for individual people and the calculation of the planetary positions at the time of birth became widespread.

The first astrologers, the Chaldeans, mapped the stars and later passed this knowledge and wisdom on to the ancient Greeks, who, during the third century BC, developed astrology into a science with the use of mathematical aids and instruments to measure planetary movements. The Greeks were the first to cast individual horoscopes. And it was the Greeks who associated the four elements with the signs of the zodiac. The word "zodiac" can be translated from Greek to mean the "circle or path of the animals." The Greeks not only had names for the twelve Solar phases but had symbols for each, and many correspond with the ones we use today.

The Greeks passed on much of their knowledge to the Romans. During the second century BC, Roman astrologers were primarily forecasters who were consulted frequently by rulers of the church and state. By the early third century AD, astrology co-existed with early Christianity. This harmonious co-existence was possible because it was considered that celestial bodies could foretell events, but did not determine the future - indeed, the stars seen by the shepherds at the time of Christ's birth were only predictors of his arrival. After the fourth century AD, Christianity strengthened and the popularity of astrology declined as Christian reluctance to support 'pagan' or 'superstitious' beliefs became more prominent. The Middle Ages saw a revival in astrology, with courses being taught in universities and other educational establishments, and connections were made between the zodiac, alchemy, herbs and medicine. Astrology was once again able to exist alongside the Church, although many remained suspicious of astrologers.

Around the beginning of the fifteenth century, academics of the Renaissance movement examined the past for knowledge, and ancient philosophies, including astrology, flourished; this coincided with arts and science movements developing. The famous prophet and astrologer Nostradamus lived during this period. Leonardo da Vinci depicted aspects of astrology combined with geometry in his art. Writers and poets of the time, including Shakespeare, alluded to zodiacal influences in their work.

During this period, astrology had numerous practical applications. Agricultural calendars were introduced, indicating favourable planting times according to the phases of the Moon; health and illness were linked with movements of celestial bodies; and emotional states and mental health afflictions correlated with the planetary positions.

Eventually, new ways of thinking led to a split between astronomy and astrology, and by the seventeenth century, the realm of science had developed to such a degree that astrology was no longer taken seriously.

The study of the sky above us has been charted for more than 5,000 years. This fact is known because ancient 'horoscopes' imprinted on clay tablets have been unearthed, dating back almost 5,400 years ago. However, no one knows for certain just how, when and where astrology first began, although it is known that it flourished in ancient Chaldea, Mesopotamia, Babylon and Egypt.

Astrology is a science which has spanned many centuries and still remains extraordinarily popular, and its truths have the potential to speak to and *through* all of us. Long before today's interest in it, men of great vision such as Ptolemy, Hippocrates, Plato, Galileo, Jefferson, Franklin, Newton, Columbus and Jung respected its inherent truths, mythology and eternal knowledge. Furthermore, astrology predates many other 'sciences' - for out of it grew religion, medicine and astronomy, not the other way around.

The discipline of astrology is ultimately a study of the interlocking and interrelated forces of the twelve zodiacal forces, or constellations, that grace the heavens, as they pour their energies into the Earthly kingdoms below. As these various energies circulate throughout the etheric realm of our Solar system, these zodiacal entities and archetypes imprint their vibrational frequencies and harmonic resonances upon our bodies, minds, souls and spirits.

ASTROLOGY & THE INDIVIDUAL

Since the earliest period of the history of humankind, people studied the starry vaults of the heavens and conceived that their presence, movements and positions endowed planet Earth's inhabitants with Divine influence. There is much evidence that positions and movements of the planets as seen from Earth at the time of a birth are linked to personality characteristics of individuals. Human energy and emotional cycles are governed by the forces and networks of magnetic impulses from all the planets. Of all the heavenly bodies, the Moon's effects and power are the most marked and visible due to its close proximity to Earth. But the Sun, Venus, Mars, Mercury, Jupiter, Saturn, Uranus, Neptune and Pluto exercise their influences just as surely. In fact, scientists are aware that plants and animals are affected by natural cycles which are governed by forces such as fluctuations in barometric pressure, the gravitational field and electricity in the air. These Earthly dynamics are originally triggered by magnetic vibrations from the atmosphere, or outer space, from where the planets send forth their unseen waves. No living organism or mineral on Earth escapes these immense, if unseen, influences.

The geomagnetic field seems to affect life on Earth in certain observed ways, and these influences appear to correlate with planetary positions. It has been suggested that the fluctuations of the Earth's magnetic field are picked up by the nervous system of the in utero infant, which acts like an antenna, and these synchronise the internal biological clocks of the foetus which control the moment of birth. The foetal magnetic antenna therefore, is sensitive enough to sense these planetary vibrations and fields, and through a combination of inherited genetics and the positions of the planets at birth, they are imprinted with certain basic inherited and 'absorbed' personality characteristics.

Carl Jung, the Swiss psychiatrist and psychological theorist, suggested that the inherent disposition of the individual is present at birth, and is reflected in the patterns of his or her natal chart. Further, he theorised that there is a 'priori factor' in all human activities, namely the inborn, preconscious and unconscious individual structure of the psyche. The preconscious psyche, for example that of a newborn baby, is not simply an empty vessel into which practically anything can be poured, but rather it is this preconscious psyche that gives us the free will to become what we are instead of what others or our environment makes us. The child is not merely a receptacle for the psychic life of those around him or her, albeit sensitive and susceptible to the surrounding unconscious forces in childhood; for he/she also brings something of his own to his experience of them.

Further, Dr Harold S. Burr, who was a Professor of Anatomy at the Yale University School of Medicine, and author of *The Nature of Man and the Meaning of Existence* (1962), asserted that there is order in the Universe, unity in the organism and man is endowed with a soul. He stated that a complex magnetic field not only establishes the pattern of the human brain at birth, but continues to regulate and control it through life, and that the human central nervous system is a superb receptor of electro-magnetic energies, indeed the finest in nature. He contended that the electro-dynamic fields of all living things, which may be measured and mapped with standard voltmeters, mould and control each organism's development, health and mood, and named these fields 'fields of life'.

It can therefore be suggested that astrological and planetary influences endow us with the majority of our characteristics at birth, characteristics bestowed upon us according to our Sun sign and other planetary forces. Other parts of the chart are also highly significant and need to be integrated for a 'whole' picture to form, however the Sun sign is an excellent starting point.

The ancients taught that astrology was one of the keys to the many enigmas that plague humans in their unceasing quest to determine what the meaning of life is, and what their role and place in the Universe is - and this quest still persists today. Astrology, which dates back over 5,000 years, is indeed one such key to unlocking the many secrets of the Universe - and ultimately, the individual self.

"KNOW THYSELF"

Man, know thyself. All wisdom centres on this.
Carl Jung

Before the temple of the Oracle at Delphi, the ancient Greeks imparted a special piece of advice that was carved onto one of the portals: "Know Thyself."

These two powerful words are easy enough to understand, but much more difficult to apply. Throughout life's inner and outer journey, astrology can provide us with an inner navigational system by which we can be guided towards our highest potential, and closer towards the eternal quest of 'knowing thyself'. It provides the hope that this higher spiritual plane exists and that if we can 'read' and therefore be guided by the unique inner blueprint that our individual birth chart has stamped upon us at the moment we take our very first breath, indeed we can reach this higher spiritual plane and realise our innate potential.

Always remember that astrology is not fatalistic. The stars may incline, but they do not compel. Astrology simply provides us with an inner guide, a blueprint, for our journey through life and the finding of our true selves - and what we do with the resulting knowledge is entirely up to us.

Good luck on your journey!

THE ZODIAC & YOUR PLACE IN THE SUN

The zodiac is a circle of 360 degrees, consisting of equal segments of 30 degrees each. These represent the twelve houses of the twelve astrological signs. This zodiac is how the early astrologers imagined the Solar system to be, a perfect circle with the Earth at its centre, around which the Sun, Moon and the planets revolved. Each sign of the zodiac corresponds to one of the twelve segments, following a chronological order and established according to the rhythm of the seasons and cycles of the Sun and the Moon. But the zodiac itself, or the band of constellations which comprise it, has shifted over the millennia, creating division between astronomical and astrological schools of thought. It has been said that due to this shift over time, one who once considered themselves as an Aquarian, is actually a Capricorn, the sign before it, and a Leo is actually a Cancerian, its preceding sign. This is the result of misunderstandings and differences in perspectives, and explanations around it are beyond the scope of this book, but can be researched further should you wish to delve a little deeper. From the astronomical point of view, it is true that the zodiac to which we refer today is not situated where it 'should' be, but indeed, nothing is fixed under the celestial vault. And so the starting point of the ancient zodiac does not correspond exactly to the one we can observe today. But for the purposes of increasing your power and luck, let's keep things simple and enjoy the ride; after all, astrology - while based upon many scientific theories, mysteries, scepticism, superstitions, facts, measurable patterns, ambiguities, correlations, paradoxes, contradictions, links, stigmatisms and observations that seek to support, refute, prove and disprove this ancient art time and again - is ultimately meant to be *fun* too.

THE SUN

Earth's Luminary ★ *Our Brightest Shining Star*

Our Centre, Core Self, Identity & Inner Guiding Light

"Perfect is what I have said of the work of the Sun."
Hermes Trismegistus, *The Emerald Tablet*

The Sun is our essence, centre, source, ego strength, power, life force, will, vitality, creative expression, purpose, life's direction, our sense of identity, and who we really *are*. Our brightest star is the core of our individuality, our inner guiding light. The Sun is externalising, and represents totality, infinity, eternity, the striving toward and ultimate reaching of one's personal destiny, and *completion* in all areas. It is the creative energising giver of life and the 'father' of the zodiac. It endows us with our inherent creative potential and personal identity - our urge to *create* and to *be*. The Sun is our core self, conscious purpose, our sense of creating something out of our own being. It is the integrated personality and represents the *present*, our greatest Gift. The Sun rules the heart and is thus symbolically the centre of self. Indeed, the Sun *is* the heart and the most commanding presence in our birth chart; the luminary Ruler who governs our essential self and wants to be noticed and appreciated, and above all, to *shine*.

★ KEY WORDS ★

Identity, core self, spirit, life force, power, essence, creativity, higher self, the Father, ego, vitality, pride, individuality, leadership, majesty, inner authority, will, expression, willpower, purpose, the journey, the path and the destiny.

THE SUN ★ THE ULTIMATE SOURCE OF LIFE ON EARTH

Throughout the ages, and indeed since life forms began, the electromagnetic waves generated by the Sun have kept planet Earth habitable for humans, animals, plants and minerals. The Sun is, in fact, the only true source of energy on planet Earth. It provides the perfect amount of energy for plants to synthesise all of the products required for growth and reproduction, which is then stored by plants and ingested by humans and animals who, through many complex processes, utilise these various forms of encapsulated Solar energy - and so the cycle continues. Wood, fuel and minerals (crystals included), too, are merely various forms of this encased Sun energy. In fact, all matter is essentially 'frozen' light. Human body cells are bundles of Sun energy; we couldn't conceive or process a single thought without the molecules of Solar-energised oxygen and glucose.

In essence, the Sun supports the growth of all species, including human beings and microscopic life forms, and without it life on Earth would simply not be possible. The mathematical and metaphysical complexity that stands behind a system of organisation and order so infinitely diverse and intricate as planetary life cannot be truly fathomed, but unerringly and miraculously, the Sun instinctively knows what each species, from a tree to a human, intrinsically needs in order to fulfil its evolutionary purpose and cycles.

Ultimately, the electromagnetic waves generated by the Sun come in a variety of lengths, which determine their specific course of action and responsibility. There are gamma rays, x-rays, cosmic rays, various kinds of ultraviolet rays, infrared, short-wave infrared, radio waves, electric waves, and of course the visible light spectrum, consisting of the seven colour rays.

Most of these energy waves are absorbed and used for various processes in the layers of atmosphere that encircle the Earth, and only a small portion of them - the electromagnetic spectrum - reach the surface of our planet. Although the human eye is only able to perceive about one percent of this spectrum, the waves exert a very strong influence upon us. The waves and rays which do affect us so profoundly, allow all life forms to undergo constant cycles of change necessary for growth and renewal. Physically, we can observe this, but on a deeper, more spiritual plane, we can even *feel* it and allow its radiance to permeate our very souls. Such is the might, force and power of that astonishing ball of fire in our sky: the brilliant, ever-shining Sun.

THE SUN ★ WHAT IT REPRESENTS IN THE HUMAN PSYCHE & NATAL CHART

"The Sun is the most powerful of all the stellar bodies. It colours the personality so strongly that an amazingly accurate picture can be given of the individual who was born when it was exercising its power through the known and predicable influences of a certain astrological sign; these electromagnetic vibrations will continue to stamp that person with the characteristics of their Sun sign as they go through life."
Linda Goodman's Sun Signs, Linda Goodman, Pan Books, 1968

The Sun is our essence, our core self, conscious purpose and sense of identity, our creative potential, our spirit, the integrated personality that shines outward from within us. It is concerned with the present. It is our centre, source, power, life force, will, vitality, purpose, life's direction, what and who we *really* are.

The Sun represents our basic urge for self-expression. It is the 'Solar energy cell' in a person's character, the Lord and giver of life, and symbolises the way in which an individual will shine out to the world. Our Sun is our personal identity and aspects to it from other components in the chart show the ease or otherwise of assuredness and confidence with which one will project and express one's individuality. The Sun sign will also show how an individual bounces back from setbacks and disappointments, their resilience and their general outward expression of energy.

The Sun is the archetype of the Father and represents the primary masculine principle in the natal chart. It indicates how we express and experience our masculine side, or animus, our conscious self, how we express ourselves creatively, our personal potential, individuality, self-expression and personal power. It has to do with courage, power, generosity, creativity, vitality, self-confidence, nobility, self-worth, dignity and strength of will. It symbolises authority and purpose, the *ruler*, and its potential is the peak of constructive maturity. It signifies self-sufficiency and abundance, containing enough energy to radiate warmth and give life to everything around it.

The sign in which one's Sun is posited, and its placement in the birth chart, strongly indicates the level and type of vitality available to the personality (the sign), and in which area of life this may be most strongly directed (the house).

The Sun in a natal chart is a powerful symbol because everything is filtered, at a conscious level, through it. It tells us what we need to do to feel fully alive, the type of engine 'driving' us, what we need to do to be authentic and to be fully functioning. Listening to the special message of one's Sun sign can provide one with greater direction, and a more dynamic energy and life purpose.

The symbol for the Sun ☉ depicts a circle with a dot or 'seed' at its centre, from which the core self, power, creativity and the first sparks of life can spring. The circle around this 'seed' represents spirit, symbolising wholeness, eternity and the never-ending flow of energy.

While the Moon, the night sky's luminary, represents the *soul*, the Sun, the day sky's luminary, represents our *spirit*.

There is a reason your Sun sign is otherwise known as your Star Sign - it's because, quite simply, the Sun *is* a star; in fact, it's the largest, brightest, shiniest one in Earth's known visible Universe. This book is about your Sun sign and how you can become much larger, glow with far more brilliance, and shine brighter than you ever dreamed possible. I wish you all the magic in the galaxy for your dreams to come true and your deepest wishes to become reality, through tapping into the amazing power and inherent potential of your Sun sign. So get set for a galactical ride through the lucky stars of your constellation - and may a shooting star cross the path in front of you as you go!

SCORPIO THE SCORPION

★ Fixed Water, Negative, Feminine, Feeling ★

"Extremes are purged in the fire and rise again"

Body & Health
Reproductive Systems, Pelvis, Excretory &
Immune Systems, Bladder, Prostate, Rectum.

How Scorpio Emanates its Life Force / Energy
Secretively, passionately, intensely, complexly

Is Concerned With
★ Birth, life, death ★ Sexuality, Sensuality ★
★ Passion ★ Pushing boundaries ★ Depths ★
★ Regeneration, Metamorphosis, Transformation ★
★ Finance, Investments, Inheritances, Wills ★
★ Secrets, Occult, Taboos, Magic, Hidden Matters ★
★ Defence Systems ★ Investigation ★ Personal Power ★
★ Renewal ★ Reformation ★ Change ★ Emotions ★

Spiritual Scorpio

Your Archetypal Universal Qualities
The Transformer, Seeker, Psychologist, Investigator

What You Refuse
To be shallow or to surrender

What You Are an Authority On
Death and rebirth, resilience, passion, self-mastery, fortitude, and the dark side of human nature

The Main Senses Through Which You Experience Your Reality
Smell, taste, desire, possession, death, reformation

How You Love
Possessively, Intensely, Passionately

Positive Characteristics
★ Penetrating and Investigative ★
★ Passionately Caring ★ Hypnotic ★
★ Tenacious ★ Intensely Focused ★ Persuasive ★
★ Protective ★ Dynamic ★ Resilient ★ Insightful ★
★ Magnetic and Charismatic ★ Loyal ★ Perceptive ★
★ Self-mastering ★ Strongly Enduring ★
★ Emotional ★ Sensual ★ Unshockable ★
★ Understands Failings ★ Intuitive ★

Negative Characteristics
★ Self-destructive ★ Controlling ★ Probing ★
★ Ruthless ★ Sadistic ★ Overpowering ★
★ Suspicious ★ Jealous ★ Possessive ★
★ Quick-tempered ★ Moody ★ Vindictive ★
★ Obstinate ★ Selfish ★ Secretive ★ Extreme ★
★ Spiteful and Vengeful ★ Cunning ★
★ Insulting ★ Cutting ★ Sarcastic ★
★ Emotionally Manipulative ★ Defensive ★

To Bring Out Your Best

Read detective novels; do a course in psychology; make passionate love; explore your spirituality;
allow yourself to be probed and share your secrets and discoveries with others occasionally.

Spiritual Goals:

To learn that true deep love involves freedom, surrendering, trusting and letting go;
to learn the beauty of forgiveness and how to sincerely accept an apology; to not misuse your awesome power or control; to give more of your secret self and to better understand your effect on others; to distinguish between proper use and abuse of your personal influence.

SCORPIO

23 October - 21 November

Fixed Water

Ruled by Pluto

"I DESIRE"

Gemstones ◊ Topaz, Malachite, Peridot

★ Passionate, intense, secretive, magnetic, penetrative, jealous, vindictive, vengeful, mysterious, investigative, psychic, suspicious, probing, sarcastic, sceptical, insightful, extreme, deep, self-mastering, pitiless, malicious, twisted, controlling, destructive, resilient, defensive, powerful, merciless, perceptive, enduring, complex, manipulative, resolute, discerning, steadfast, all-or-nothing oriented, tenacious, unflinching, power-seeking, cathartic, hypnotic, aware, ruthless, unapologetic, subtle, enigmatic, intuitive ★

"If you could kick the person in the pants responsible for most of your trouble, you wouldn't sit for a month"
Theodore Roosevelt

SCORPIO

♏

★ **Intense** ★ **Powerful** ★ **Probing** ★
★ **Magnetic** ★ **Secretive** ★ **Complex** ★
★ **Insightful** ★ **Loyal** ★

Scorpio is the sign of the Scorpion, the all-powerful stinging arachnid whose menacing presence can send others scuttling in the other direction. Intense, loyal, jealous, vengeful, vindictive, penetrative, extreme, destructive and regenerative are Scorpios' most notable traits. Being a sensitive and highly emotional Water sign, your feelings brew under the surface and although you may intuit others' feelings and even probe your loved ones relentlessly, the Scorpio character is very secretive about her own inner self. Charismatic and magnetic, Scorpio loves to have control and power over others, sometimes in tyrannical way, but mostly in a benignly, albeit fiercely protective way. The Scorpion is complex and secretive, with an inner turbulence that rarely reaches the surface; once it does, however, the Scorpion can become vindictive and merciless, plotting and exacting revenge like no other sign. Loyalty is a big thing for the passionate Scorpion's spirit, and if she senses any hint of disloyalty or infidelity, she will not hesitate to punish the offender with her powerful sting. Scorpio is transformative and regenerative, symbolically 'dying' or shedding her skin in order to rebirth herself, rising above the ashes like the powerful Phoenix, another symbol of this sign.

Scorpio is mysterious, perceptive and insightful, with an amazingly investigative and probing nature, helping them uncover what no one else can see; however, they are also suspicious and sceptical. A passionate lover, intense friend, and an all-or-nothing superpower, Scorpio is the eighth sign and the enigmatic detective of the zodiac, helping the rest of us uncover our hidden truths with their deeply aware perceptions.

KEY CONCEPTS
★ Transformative healer ★
★ Giver of strength ★
★ High-voltage intensity ★
★ Merger with spirit ★
★ Destruction and manipulation ★
★ Seducer for personal gain ★
★ Clever hypnotist ★
★ Power and passion ★
★ Enduring loyalty ★
★ Vast resourcefulness ★
★ Inexhaustible resilience ★

SOME CORRESPONDENCES THAT ARE ASSOCIATED WITH SCORPIO

Detectives, secret matters, morticians, psychic abilities, espionage, scorpions, the occult, cemeteries, private investigators, floods, autopsies, sorcery, the reproductive organs, passion, hypnotism, deceased estates, inheritance, abattoirs, butchers, legal wills, magnetism, plumbing, sewers, laboratories, rubbish dumps, surgery, embalming, treachery, cesspools, nuclear science, the bladder, executions, cremation, funeral directors, plumbers, surgeons, insurance, vice squads, underground activities, legacies, dangerous activities, death, taxation, drains, tyranny, and witchcraft. Take your pick and enjoy the ride!

QUOTES BY SCORPIONS

"Keep your eyes on the stars, and your feet on the ground" - Theodore Roosevelt (27 October 1858)

"To believe in love, to be ready to give up anything for it, to be willing to risk your life for it, is the ultimate tragedy" - Leonardo DiCaprio (11 November 1974)

"I'm a great believer that any tool that enhances communication has profound effects in terms of how people can learn from each other, and how they can achieve the kind of freedoms that they're interested in" - Bill Gates (28 October 1955)

"I am the American Dream. I am the epitome of what the American Dream basically said. It said you could come from anywhere and be anything you want in this country. That's exactly what I've done" - Whoopi Goldberg (13 November 1955)

"I took a deep breath and listened to the old bray of my heart. I am. I am. I am" - Sylvia Plath (27 October 1932)

"As a housewife, I feel that if the kids are still alive when my husband gets home from work, then hey, I've done my job" - Rosanne Barr (3 November 1952)

"I'm a Scorpio, and Scorpios eat themselves out and burn themselves up like me" - Vivien Leigh (5 November 1913)

"Believe you can and you're halfway there" - Theodore Roosevelt

"It is not the question, what am I going to be when I grow up? You should ask the question, *who* am I going to be when I grow up?" - Goldie Hawn (21 November 1945)

"It's okay to be fat. So you're fat. Just be fat and shut up about it" - Rosanne Barr

"Water at 211 degrees makes hot coffee. Water at 212 degrees becomes steam and can move a ship around the world. Move out of the hot water of mediocrity and into the steam of outstanding success" - Zig Ziglar (6 November 1926)

"I am a victim of introspection" - Sylvia Plath

"I see music as fluid architecture" - Joni Mitchell (7 November 1943)

"I do believe in a lot of weird things these days, like synchronicity. Quantum physics suggests it's possible, so why not?" - John Cleese (27 October 1939)

"I consider myself to be a pretty good judge of people. That's why I don't like any of them" - Rosanne Barr

"I rant; therefore, I am" - Dennis Miller (3 November 1953)

"The power to question is the basis of all human progress" - Indira Gandhi (19 November 1917)

"Emancipation of women has made them lose their mystery" - Grace Kelly (12 November 1929)

"Sorrow is so easy to express and yet so hard to tell" - Joni Mitchell

"The thing women have yet to learn is that nobody gives you power. You have to take it" - Rosanne Barr

"I would say what scares me is that I'm going to ultimately find out at the end of my life that I'm really not lovable, that I'm not worthy of being loved. That there's something fundamentally wrong with me" - Demi Moore (11 November 1962)

"For a woman, forty is torture, the end" - Grace Kelly

"Nothing in life is to be feared, it is only to be understood" - Marie Curie (7 November 1867)

"It's an interesting combination: having a great fear of being alone, and having a desperate need for solitude and the solitary experience. That's always been a tug of war for me" - Jodie Foster (19 November 1962)

"Let them eat cake" - Marie Antoinette (2 November 1755)

"There is no duty we so much underrate as the duty of being happy. By being happy we sow anonymous benefits upon the world" - Robert Louis Stevenson (13 November 1850)

"The Universe is full of magical things, patiently waiting for our wits to grow sharper" - Eden Phillpotts, 4 November 1862

"Appreciation is a wonderful thing; it makes what is excellent in others belong to us as well" - Voltaire (21 November 1694)

"Effort only fully releases its rewards when a person refuses to quit" - Napoleon Hill (26 October 1883)

"Sometimes doing (the substance) was nice and dreamy and euphoric and carefree, almost romantic-feeling. In reality, I was dying and couldn't quite see that from being so deep in my own forest" - Anthony Kiedis (1 November 1962)

"Keep your fears to yourself, but share your courage with others" - Robert Louis Stevenson

"The beginning of every great success is desire" - Napoleon Hill

"If you go on working with the light available, you will meet your Master, as he himself will be seeking you" - Eden Phillpotts, 4 November 1862

"If your dreams don't scare you, they aren't big enough" - Ellen Johnson Surleaf (29 October 1938)

THE SCORPIO CONSTELLATION

The signs of the zodiac are the twelve symbolic features that ancient people imagined while observing the heavens. They saw shapes, patterns, faces, and natural and supernatural beings in the stars, from which they established, over centuries, a kind of celestial hierarchy and system based upon their observations. Groupings of stars became constellations, and twelve of these constellations make up the zodiac, a Greek word meaning 'circle of animals', that we know today.

Star constellations are not really self-contained groups but are particularly bright stars that give the appearance of being close together and form distinctive patterns. These are the patterns that over the ages have been identified as animals, deities or mythological figures and heroes. The stars are the living past. We receive their light long after it has left the star itself and so they are a good focus for escaping from the parameters of time. Their stellar influence is analogous with the aura, the bio/psychic energy field surrounding humans, animals, plants, crystals and even places. These individual energy systems interact with the energy waves emanated by other people, and even the cosmic rays emitted by planetary bodies, for psychic energies are not limited by time or distance.

The cluster of stars we know as Scorpius, or Scorpio to astrologers, is aptly named, for its brightest stars resemble a Scorpion poised to inflict its sting. Scorpius is most easily seen in the Southern

Hemisphere. It is directly overhead Sydney at about 10 p.m. in July. In the more northerly latitudes only some of its body can be seen, for it is best observed in the southern United States, Mexico and the Caribbean Islands.

At its heart, Scorpius contains a bright red star called Antares, which lies at the approximate centre of the enormous Cloud Nebula in Scorpio. Although Scorpius contains many bright stars, this brightest one, Antares, also called the Heart of the Scorpion, is distinctly reddish. The beauty of this constellation is increased by virtue of the fact that it lies in a part of the Milky Way which is thick with fainter stars.

One of the most easily distinguishable constellations, composed of notably bright and large stars, Scorpio is among the largest of the twelve constellations. Scorpio is known for its secrecy, and this characteristic seems to correspond with only the tip of its fore claws peering above the ecliptic, the circle which defines the boundaries of the zodiac. The rest of the Scorpion's body and long, arched tail is 'hidden' (although visible) against the backdrop of the Milky Way's multitude of stars.

WISHING UPON YOUR STAR

The practice of wishing upon a star is familiar to most of us, and is a mystical superstition that is ingrained in many of us from childhood. As a night-time ritual, you can wish upon your own sign's constellation or that of the sign whose energies you wish to call forth; indeed, you can wish upon any constellation you feel an affinity with. If you can't see a particular constellation in your night sky, you can always meditate on it in your mind, or you can use the traditional technique of wishing upon the first star you see, while reciting the popular rhyme: *Star light, star bright, first star I see tonight, I wish I may, I wish I might, have the wish I make this night!* Any one of the three rituals will hold power for your own special wish. Good luck!

THE SCORPIO SYMBOL ♏

Astrology uses symbols or 'glyphs' to represent the planets and signs. The glyph is made up of shapes representing the energy and physical matter of which the Universe is composed, and how these shapes are used in each symbol provide hints as to the properties of the sign or planet it represents.

The ancient view was that there were five elements: Fire, Water, Air, Earth and Ether (or Spirit). Ether is invisible energy, while the four tangible elements are known as 'matter'. Ether, as pure energy, cannot be influenced by any of the physical/matter elements, although it surrounds them and indeed fuels them. The Greek philosopher and scientist Aristotle regarded this idea as a circle (Ether/Spirit) with a cross (matter) in the centre. This glyph is used in astrology as a symbol for Earth, and the cycle of life. All the symbols used in astrology represent the relationship between energy and the 'matter' elements.

Scorpio is symbolised by the tail of the Scorpion. Its three lines represent three levels of consciousness: the first representing the lower mind, the second the higher mind striving to evolve, and the third its regenerative or super-conscious abilities. The last stroke ends with a barb and arrow, which hold it back and imbue it with Earthly desire. The three lines could also be interpreted to symbolise the coils of the serpent, a creature closely associated with Scorpio.

Scorpio's glyph depicts the sting in the tail, but can also be seen as phallic. This symbol is very similar to that of Virgo, being based on the same Hebrew letter, Mem, to which is added a barb, reminding us of the sting in the Scorpion's tail, instead of the fish symbol. This barb may be regarded as Cupid's dart, emphasising the lure of the senses. In Scorpio the female principle has now the power to destroy (ideally to make way for a new and better creation). The Phoenix, the mythical bird that was consumed by fire and rose again from its own ashes, and the soaring eagle, are alternative symbols for the sign. Scorpio is a Fixed Water sign. Water in its fixed state is ice, which it shares with the Scorpion an extreme susceptibility to heat.

THE SCORPION ANIMAL

Along with cockroaches and ants, scorpions are among the world's great survivors. Scorpions are ancient animals that have survived with little structural change since up to 360 million years ago (170 million years before dinosaurs began). Ancient scorpions were more diverse and much bigger than today. Some were giants a metre long, compared with 30 centimetres for the longest alive today.

Scorpions are classified as 'arachnids', the same class to which spiders, mites and ticks belong. All scorpions have eight legs, as well as the famed pair of claws at the front, and a sting on the tail, which can strike forwards over the scorpion's back, or at prey held in its claws.

Worldwide, there are nine scorpion families occurring in warm and temperate climates. Prominent in legends of early Mediterranean, scorpions have always had a fearsome reputation, which is certainly deserved in Africa, the Middle East, Central and South America, and parts of Asia, where deadly species threaten humans and animals. All scorpions are carnivores and will eat practically anything that is alive and the right size.

It is rare to encounter these elusive creatures in the wild, even though there are plenty of them, living in various habitats from desert to rainforest and sea-level to mountains. They are seldom seen because they are mainly nocturnal. There is a great way of spotting them that depends on a remarkable property of scorpion cuticle: they fluoresce under ultraviolet light.

THE AGE OF SCORPIO ★ 16,000 - 14,000 BC

The Age of Scorpio lies deep in prehistory, and saw the development of tools and weapon-making in early human societies. Humans began to develop more specialised tools such as needles for making garments and harpoons for hunting. Blades made from stone also became more sophisticated in this period. These early creations reflect the association of Scorpio, the Scorpion, with piercing and tool- and weapon-making. A desire to probe into and unravel some of the great mysteries of the Universe is also indicative of Scorpio's influence, Scorpio being a sign which seeks to understand both how and why things work. During this period, detailed astronomical observations began to be made in China as humans sought to understand the workings of the wider Universe. The earliest date suggested for the creation of the Zodiac Wheel is 15,000 BC, falling in the Age of Scorpio. Cave paintings of this time show evidence of religious cults, which have been allied with the search to find a deeper meaning in life, reflecting perhaps one of Scorpio's greatest quests. During the Age of Scorpio, a Water sign, a notable increase in rainfall turned the Sahara Desert temporarily into savannah grassland, and many early settlers in Egypt moved away from the Nile to hunt. Also, people began to collect seeds from wheat and barley, and as barley is one of the main cereals used in beer fermentation it seems likely that alcoholic drinks were first produced during this period.

THE RUNDOWN & LESSONS
SOME QUIRKS, ODDITIES, UNIQUE CHARACTERISTICS AND IDIOSYNCRASIES OF SCORPIO

"Scorpio can do just about anything he wants to do. If he *really* wants it, it's most definitely no longer a dream. The dark, magical and mysterious power of Pluto turns desire into reality with cool, careful, fixed intent."
Linda Goodman

There are two types of thinkers: what I like to call 'right-brainers' and 'left-brainers'. The left hemisphere of the human brain deals with things such as control of speech, verbal functions, logic, reason, mathematics, linear concepts, details, sequences, the intellect and analysis; the right hemisphere is concerned with spatial, music, holistic, artistic concepts, as well as simultaneity and intuition. You could go on to say that the left brain is masculine or yang in quality, and the right brain is feminine or yin in quality. Based upon these very simplistic outlines, it can be further stated that Water sign Scorpio dwells mainly in the right hemisphere, with a little bit of left thrown in for good measure.

The essence of Scorpio is self-mastery, the understanding of its own transformative powers. The keys to a Scorpio's psyche are trust, secrets and privacy. This sign contains things on a deep level, is psychologically penetrative, and awakens to consciousness through betrayal - essentially, they must go through the 'death' of something to re-emerge transformed. Indeed, 'deaths' and 'rebirths' are what bring out Scorpio's best. You were born instinctively knowing the secrets of life and death, as well as being gifted with the ability to conquer both if you so choose. Betrayals usually occur through sex and money. The typical Scorpio wants to be acknowledged on a deep level and you have an urge for self-understanding, emotional insight, commitment from another, and overall healing and transformation. Your best comes out when you are in danger or crisis. Technically, the only way Water can be Fixed is when it is ice. Scorpio can certainly be seen as a metaphoric iceberg, revealing little of yourself, with your greater parts and more substantial self being submerged and often treacherous. Some Scorpios can be cold and hard, but another interpretation of Fixed Water is that the feelings and emotions are unbending, determined, strong, solid and intense. Scorpio embodies extremes, being the sign of heights and depths. You can be the most loyal of friends or the most avenging of enemies. Everything must be experienced, probed, examined and penetrated, even down to the darkest caverns of human experience. Scorpios may struggle with the use and abuse of power and are often tempted to try and control others - through sex, mind games, magic, hypnotism, or just in the daily battlefields of work, love, pleasure and leisure.

The word most associated with Scorpio is passion, for she can do nothing by half measures; it is all or nothing to this fearsome character. You are a staunch and faithful friend, a tireless worker, a demanding lover and an implacable enemy. But despite all appearances, reputations and associations, Scorpio is not the big bad guy of the zodiac. Like the Phoenix who rises from the ashes to seek the embodiment of perfection in another form, Scorpio is compelled by Pluto to evolve ever onwards and upwards.

With Scorpio, it's all in the eyes. With a piercing, hypnotic intensity, you have the power to make others feel nervous and uneasy under your gaze and in your presence. Perhaps astrologer Linda Goodman summed it up best when she said, "You'll have to break the spell and look away first. He'll outstare you every time. It's a foolproof identification of the Pluto personality. Scorpio eyes bore deeply into you, mercilessly, as if they're penetrating your very soul. They are." Indeed.

Scorpio works out the often hidden issues that arise from partnership, especially those related to shared resources or property due to needs for security and self-empowerment. Emotions can be suppressed in your sign more than any other, and this conflict between expression or repression often predisposes you to emotional energy which can manifest as complexes or unhealthy obsessions. It also makes you difficult for others to get to know (which is usually the way you like it). The fact that you maintain an air of secrecy seems to add to your already alluringly dangerous charm.

Scorpio is associated with the underworld, and when one examines the mythological and traditional associations of the time of year during which its influence is strongest, it is easy to see why. During the month of Scorpio, the leaves fall from the trees and the Earth begins to 'close down', to prepare for the long slumber of winter. In the ancient nature religions, this was the time in which the goddesses and gods actually journeyed into the underworld; everything above would be empty, dark and cold until the winter solstice marked the beginning of the process of return, leading finally to the resurgence that is spring. For most of us, this symbolism is connected with a journey to the very depths of our being - an inevitably painful journey, for it forces us to confront our psychological complexes, oft rampant emotions and inner demons. But Scorpio also offers the promise of resurrection, restoration, an arising of the self-anew, a return to the light. Therefore, your sign is regarded as one of transformation.

Certainly, Scorpio has long been associated with occult wisdom and knowledge. Some esoteric astrologers offer the analogy of a fourfold process to describe the Scorpio experience: from raging primal Scorpion to introspective lizard (the underworld journey) to soaring eagle (rebirth) to white dove (the highest spirit). As already mentioned, Scorpio has also been linked to the phoenix, the mythical Egyptian bird which succumbs to the flames of a fire, only to rise reborn from its own ashes.

Indeed, there are two main types of Scorpios: The Eagle and the Scorpion, and a third class: The Phoenix or Dove. Only those who are living the mystery of the Scorpio experience will know instinctively which separate class of 'soul' they belong to. You can be either the healer, the transformer, the mystic or the vampire. The latter is the pure Scorpion type, who sucks the lifeblood from her victims through her hypnotic powers, leaving her prey either dead or with just enough life to be a slave to her will. Interestingly, the spider is also ruled by Scorpio, and its nature is analogous with the Scorpion nature, that is it weaves a web and awaits prey to stumble upon its intricately woven construction and fall into its trap. And we all know what happens next!

The rarest type of Scorpio is the Dove, and if you are one of these, you will recognise yourself in the following words by astrologer Alan Oken: "Like his name, Dove-Scorpio has completely transcended all personal and egocentric desires, he works to bring joy to his fellow man and to absorb sorrow and pain from others and replace them with Universal love. He is the natural healer and mystic and is often the solitary ascetic. Most Scorpio natives are an active combination of the Eagle and Scorpion types but all are also latent Doves." He goes on to say that no matter what your present state of being, all Scorpion types have to constantly choose between rising high into the Light, or falling into the Darkness of oblivion.

Inside anyone who has a strong Scorpio influence in their natal chart, is someone who is impenetrable, so the secret Scorpio usually remains just that - a *secret*. You rarely hesitate in probing others and getting to the core of complex issues, for yours is a highly intuitive personality that understands others very well, and you seek to use any knowledge gained through insight in order to manipulate people for your own ends. In fact, your sign goes where others fear to tread, and you will *always* use this power to your advantage. You are both fearless and feared, and revel in your status of Powerful One and controller. You can even hypnotise other people into doing exactly what you want them to do and do this with such instinctive, expert efficiency that the recipient does not even realise he is under a spell.

As a Fixed sign, you have a somewhat change-resistant character, and hold rigid and unchanging opinions. Your viewpoints can be extreme and unconquerable, your thinking patterns direct and determined. You are not a daydreamer: you always know exactly what you want and never get side tracked from your path. But you are also vulnerable underneath your intimidating shell, and can be ruthlessly critical of yourself. You have a suspicious personality, arguably based upon hidden insecurities and personal complexes, that dwells on past hurts and allows vengeful and vindictive thoughts to fester. Everything that happens to you is judged on the basis of feelings and emotions; slow to trust, if you are betrayed, the pain can be so great that you will never forgive nor forget. Not that the betrayer may ever know, for you keep your emotions firmly under wraps and resentment will simmer and smoulder but rarely boil over - your sense of self-control is all-powerful. Your ego is equally as solid as your self-control, and it is a rare Scorpio who is nervous, fidgety, jumpy, aimless or restless. Your sense of self is robust and unbreakable; you know what you are and you know what you are not; similarly, you know what you want and what you don't want. You require no validation from anyone else but your own self, and certainly need no one to tell you of your vices or virtues. You already know. Such mastery of character has to be envied, and often is. But it is also feared. Your smiles are rare, but genuine. But when you are not smiling, others should be advised to be on their guard, for you pack a powerful punch. You tell the truth and you tell it fast; you are nothing if not incisive. There are no in-betweens with your truth, and although you may unsettle more sensitive types with your oft sought opinions or advice (they asked, after all), you could never be accused of being dishonest with your answers or viewpoints. You are not afraid what anyone else thinks of them either.

Scorpios also enjoy a vivid fantasy life but when used in a characteristically self-destructive or menacing manner, these fantasies can often dip into the darker side of human nature - experimentation with black magic, the occult and other things which others may find disturbing, for example - which the Scorpio will usually keep to herself, not for not wanting to shock others, but because they have an almost perverse need to keep their depths mysterious, their true nature hidden, and one piece of their personal puzzle perpetually missing.

Perhaps as a legacy or remnant of the many centuries Scorpio was ruled by Mars, you tend to be a bit of a daredevil, undertaking extreme or risky or downright destructive behaviours. But what these seemingly obsessed and possessed Scorpios really seek is not the demolition of the physical body, but rather the death and rebirth of their consciousness. You may pursue adrenalin sports such as race car driving or bungee jumping, or try to lose yourself in sex, drugs or fame, but at your very core you are actually seeking transformation and personal empowerment.

Much of Scorpio's nature is hidden under a veil of secrecy; your motives are rarely open. To you, knowledge is power, and for this reason you will not reveal too much for fear that others may gain the upper hand and attempt to manipulate *you*, for you have a fundamental need to stay in control at all times and of all circumstances.

Scorpio has a reputation for being highly sexed or at least concerned with sex on a spiritual level. This reputation is justified, as Scorpio has much to do with the 'urge to merge'. To Scorpio, the idea of a complete joining of forces with a person or sometimes with a higher realm, is of utmost importance. This union is perhaps even more vital to you than its primal purpose of producing offspring. You don't seek to give birth to a new creation as much as you desire to rebuild on an already existing entity into a more refined, uplifted, renewed and exalted state. And this you will do through the use of other people's (sexual) energies or resources. Ultimately, you seek to make your own being more powerful through using these forces and energies to your advantage, no matter what the cost to anyone or anything else. Overall, through your sexual force, you can either by the tempter or the stealer of souls. You can also be the catalytic agent who gives others a way towards growth and renewal.

There is certainly nothing shallow or wishy-washy or vague about the Scorpion. Your willpower is phenomenal and you are extremely purposeful in all that you do and say - or *don't* say. The force of your character is such that it can zap the energy right out of you, leaving you drained, or it can inspire you to unscaled heights. In any case, the experience of being a Scorpio will not leave you unchanged.

In relationships you are as intense as you are in every other area of your life. As a Water sign, your emotions run deep, and as a Fixed sign, they are likely to remain constant until or unless something happens to destroy your trust - a sin you will never forgive, nor forget. Hate and love are extremes of passion and you know this better than anyone else; you feel this polarity with an unmatched intensity. Your sheer devotion to a person or cause is undying, as is your enmity. A great source of power but an ever menacing danger, your memory is longer than an elephant's, and you will forget neither a kind gesture nor a hurt. If you see something heading for ruin, you will try to take everything out in your path along with you. Others should cross you at their peril, for you have great staying power and are willing to wait until the end of time to exact revenge if that's how long it takes. Your need to control everything may manifest itself as unreasonable possessiveness and you can be extremely jealous.

This possessiveness can extend to things aside from people, too. You are fiercely protective of what you believe to be yours, including success, but your ambition is never obvious.

Scorpio has the ability to inspire fear or awe in others, often both, because of the overwhelming force of your personality. But forcefulness does not necessarily mean harshness, for beneath your surface lies a rich vein of compassion, albeit for the most part untapped. Although your greatest strength lies in your ability to impose your will upon others, you give very little away of your vast pool of resources - or at least only enough so that you may control others. You have an innate gift of raising people up and infusing them with just enough spirit to keep them right at the level on which you want them. You can bring out abilities and talents in others, changing them to suit your own ends, needs and desires, and will only ever become personally entangled in someone else's hype if it suits your purposes. The Eagle type particularly, will be incredibly incisive and discerning, swooping down swiftly and surely after consciously zoning in on the situation from above. This type does not involve herself with petty emotions, her aims are high and her feelings are under tight control. You fly above jealousy, anger, resentment and tempests, for you are possessed by pride and restraint.

The most powerfully emotional of the zodiac, your fixed intensity of feeling usually makes you a physical powerhouse as well, driven by your determination and persistence. Magnetic and potent, this passion can also turn into possessiveness, raging jealousy and revenge, as you easily span both light and dark emotions. Being so 'hidden' and penetrative, you are able to search the depths and then rise transformed and renewed. Your transformative experiences are seldom undertaken willingly. After all, you are Fixed Water and thus do not usually welcome change. The serpent has to bite you first, and only then your atomic reactors are ready to fire on all cylinders. Once you have discovered, recognised, slain, and accepted your inner demons, you allow your former demons to become totems of empowerment for your own self-healing processes. But there are some Scorpios who have trouble slaying their dragons for whatever reasons. The wrestling with emotional depths and excesses is encountered in Scorpio as in no other sign, and can manifest in the already mentioned self-destructive behaviours you are so well-known for.

The separation and regenerative processes that are so closely linked with your sign reflect their rulership in the body as well. In medical astrology, the sex organs (procreation, regeneration) and the eliminative organs (colon, bladder) are ruled by Scorpio, making it an analogous with you finding it challenging to eliminate the old emotional garbage in your life, which can have serious repercussions for your body's *physical* elimination processes as well.

There is also an intimate link between Scorpio and the mysterious life-force known as *kundalini* (the Serpent Power) in Sanskrit. Regarded as an essentially potent sexual energy, the kundalini is the vital, animating force within us. It 'sleeps' at the base of the spine, and esoteric astrologers believe that the glyph for Scorpio itself - ♏ - represents this Serpent Power - coiled, sleeping, but ever ready to arise. Traditionally, an imbalance in the kundalini produces all kinds of sexual issues and deviant behaviours - concepts usually associated with an afflicted Scorpio placement in the natal chart.

Your ruling planet Pluto endows you with your famous intensity and willpower, and when combined with your traditional or secondary ruler Mars, your passion and power are increased immensely. Pluto, the Greek god of the underworld, ruled hidden riches and gained his power from a helmet which made him invisible. You too passionately desire power, control and security and like to know the secrets and motives of others, without revealing yours.

Ultimately, Scorpio represents the descent of consciousness into its deep personal underworld and there, in the depths of our souls, our old ego-consciousness dies so that we may be reborn. Therefore, it can be said that Scorpio is the deepest and most complex of the signs. If you can use your extraordinary powers of magnetism, power and influence for the good of all and not just for the slaying of your *own* dragons, the world would be a much richer - and empowered - place, for having you in it.

LESSONS TO BE LEARNED FOR GREATER POWER, ENLIGHTENMENT & LUCK

Scorpion problems and ultimate undoings arise through your compulsiveness, over-sensitivity, obsessiveness, sarcasm, extremism, and control issues. Scorpio has a tendency to abuse their power through controlling others in the form of possession, manipulation, jealousy, or plain sulking and withdrawal. If this abuse of power is taken to extremes, Scorpio can be sadistic and can use their innate charisma and magnetism to draw those who are vulnerable into their lives. You can be spiteful, venomous and hold a grudge like no other sign. Self-destructive, uncompromising and stubborn, Scorpio needs to learn how to find the hidden treasure in the traumas of their past, the biggest one being the strength and magnitude of the powerful, resourceful and resilient personality that has emerged as a result. If you can uncover those lessons learned, you will see that the mere fact you have survived through it all is testament to your emotional strength, hugely transformative nature and capacity for change.

Your propensity for regeneration and for bettering yourself under even the most extreme and adverse of circumstances, coupled with your deep reverence for life's mysteries, are your greatest strengths. When you focus upon using your power to positively influence, enrich and guide others, you are living up to your optimum potential and will be richly rewarded for your efforts. When you uplift rather than force other people, your exercise of self-control and self-mastery inspires them to morph into a better version of themselves also - and then you are the *true* eagle. You are able to enjoy the fullness of life, yet have the ability to reject everything you know to be destructive to yourself. If more negative forces prevail however, self-damaging behaviours, toxic patterns, implicit selfishness, dark broodiness, and cruel vindictive actions can replace that lofty Scorpionic purpose. The same strong willpower can pull you down with just as strong a suction, and there is the ever present danger of destroying yourself with addictions, obsessions and compulsions. You, of all the zodiac signs, know life's extreme highs and lows, peaks and troughs, valleys and mountains - and because of this profound inner wisdom, you have the capacity to chart the inner darkness and demons to emerge victorious. After all, rising above it all is what Scorpio does best.

A NOTE ON DEATH

Many esoteric, occultist, shamanic and healing workers take a rather spiritual view on death. They believe that if we die young or before our 'time', it may be that we feel we have learned all we need to learn this particular life experience and Earthly plane has to teach us, or that we have chosen a situation which is not likely to teach us what we most need to learn. If we live long, tedious, miserable lives praying for deliverance from a cascade of tears and pain but are still being impelled by something inside ourselves to struggle for existence, then we can be sure the Life Force is trying to pound something into us that we are perhaps stubbornly refusing to know or learn. Scorpio acknowledges this concept on a profound level and indeed at *all* levels - physically, mentally, emotionally, psychically and spiritually - and as such most true Scorpios experience many deaths in many forms every single day - for yours is the zodiac sign who instinctively knows that to die is to be reborn anew in a different state, another life, a higher stage, or an entirely new plane of existence. You, more than most, also know that matter and energy can never essentially be created or destroyed, but merely *transformed*.

THE THREE DECANS OF SCORPIO

Decans are thirty-six groups of stars that rise in a particular order on the horizon throughout each Earth rotation. These decans were developed in Egypt thousands of years ago. The rising of each decan marked the beginning of a new 'decanal hour' of the night for these ancient people, and eventually three decans were assigned to each zodiac sign. Each decan covers ten degrees of the zodiac wheel, and is ruled by different planetary rulers that rule over the other two signs of the same element (and a traditional ruler, when only seven of the planetary bodies were known). Decans continued to be used throughout the Ages, in astrology and in magic, but many modern astrologers, for whatever reasons, tend to disregard them. Following are brief descriptions for each decan of Scorpio. Which one do you belong to? Can you relate to the description and the energies of your decan's ruling planet?

FIRST DECAN SCORPIO ★ October 23 - November 2

Ruler ★ Mars (traditional *) / Mars (modern)

Keyword ★ Vital

First Decan Scorpios' Three Special Tarot Cards
Death, King of Cups & Five of Cups

Birthdays in this decan range from 23rd October to November 2nd. This is the Scorpio decan, ruled by Mars *. Scorpios born during this decan possess a great wealth of vital and mental resources. Your impulses are strong and essential, and instinctive forces dominate your drive. Strong-willed, ambitious and driven, you focus on what you want and achieve almost everything you set your vision upon. The power to act is strong, tenacious and resistant, and you have a robust propensity for creativity. Powerful and influential, you like to control others but also yourself - you are extraordinarily self-disciplined and resilient. By nature, you are secretive, magnetic and mysterious, passionate to the core and dedicated to your convictions, which you don't change to suit anyone. You are loyal to your partners, and demand the same fervent love in return; you detest betrayal of any degree, and will easily become vindictive and vengeful if you have been wronged. You may come across as intense or brooding to others, but you always live truthfully and unwaveringly by your own code.

SECOND DECAN SCORPIO ★ November 3 - 11

Ruler ★ Sun (traditional *) / Jupiter (modern)

Keywords ★ Soulful Non-conformist

Second Decan Scorpios' Three Special Tarot Cards Death, King of Cups & Six of Cups

Birthdays in this decan range from 3rd November to 11th November. This is known as the Pisces decan and is ruled by the Sun * and Jupiter. Your personal style is one of great depth, and your mottos revolve around 'transmutation'. The influence of Jupiter may prompt you to over-indulge in all manner of things, from food and sex, to alcohol and other drugs, to exercising control and power over others. Beneath a hardy and resilient exterior, your heart is actually very tender and sensitive, needing careful handling, and you will go to great lengths - and some of you will make it your life's mission - to find your soul mate. Although energetic and ardent, you possess a moderating streak of charity and generosity. Passionate and extreme, you make an exceptional friend or lover to those you choose to give your heart and soul to. Indeed, you do not do anything by halves.

THIRD DECAN SCORPIO ★ November 12 - 21

Ruler ★ Venus (traditional *) / Moon (modern)

Keyword ★ Intuitive

Third Decan Scorpios' Three Special Tarot Cards Death, Knight of Wands & Seven of Cups

Birthdays in this decan range from 12th November to 21st November. This is the Cancer decan, ruled by Venus * and the Moon. Scorpios born during this decan are characterised by strong instincts, intuitive impulses, powerful feelings and raging emotions. Venus stimulates and exacerbates your sensitivity and vulnerability, making you clingy and possessive and possibly moody, particularly when feeling threatened. Caring, devoted and with a deep need for security, particularly in relationships, you may wrap yourself up in illusions and fantasies as a self-protective mechanism - or worse, indulge in comforting substitutes such as food, promiscuous sex or over-spending your money. In any case, you don't have the same level of self-discipline and self-control as the other Scorpio decans. Your psychic powers, imagination and personal magnetism are also heightened with these influences, giving you a mysterious, almost ethereal charisma that others are drawn to but can't seem to explain why. You are sensually intense, seductive and in a word, magical.

* The decan's traditional ruler based on the Chaldean order of the planets

YOUR ELEMENT ★ WATER

According to the *Oxford English Dictionary*, the word *element* has a mysterious origin, and was first found in Greek texts meaning 'complex whole' or 'a single unit made up of many parts'. From the ancient up to medieval times, there were only four elements - Earth, Air, Fire and Water - and the occult-oriented also believed in a fifth: Spirit, or Ether. (Cornelius Agrippa called Spirit the 'quintessence'.)

Alchemy is a tradition of visions and dreams, and images can combine on different levels of reality. Alchemists have long used images in their illustrations to express the enigma and mystery of their art, and to include all dimensions of our experience. The traditional worlds of Earth, Water, Fire and Air symbolise these dimensions very well. Broadly speaking, and in human terms, Earth corresponds to the level of the body and the senses, Water to the flow of thoughts and feelings, Fire to inspiration and energy, and Air to the world of the higher mind and intellect. Each of these worlds has its own realm of imagery. Scorpio belongs to the realm of the Water element.

★ The Emotional Group ★

The Path to SPIRITUALITY

Focused on Emotion and Feelings

Alchemical Associations ★ The Subconscious, Quicksilver and the Colour White

Key Attributes ★ Sensitivity, Flexibility, Intuition, Creativity, Feeling

Symbolism ★ Healing, Reflection and Cleansing

Governed by ★ The Soul and the Feelings

Water Characteristics ★ Subjective, Emotional, Intuitive, Sensitive, Imaginative, Receptive

★ THE MAGIC OF WATER ★

Water is the flow of emotions, the tide that carries you out to sea and will bring you back to a safe shore after your whimsical adventures. It can be placid or tempestuous, and without it life cannot flourish. It can cause your dreams to carry you away on the waves, without anchoring your aspirations. You can sink or swim in Water, having nothing to cling to for support, as it has no form, shaping itself into its surroundings. It needs a container to prevent your dreams being swept away; cups, goblets and bowls are often associated with water, and the term 'Holy Grail' describes your greatest desires.

The sage is like water.
Water is good, nourishes all things,
and does not compete with them.
It dwells in humble places that others disdain;
hence it is close to the Tao.
In his dwelling, the sage loves the earth.
In his mind, he loves what is profound.
In his associations, he is kind and gentle.
In his speech, he is sincere.
In his ruling, he is just.
In business, he is proficient.
In his action, he is timely.
Because he does not compete,
he does not find fault in others.
Lao Tzu (604-517 BC)
***Tao Te Ching,* VIII**

★ KEYWORDS ★

Impressionable, compassionate, reflective, insightful, merging, fertile, receptive, absorbing, responsive, habitual, perceptive, secretive, submissive, possessive, nurturing, sensitive, clingy, dependent, instinctive, emotional, sympathetic, intriguing, protective, empathetic, psychic, mysterious *

* All these words don't necessarily describe all three Water signs. Pisces, for example, is not possessive, and Scorpio is not submissive.

Water is the most important element of all, for without it there would be no life on planet Earth. Without Water the land would not be fruitful or fertile, but dry and sterile. It has long been revered as the wellspring of life, enabling human civilisations to grow and flourish across the planet. The ancients understood the generative energy inherent in Water, and it has given rise to many myths, stories, superstitions and symbolism. For example, the chalice, a vessel for holding this element, is a legendary symbol of abundance and spiritual power. The Moon and its compelling influence on the seas and female reproductive cycles, is strongly linked with the Water element and its deeply feminine nature.

As the ultimate source of life and growth, Water is the most significant element in terms of regeneration and metamorphosis. Water follows a relatively unchanging cycle, going from a liquid state to a solid state, and according to scientific observations, reproduces itself around thirty-four times in the course of the terrestrial year. Under the combined influence of the movement of the Earth's rotation upon itself and of gravity, water shapes the Earth's surface. The perpetual motions and meandering courses of all the bodies of water on the surface of the globe, as well as the numerous currents, are caused by this terrestrial rotation, and also by the movements of the Moon around our planet. By the same token that water is the source of life - by drinking it or immersing yourself in it, you can regain your strength, satisfy a primary need, quench your thirst, be regenerated, and be washed and cleansed.

Water is the Universal Solvent, and the Universal Coagulant in the alchemical laboratory of nature. The Sun of Life, the Ego, passes through the waters of parturition in three definite stages symbolised by the Watery signs. They are the most primitive of all the animals depicted in the zodiac: the scorpion, the fish and the crab. The different astrological animal and human symbols, are said to represent the hierarchical instincts (e.g. aquatic, deep, dark) and the temperament of each creature or human type - our primal, instinctive and unconscious sides. Two of the Water signs - Scorpio and Cancer - are symbolised by half land-half water creatures, amphibious and flexible, but the Fish that represents the sign of Pisces can't breathe air and must live eternally in the cool water, sometimes muddy, sometimes clear, but always flowing.

In Greek mythology, Poseidon (Neptune to the Romans) rules the oceanic and water domains. Symbols and images most associated with the Water element include mermaids, wells, reservoirs, swimming, fish, crabs, lakes, rivers, dolphins, whales, diving, water-skiing and boating.

Water has long been associated with the powers of birth and regeneration, representing the feelings and healing energy. Ancient people built their settlements close to the life-giving rivers, streams and springs that became the source of several magical traditions and beliefs. In most cultures, wells, lakes and ponds were worshipped and venerated. Offerings were dropped into the watery depths in return for blessings - a ritual that survives today in the form of a wishing well.

Pulled by the Moon, the tides of Water can help you attune to change. The unpredictable nature of the waves and tides can be overwhelming however, and it's for this reason that Water brings powerful emotions to the surface, where they can be purged. Working with Water in your daily magic rituals can restore your spirit, increase your sensitivity, awareness and receptivity, and gently renew your faith in the flow of the Universe.

Astrologically, Water is associated with the feeling principle and function, representing the emotional realm. Its primary motivating force is deep yearnings. It is characterised by emotional depths, compassion and perceptions. Water signs are sensitive, experiencing life through their feelings. Attuned to delicate nuances, they can be dependent and vulnerable, often misinterpreting signals through the bias of their own feelings. When the intuitive function is working well, Watery signs can access an inner level of knowing that goes beyond the five physical senses.

Water is a paradoxical element and represents integration, dependence, merging, blending and union. Cancer represents personal development, Scorpio represents interpersonal development, and Pisces represents transpersonal development. The Water signs, living in the fluid world of emotion and feeling, express themselves in these differing ways: Cancer, through a great nurturing compassion, especially in home and family affairs; Scorpio, through its enormous sexual intensity and capacity, and its fascination for, and immersion in, the ultimate forces of life and death; and Pisces, through its acute sensitivity to the environment and its strongly developed depth of subconscious Universal undercurrents. The Water signs are feminine in polarity, introverted in expression.

Water signs are empathetic, attuned to others' feelings, and reflect the world around them as a reaction to how they feel. They experience the world subjectively. Water knows no boundaries and locates itself in the past, giving it a strong sense of memory and past experience. Often vulnerable to and overwhelmed by their emotions, their most appropriate outlets are expressed spiritually and artistically, or alternatively, to withdraw, hide, protect, deny, escape or defend.

Water, symbolic of the 'Great Mother', is the fountain of life and the source of all things, associated with birth, transformation, purification and movement. Deep, purifying and cleansing, it can symbolise the unending cascade of spiritual energy. But this movement can have its downside: although on the surface Water signs may appear calm, docile and placid, underneath there can be restlessness and deeper motivations brewing, for like the ocean, Watery people have many cross-currents. They are fearful of any form of confinement, and can therefore be extremely secretive about their true intentions or emotional undercurrents, making them at once enigmatic and mysterious.

As the element suggests, Water is sometimes turbulent, sometimes flowing, sometimes deep and murky, merges with its surroundings, and almost always fluid. Psychic, penetrative and intuitive, Water signs rely on instincts rather than logic. Acutely aware of the pain, feelings, suffering and thoughts of others, they are extremely sympathetic and will often put others' needs ahead of their own. Indeed, Water signs have an immense insight into human nature, making it hard for others to 'hide' around them; they dig, probe and 'feel' around to get to secrets and hidden matters. Although inherently private, Water signs can always be counted on for emotional support, sound advice and a receptive ear. Given that their self-expression is quite subtle, truly knowing a Water sign often involves a long but worthwhile learning process. Whether a nurturing Cancerian, intense Scorpio or an empathetic Piscean, Water signs are complex, deep, introspective and anything but frivolous. While Water types can be moody, changeable, over-sensitive and irritable, they can also be affectionate, playful, humorous and loyal.

The Water element is connection-seeking, fluid, and paradoxically powerful yet powerless, representing the strongest and weakest traits of the human experience, moves around obstacles, is chaotic by nature, has a sense of oneness, is life-giving and life-sustaining, purifying, rebirthing, feels 'in the moment', is wise and understanding on deeper levels, is boundless, aroused by empathy and passion, is never the same, feels others' feelings, can be a curse or a blessing, absorbs feelings and can lose itself in its response, can operate out of others' feelings, is generally unconditional, is creative, past-dwelling, nurturing, sensuous, surrendering and sacrificing, has depth of self, has emotional integrity, contains itself or allows its feelings to gush forth depending on the situation, can idealise suffering, shies from the mundane world, is relentless, eroding, nostalgic and sentimental, and has a great capacity for depth in union. Watery temperaments have an innate capacity for sympathy, protectiveness, romance, empathy, intuition, psychic insights and sensitivity, but can be subject to secrecy, and can suffer mysterious, unfathomable moods. They can also be hidden, escapist, evasive, dependent, manipulative, 'slippery' and elusive.

The Water element puts a strong emphasis on relationships and they are compassionate and responsive to others' needs, especially if Cancer or Pisces predominate. Scorpio is a little less subtle than the other two, being ruled by Pluto and having a tendency towards more hidden, penetrative and occasionally explosive behaviour; passion and intensity are also Scorpio traits which the other two express much more gently.

Overall, Water is the cleansing, purifying element, necessary for all life. It is the major component of the human body and is associated with our lymph systems. In the form of rain, it nourishes the Earth, promoting and enabling fertility and growth. Water is formless and meandering, and it connects, enters and merges, while still retaining its own essence. It needs the freedom to flow and like the tides, it has its own behaviours and rhythms. Sensitive to stimuli, it is highly receptive, absorbing that which comes into contact with it, and often encompasses or envelopes those things. Self-contained and protective, Watery types are able to experience the contentment of simply being, continually replenishing themselves from their inner reservoirs. These types are flowing, and oriented towards forming connections and blending with their surroundings. Highly instinctive and feeling, they are attuned to unseen realms, and possess a psychic sensitivity which enables them to excel at nonverbal communication and to hear and receive unspoken emotions. They are also imaginative, dedicated to their ideals, introspective and creative. Although some Watery types may not consider themselves religious, they have a heightened sensitivity to spiritual disciplines and forces, and so are naturally drawn to these areas by their very natures.

Water is encouraged to experience emotions without repressing or being overwhelmed by them, achieve inner emotional security, and to handle intuitive and psychic sensitivities adeptly, that is, without becoming engulfed by them and through being both open and self-protective.

Positive Water Qualities ★ Empathic, feeling-oriented, flexible, compassionate, sensitive, responsive, deep, intuitive, receptive, nurturing, adaptable, caring, devoted, self-contained, retentive, protective, attuned to the unseen, imaginative, private, introspective, idealistic, flowing, understanding, resourceful, spiritual, psychically aware

Negative Water Qualities ★ Secretive, wallowing, evasive, closed, cynical, overly subjective, brooding, self-absorbed, oversensitive, disillusioned, elusive, overly emotional, passive, waterlogged, clingy to past, moody, gullible, self-pitying, overwhelmed, inaccessible, hidden, manipulative, resigned, withholding, timid, expect too much, irrational, muddled thinking, directionless, devitalised by fears which focus on negatives, takes everything personally, blaming, indecisive, insecure, vindictive, unrealistic, confused, dependent/co-dependent, symbiotic, compulsive, drifting, regressive, impressionable

THE ARCHANGEL OF WATER ★ GABRIEL

An archangel is an angel of greater than ordinary rank. They possess a stronger, more powerful essence than the guardian angels, through overseeing and guiding the other angels who are said to be with us here on Earth. The word 'angel' derives from the Greek word *angelos* meaning 'messenger'. To humans, angels are often seen as bringers as all sorts of messages. Angels in all their forms are believed to bring the message of 'spirit' into matter, carrying the blueprints of creation and the Source from the Divine into the manifest world. Angels are not and never have been human; they, like fairies and nature spirits, are part of a different evolutionary pattern – but they do appear to us in human form (usually with wings) because that is what we understand. An angel can be in many different places at once, and with the same intensity and concentration, and wish for us to be aware of them and benefit from them.

There are said to be three categories of angels in the cosmos, each with three subdivisions *. 'Angel' is the generic term and also relates specifically to those closest to the physical. Similarly, archangel may be taken to mean any of the higher orders, and indeed signifies the order just above ordinary 'angel'. Found in a number of religious traditions, the word 'archangel' itself is usually associated with the Abrahamic religions. The word archangel is of Greek origin, and means literally 'chief angel'. All archangels end with the 'el' suffix, 'el' meaning 'in God' and the first part of the name meaning what each individual Angel specialises in. The archangel who rules your sign will be the one with whom you most resonate. The astrological sign is an energy signature, a matrix of a specific stellar pattern that will subtly affect and influence you. Although there are many associations for the great archangels of the Universe, we must keep in mind there is great overlapping in their duties and guidance. For example, we may say that one is for healing and another for protection, but they can all perform the functions of the others, and each has only areas of greater focus and responsibilities. Four of the multitude of archangelic beings work intimately with the Earth. These are Raphael (Air), Michael (Fire), Gabriel (Water) and Uriel (Earth). Associated with each of these archangels are one of the four elements, specific colours, one of the four directions or quarters of the Earth, three signs of the zodiac, and a variety of other energies and powers. Understanding these associations and considering them in relation to our own paths, can help us determine with which of them we are more likely to resonate. Your sign, being of the Water element, vibrates to the essence of Gabriel.

* The first sphere, the *Heavenly Counsellors*, comprises Seraphim, Cherubim and Thrones. The second sphere, the *Heavenly Governors*, comprises Dominions, Virtues and Powers. The third sphere, the *Heavenly Messengers*, comprises Principalities, Archangels and Angels. Of course, all such classifications are a human construct, a way of placing order upon the unknowable and allowing us to perceive something about which we have no words to express. However, as long as we think of angelic hierarchies as a way of working with celestials, of remembering important attributes, and we are able to imagine and experience these beings, this order of angels will prove useful to those wishing to draw upon their messages and assistance.

★ ARCHANGEL GABRIEL'S ASSOCIATIONS ★

Element of Water
The Western quarter of the Earth
The winter season
The colours emerald, silver and sea green
The crystals opal, fluorite and moonstone
The astrological signs of Cancer, Scorpio and Pisces

Gabriel, meaning "Strength of God" or "The Divine is my strength," is known as the messenger and can help us to find our true soul's purpose. As archangel of the Moon and ruler of dreams, Gabriel is chief archangel of the night and the alter ego of Michael, the Sun archangel. Some consider Gabriel a feminine energy. The archangel of life, hope, truth, astral travel, unconscious wisdom, illumination and love, he inspires and motivates artists and communicators, and delivers important prophetic messages to people. He guards the sacred places of the world and the sacred waters of life. Gabriel provides intuitive teaching, guidance, mystical experiences, inspiration and enlightenment of spiritual duties, including awakening within us a greater understanding of dreams. He can be called upon when you are feeling alone, afraid or vulnerable. Gabriel is said to be the angel who chooses the souls to be born and cares for them in the womb. He is also an angel of death, but a gentle one, bringing release from sorrow and pain.

SCORPIO'S ZODIAC ARCHANGEL ★ RAZIEL

Additionally, each sign is associated with a particular archangel. Such knowledge can help you to build up a relationship with these beings, based upon your strengths and needs. However, no link is rigid, and as you work with angels you will come to develop your own affinities. When invoking a specific archangel, a useful ritual to draw them closer is to light a candle in that angel's colour, burn some oil or incense of its scent, and hold the appropriate crystal while focusing on what you are needing guidance on.

YOUR ARCHANGEL ★ Raziel means 'secret of God' and he is lord of the mysteries of life. He awakens the spirit so that it can comprehend things which cannot be understood by the intellect. The insights of Raziel run deep and can be life-changing and difficult to express or explain to others, but ultimately these insights can bring about profound transformation. Raziel's gifts include self-awareness, release of obsessions, inner peace and harmony, and the clearing away of mental chatter to make way for true knowing.

SCENT/OIL ★ Neroli

CANDLE COLOUR ★ Indigo

CRYSTAL ★ Garnet or electric blue obsidian

THE DEVIC REALMS & WATER ★ WEST: REALM OF THE UNDINES

"Through magick we do conjure the Elements, evoking unto us the special properties of the Life-force for our learning and our coming-into-light. And yet are there secret paths of knowledge that have fallen from the minds of men ... For the way of Magick is a path to sacred knowledge, of reverence and humility - and the world is a wondrous place. Yet how many amongst us have fathomed these depths?"
***Merlin's Book of Magick and Enchantment*,
Nevill Drury**

Deva is a Sanskrit word that means 'shining one'. Devas are the life force within nature, and there are four devic realms - Fire, Earth, Air and Water - which contain ethereal elemental spirits or sprites. Elementals are the building blocks of nature, and close to being true energy and consciousness. The four elements correspond to four different states of matter: energy/transmutation (Fire), gas (Air), liquid (Water) and solid (Earth), which are linked to the four human states of consciousness: inspiration, thought, feeling and practicality. There are four spirits, or elementals, which reside in the devic realms, associated with each element. People have been painting pictures, telling stories and writing about these devic realms for hundreds of years, albeit sometimes through disguised mediums such as fairy tales or children's fantasy stories like Tolkien's *Lord of* *the Rings*. The power of the natural world is easily observed and since ancient times primal forces have been ascribed to various spirit beings. Belief in nature spirits is of such ancient origin and is Universal; cultures everywhere have names or words to describe them. In the sixteenth century, a famous Swiss physician, alchemist and mystic called Paracelsus * defined these beings as 'Elementals', classifying them according to the element of nature they inhabit. There are four main levels of elemental beings: Gnomes (Earth), Undines (Water), Sylphs (Air), and Salamanders (Fire). The fifth element of Ether is the element from which came forth the other four, and Ether, or Spirit, has never been defined in any particular category, and encompasses the aspects and beings of all the other elements.

Elementals are usually benevolent guardian beings or spirits that look after nature's secrets and treasures in whatever part of the natural realm they occupy. They can only be seen or 'felt' by those possessing heightened psychic abilities, yet they can be summoned by those practising alchemy, spells and magic in order to harness the forces of nature for their own particular intentions. In our modern lives, it may seem as though this magic doesn't exist, but the truth is that most of us are simply less in touch with it than ever before. The consequence of this is that we are destroying vast areas of land, polluting waters, creating toxic landscapes, and disrespecting the laws of nature, which often whisper their messages softly. It is therefore important for us to look at the beauty that surrounds us with true appreciation and genuine regard, and to open ourselves up to the magic resides within it. The four devic realms can teach us much about nature; they act as custodians for the four elements, and learning to work with them is a way of attuning to all the energies and beings of nature. Elementals are four-dimensional, and have nothing to obstruct their movements. Therefore, they move as easily through matter as we do through air and space. They do require some contact with humans for their own evolution. Helping to direct them is an overseer, traditionally called the King of that element, and an archangel. Each of these elements is affiliated with one of the four directions and each elemental spirit embodies its own special energy. If you wish to re-connect and re-harmonise yourself by working with nature and its messages and lessons, you could begin by learning a little about your element's realm: Your element is Water, which is connected with the West direction and the realm of the Undines.

* Paracelsus is considered the most original medical thinker of the sixteenth century. His belief in supernatural beings, intuition and the invisible causes of illness helped him discover hydrogen and nitrogen. Paracelsus believed that "Elementals are unlike pure spirits for they are mortal, but they are not like man for they have no soul."

★ UNDINES ★

Undine is from the Latin *unda*, meaning 'wave', and therefore these spirits are said to control the waters of the Earth. Undines are perhaps the best known of the four elementals as they appear frequently in stories and legends. Usually female nymph-like beings, they are beautiful, eager to tempt, and enjoy associating with humans. They like to lure with their musical enchantments, creating sweet, intoxicating melodies with their harps, or singing pure, uplifting songs for those who are still and near enough to listen. Found wherever there is a natural source of water, the undines are responsible for the vitality within liquids and they also work with plants that grow underwater. All water upon our planet - rain, rivers, oceans, lakes, et cetera - has immense undine activity. Undines, like the gnomes, are subject to mortality, but they are more enduring. They are dependent upon humans for growth, and as we evolve, so do they.

One of the most famous of the Water elementals is the Lady of the Lake who features in the legends of King Arthur. This undine beauty rose from her lake to present Arthur with the sword Excalibur and captured the hearts of many of the Knights of the Round Table. The undines govern the realm of autumn and Water, the west, and the Cups in the Tarot deck. In many religions, water symbolises the initiation through baptism in the 'waters of life'. In ancient times all great rivers were considered holy and sacred, without which nothing could prosper; springs, wells, ponds, pools and fountains were regarded as holy places where great healing properties and energies could be found and prophecies foretold.

The Undines work to maintain the astral body of humans and to stimulate our feeling nature. This is associated with heightened psychic functions as well as emotional ones. Theirs is an energy of intuition, creation and birth. Undines guard and carry the secrets of the Dreamtime, inner visions, emotions, feelings and journeys.

Water is the spring well of life, and these beings are essential to our finding that spring well within. Essential to the gifts of healing, purification and empathy, they work with humans to help us discover both our inner and outer beauty. Human beings are made of around 75 per cent water, which acts as a channel or stream for all physical and chemical changes to occur; and the same percentage again is echoed by our planet's water composition - three quarters of the Earth's surface is covered by seas, rivers and oceans, which are governed by the Moon, which provides a natural rhythmical rulership over planetary phenomena. Folklore says that water gives to us what we give to it. The undines, who dwell in the Watery realms, will indeed do the same. The King of Water is Llyr or Niksa, its archangel is Gabriel, its magickal tool is the Cup (which calls down the spirits into form), and its sacred ceremonial stones are Amethyst, Moonstone and Pearl.

INVOKING THE WATER DEVAS

Water represents flow and change – in many myths crossing a stream signifies a shift in consciousness, all cultures regard water as the biggest life-giving source, and baptism is a rite of passage in some religions. Water is mysterious, moody and changeable. Water devas embody all of these attributes and most are hauntingly beautiful. Water can be a tricky medium to work with, but overall they help to connect you with the wellsprings of your feelings, bringing sympathy, empathy and the bonds of human love. If you are feeling raw, lonely, sad, uncared for or buffeted by life, ask the water devas for their help. Undines will give you blessings when you are going into any situation that requires deep emotional strength. They can be found in any body of water, the tides and rains, in mists and in fogs, and are purifying, healing and cleansing.

THE WEST DIRECTION'S CORRESPONDENCES

If you wish to work more with your particular element and direction, the following may help propel your wishes and magical journey:

Time of Day ★ Sunset
Polarity ★ Female, negative
Exhortation ★ To know
Musical Instruments ★ Strings, bells
Colours ★ Blue, green
Season ★ Autumn
Magical Instrument ★ Cup
Altar Symbol ★ Chalice
Communion Symbol ★ Wine, water
Archangel ★ Gabriel
Human Sense ★ Taste
Art Forms ★ Music, song
Animals ★ Fish, whales
Mythical Beast ★ Sea serpent
Magical Arts ★ Healing

Guide Forms ★ Moon, water goddess
Meditation ★ The ocean, rivers
Images & Themes ★ Lakes, pools, living underwater, healing, calm, the setting Sun

HOW YOU CAN GET IN TOUCH WITH YOUR WATER ENERGY

"Water flows on and on ... It does not shrink from any dangerous spot nor from any plunge, and nothing can make it lose its own essential nature. It remains true to itself under all conditions."
I Ching, hexagram 29, k'an/k'an

★ Use Water energy when making wishes around the following: Healing, spiritual and psychic development, relationship harmony, emotional issues, psychosomatic illnesses, dreams and trust

★ Spend time in and around water - oceans, rivers, streams, lakes, waterfalls

★ Install a water fountain in the space in which you spend the most time

★ Carry a small spray bottle of water with you and spritz yourself with it throughout the day

★ Float in the water - surrender to its unerring support and let it keep you afloat

★ Research, make and use gem (crystal) essences

★ Try to take a bath rather than a shower; you can linger for longer, and even meditate more effectively, in a still bath

★ Engage in water sports (not too extreme though, unless you're a Scorpio!), such as water skiing, swimming, kayaking, surfing, yachting, scuba diving, canoeing, sailing, or water volleyball

★ Drink lots of water

★ Meditate on the Cups suit in the Tarot (the Cups suit represents the Water element)

★ Eat watery, water-based foods, such as brothy soups, watermelon and juicy fruits

★ Purify and cleanse your body occasionally, by undertaking a day-long fast / liquid diet

★ Sleep on a waterbed

★ Green-coloured crystals will activate your connection with the element of Water and enhance hope, healing, love and creativity.

★ Join an emotional support group - or facilitate one

★ Install a water fountain in your home, garden or office - water features, placed strategically, are believed in Feng Shui tradition to attract certain desired things into your environment and experience

★ Wear and surround yourself with the colours blue, silver and green

★ Decorate your home or office with soothing watery images, such as scenic lakes, panoramic beach photographs, ocean-side postcards

★ Listen and meditate to ocean waves and bubbling brook sounds on an audio system

★ Walk in the rain, jump in puddles

★ Visit a spa regularly, and indulge in saunas and Jacuzzis - better still, install one in your home

★ Learn and practice graceful, flowing forms of movement, such as Tai Chi

★ Express your emotions fearlessly; try to use them as your ally

★ Nurture others and inspire them to nurture themselves

★ Express your feelings through art, poetry and drama

★ Cultivate a spiritual practice

★ Develop your counselling and listening skills so you can help others - and yourself!

★ Meditate regularly. Embrace your inner silence, peace and spiritual essence

★ When working with the Water element in magical practice, stand at the West quarter of your magical space, as the West is its domain, and invite its living essence into your 'circle'

★ Use chalices, bowls, crystals, blue or silver items, and cauldrons to represent your element. If you are fortunate enough to live near the ocean, its tides can be a great energising force that evokes dramatic magical transformations. When the tide goes out, visualise your worries being drawn away. High tide is an optimum time to focus on wish magic, and as the waves move in closer, imagine your dreams coming towards you. Spells cast on a riverbank or near a spring will also be empowered by the moving energy of Water

★ The best days on which to employ Water magic are Monday, ruled by the Moon, and Friday, ruled by the planet of love Venus

★ Water spirits are also known as sea nymphs, naiads, undines or sprites. They are responsible for the cleansing, refreshing and clearing of our spirits, so Water signs would be wise to adopt one (or all) as their very own spirit guide!

YOUR MODE ★ FIXED

Each sign belongs to one of the three quadruplicities, Cardinal, Fixed and Mutable. If we closely examine the Earth's yearly cycle, we can form a very accurate picture of the nature of these quadruplicities, for they correspond directly with the manifestation of the seasons. Each season has three months: the first month brings the new phase of the cycle, the second month brings a concentration of the season's energy to its fullest expression, and the third month represents the transition from the current season to the next one. The astrological quadruplicities represent the three basic qualities in all life: creation (Cardinal), perseveration (Fixed) and destruction (Mutable). Everything that is born, from a period of time to a human being, experiences a life and then dies. In this context, death can be taken to mean that the form of the energy changes; but the energy itself can never be annihilated, for form is mortal, whereas essence is immortal.

The Fixed mode covers the signs Taurus, Leo, Scorpio and Aquarius, and is the most determined and unshakable of the three qualities. The positive side of the Fixed signs is stability. You are the builders, whether of Earthly creations (Taurus), artistic endeavours (Leo), occult powers (Scorpio), or world-changing visions and ideas (Aquarius).

The Fixed mode signifies the manifestation of purpose and its subjects are concerned with ownership, concentration, stability, fixation, and working with a cool head and calm demeanour under pressure. The Fixed quality is associated with stabilisation, depth, preservation, persistence, loyalty and strength of will. You operate with purpose, dedication, self-reliance and determination, happy to forge ahead, through calmly working away, until you have achieved your ultimate goals. Fixed signs are a fearsome, formidable and quietly forceful group, able to follow their will and demonstrate fixity, often to the point of being stubborn, win-at-all-costs and wilful. Rarely are you distracted in your quests, for you have the ability to stay on firm course and track until a project's end. You are enduring, deliberate, steady and stable, but may be rigid and single-minded. You have a strong sense of routine, ritual and control. You work hard to consolidate and preserve the things that matter to you, but you can also be inflexible and resistant to change. You stick with situations even when they are outworn, uphold the status quo, and are loyal and dependable, but hate to give in and may lack spontaneity. Your energy and nature is powerful, robust, concrete, limited, set in its ways, purposeful, conscientious, slow, consistent, enduring, stubborn, innately cautious, rigid, unimpulsive, opinionated, unchanging, and you are generally strong in opinions, habits, likes and dislikes. Not easily distracted, you always keep your eyes on the prize, but you have a tendency to brood or to become stuck in a rut. You also project an image of strength as an effective shield against your considerable vulnerability. The Fixed mode indicates the midpoints of the seasons, which are very strong ritualistic times and 'fixed points', signifying points of power in the zodiac. Because Fixed signs fall in the middle of the season, this term signifies that the season is firmly established - fixed - by the time the Sun enters these signs.

Scorpio is the most fixed in its emotions and beliefs of the Fixed signs, and is unshakable and immovable in the face of opposition or conflict. Your Fixed quality is firm and resolute and you would sooner put your life on the line than give away your power or back down in the name of your convictions.

YOUR RULING PLANET ★ PLUTO

The Powerful Undercover Agent of Change, Transformation & Regeneration

Planetary Meditation
I am my Earth (my body),
and my Sky (my transcendence)
I am my Sun (my spirit),
and my Moon (my soul)
I am my Venus (my pleasure),
and my Jupiter (my faith)
I am my Mars (my courage),
and my Saturn (my lessons)
I am my Mercury (my thoughts),
and my Uranus (my truth)
I am my Neptune (my dreams),
and my Pluto (my transformation)

Each planet has its own distinctive and original meaning which, according to its position in the zodiac, combines with the qualities that are inherent in each of the twelve astrological signs. If a planet is your sign's ruler, however, it exerts a significant influence upon your life, regardless of its birth chart or zodiacal position.

Errant ★ Associated with Death, Rebirth, Transformation, Elimination, Eruptive Change
★ 248 Year Cycle

★ KEY WORDS ★

Regeneration, Transformation, Power, Death, Rebirth, Renewal, Wealth, Riches, Yearning, Elimination, Control, Metamorphism, Eruption, Compulsion, Passion, Penetration, Insight, Self-mastery, Occult, Hidden Secrets, Obsession, Transmutation, Charisma, Magnetism, Subversion, Depth, Darkness, Psychoanalysis, Research, Sex

★ KEY CONCEPTS ★

★ Elimination ★
★ The Reformer, the Purger by Fire ★
★ The Passage to the Other Side ★
★ Changing from One State to Another ★
★ Mining, Excavation & Archaeology ★
★ Wills, Legacies & Taxes ★
★ The Redeemer, the Master Builder ★
★ The Beginning & the End ★
★ Transmutation of Energy ★
★ Psychiatry, Unlocking the Unconscious ★
★ Investigation, Research, Espionage ★
★ Regenerative Principles of Death ★
★ The Annihilator, the Eliminator, the Transformer ★
★ Renewal of the Life-Force, Redemption ★

Basic Energy & Magic ★ Transformation, Personal Power

Colours ★ Dark Reds, Dark Purple, Magenta, Violet

Gems/Minerals ★ Jade, Pearl, Beryl, Smoky Quartz, Black Obsidian, Jet, Kunzite

Metal ★ Plutonium

Flowers ★ Narcissus, Daffodil

Tree ★ Cypress

Zodiacal Influences ★ Rules Scorpio; Exalted in Aquarius; Detriment Taurus; Fall Leo

Discovered in 1930, Pluto is the most distant known planet, and hence the most mysterious. A small, solid body, it may once have been a satellite of its neighbour Neptune. Pluto is so far from the Earth and its cycle so long - 248 years - that its influence is seen as largely impersonal and having more of a mass, or generational, effect * (unless it is prominently placed in a birth chart). Being the slowest moving of all the planets, and as one of the outer planets, its influence applies more to generations and large groups of people, and is less relevant to individuals. Accordingly, only the house placings of Pluto can help decipher the individual psyche.

For eighteen years before it was discovered, Pluto was called planet X, a factor which was known to exist but could not be found. The name Pluto was apparently proposed by an 11-year-old girl who was thinking of the Disney dog.

Pluto, or Hades as he was known to the Greeks, was the ruler of the dead and the underworld. He was the son of Saturn and brother of Jupiter and Neptune. Jupiter came to rule the skies and Neptune inherited power over the oceans, leaving Pluto to rule the underworld. The ancients associated Pluto with wealth and riches because underground gold and other precious stones and minerals were said to dwell in his domain and therefore to be in his custody. Greek mythology thus depicted Pluto as the god of wealth and buried treasure, and the word 'plutocracy', which refers to a government ruled by a group of rich men, derives its title from Pluto. But when one's life is unbalanced and there is a total and absolute focus on the attainment of material wealth without the development of the spiritual wealth inside, Pluto can see to it that the slate is wiped clean, and in doing so, can have devastating effects on the tides of fortune.

A commonly used glyph (or symbol) for Pluto is monogram P with a horizontal line extending out under the upper semi-circle of the P. This is simply a combination of the first two initials of Percival Lowell, the astronomer whose calculations led to Pluto's discovery.

Another glyph of more recent origin for Pluto is three-fold: the circle of spirit sits inside the crescent of soul atop the cross of matter. The circle is detached from the semi-circle and hovering above it, appearing to rise up. Its esoteric meanings have very ancient roots, as it encapsulates the whole process and concept of involution and evolution. It symbolises that the energy of the spirit descends through the soul in order that continuously changing finite forms of concretised energy may manifest on the Earthly plane, signifying involution. The force of regeneration is illustrated by the reverse process: the interactions of an individual within her environment evokes an awakening of consciousness within her soul, resulting in both personal and collective evolution. The release of this crystallised spiritual energy from the matter is then cleansed by the soul and transformed into the ether (or spirit) which is then re-sent down through the soul to energise herself and the Earth, demonstrating the metamorphosis and renewal that is inherent within Pluto. (The disc rising from the crescent above the cross can also been described as an egg of rebirth and transformation rising from the cup of the Earth.)

Although it is small and far-away, Pluto has a symbolically potent effect in our birth charts. Pluto rules intense energy and describes the areas in which you consciously or unconsciously seek to exercise power or control. It reveals the areas in which you must gain the deepest level of understanding. But it can also reveal contradictions in yourself. Pluto can present us with maddening paradoxes: it is both an annihilator and transformer, constructive and destructive, a psychiatric healer and brainwashing propagandist, self-destructive and self-empowering, uses and misuses power, embodies mass communication and mass hysteria, gives rise to intense hatred and consuming love, and evokes both toxic build-ups and swift disposal. Its contradiction can be best illustrated by the concept that its era of discovery gave us the blessings of nuclear power but the curse of the atomic bomb.

Pluto tells us about our urge for transformation, penetration, power, self-mastery and how we access deep insights. Associated with renewal and rebirth, Pluto represents endings and new beginnings, as well as spiritual growth and transformative powers. It rules the inevitable changes that take place in the cycles of life, from birth to death, and is a transmutational energy, governing intense forces and signifying those areas in which you seek to exercise control. Pluto marks the known border of our Solar system and in astrology this strengthens its position as a planet of endings and beginnings, albeit sometimes hidden or disguised.

Indeed, Pluto's energy can be linked to many analogies and metaphors: a snake shedding its skin to allow its new self to emerge, the caterpillar morphing into a butterfly, autumn leaves decomposing so that a tree may grow from the resultant nutrients generated in the soil. In its role as the transformer, it brings about the end of one form so that another form may be brought to life. This sometimes requires total disintegration in order to rebuild from scratch. Pluto represents the change within - the earthquake, the volcano and the powerful seed. But first we must understand the nature of crisis, in that it is not always the disaster it may seem and often offers opportunity for upward growth. In fact, the Chinese character is the same for both words: crisis = opportunity.

Pluto rules the psychological and subconscious aspects of life, especially obsessions and compulsions, as well as phobias, fears, and feelings of alienation, separation and isolation. Cold, icy, dark Pluto is indeed distant and enigmatic. He embodies the drive to confront all that is darkest and deepest in the psyche. He rules anything that is toxic, contaminating and polluting - both inner and outer - and is the repository of all things that are deemed unacceptable or 'evil'. One of Pluto's primary functions is to transform our egos through facing ourselves, for when we do confront the secrets and complexities of our deepest recesses, we can free ourselves from the ball and chains we did not even realise we were wearing. Pluto rattles the skeletons in our closets, and challenges the inner demons to a fight so that we are forced to examine ourselves. And so it is Pluto's job to ensure that we confront our darker aspects. He will teach us that we must grow whether we wish to or not. Pluto knows that once our unconscious garbage is cleaned away then healthy new growth can start.

Pluto illustrates the extremes which exist in human nature. But he also provides the tools with which you can achieve transcendence from potentially imprisoning states of mind, for as a potent eliminator and purger, he will provide you with the loofah and bucket of water to slough away all that dirt and grime. Pluto is a master of resilience, and will help you unlock the door to self-transformation.

The sign and house that Pluto occupies in your birth chart reveals your intuitive natures and powers, how you use them, and in which area of your life you will exert them. It describes where and in what form a compulsive attitude may exist. It also shows, however, the aspects of yourself that you keep hidden from view - your compulsions, obsessions, and your self-destructive streak. But it has much to offer those who are prepared to explore places where angels fear to tread. Used wisely, Pluto can transmute dark experiences into a potent, overcoming force. The house Pluto resides in shows in what areas Plutonian qualities manifest themselves, the way in which you use your personal power and the activities that can offer an avenue for personal growth. Pluto will be forceful if necessary, and it is important to remember that he is involved in life, death and decay, so his lessons will not always be easy to bear. But to confront them, one will come face-to-face with his own potential for intense self-awareness and new life. Pluto also concerns itself with the use, abuse and misuse of power, so it is up to the individual how this potent force will be used in their expressions and behaviours. When you are feeling empowered, it could mean that Pluto is operating positively.

Pluto is the higher octave of Mars. While Mars brings the energy, Pluto directs this energy where it is needed for spiritual growth, metamorphosis and enlightenment. Mars is the aggressive force, while Pluto is the destructive Fire whose power is far mightier than the comparatively small sword Mars wields. Mars manifests itself in short, sometimes violent bursts of energy and exhausts itself, burning out quickly. Pluto, however, explodes like a bomb but his planning was done in secret and its effects much more long-lasting. Pluto often unleashes the underground turbulence of years of repressed feelings that have been left to simmer far too long. But Pluto serves in a dual capacity as both eliminator and renewer. His Fire may destroy all in its path, but it is all made worthwhile by the new life that springs up once the embers have turned to ash. Pluto stands for transcendence, and death and destruction in a broad sense mean just that - transcending through leaving behind a lower level of consciousness in order to assume a higher one; therefore, Pluto does not fear death for it knows instinctively that energy cannot be created nor destroyed, it just shifts into different forms. To deal with death in physical terms, some ancient and modern religions and philosophies have given this shift of body, spirit and soul a name. Depending on the specific culture, he has been endowed with a number of personas. An interesting example of this is that Pluto's kingdom has been called *Abaddon*, meaning 'destruction' and *Sheol*, meaning 'cave', by the Hebrews. Both terms conjure up Pluto-inspired concepts, such as underground, hidden and ruin.

Pluto reveals not only our purpose and powers of regeneration, but our style of evolutionary growth, destruction and renewal, and our interest or otherwise in the occult, black magic, release, purging, catharsis, resurrection, metamorphism, the underworld, obsessions, corruption and hidden powers.

Pluto is the 'journey to empowerment', showing the path from unresolved pain into empowerment and freedom. Pluto ruled over the underworld; nobody was ever known to have escaped transportation to his land of death beyond the river Styx. As lord of the underworld, Pluto invariably shows up on everyone's doorstep at some stage in life, and his visit will alter the course of your life forever. The underworld or inner world of your psyche often contains areas of unhealed grief, loss, pain or brokenness. By our very natures, and as a kind of self-protective survival mechanism, we tend to repress trauma, grief, loss, unresolved painful feelings or potentially damaging hidden secrets. All that is repressed is the domain of Pluto. Chaos, drama and betrayal can all ensue as a result of stored emotions. Though Pluto often puts us through this process of initiation by imposing loss, pain, grief and darkness, he also symbolises the rising up again through resurrection. And herein lies his greatest power: rebirth. The Plutonian descent is inevitably linked with a subsequent resurfacing and re-emergence.

Hades, who is associated with Pluto, is the ancient Greek word for 'underworld', and it actually meant 'unseen' or 'invisible', and that which is hidden will be exposed when you are confronted with Pluto. Pluto does have an early warning system however, in the form of gut feelings, niggling doubts, hunches, or worrisome imaginings of the mind.

Pluto is like an astrological compost heap: breaking down still-living matter and transforming it into a different form, from which will spring new life, renewed hope and refreshed senses. Pluto's methodology isn't always pleasant, however; this force is responsible for the dramatic innovations in medicine which have been coming faster and faster since the official discovery of the planet showed us that humankind now has the power and mental capacity to apply this force, but Pluto also blows things to smithereens in order to destroy so that we may see the light. Tearing down old concepts, cherished memories, barriers, and smashing illusions and ignorance to pieces so that more useful structures can be erected on the ruins, is the nature of Pluto's game.

It is worth noting that one of the meanings of Pluto is 'wealth' or 'rich man'. Indeed, the underworld may be holding ground, supporting all you have repressed, but this under-ground is also full of untapped potential. Your unconscious self is the keeper of your buried or hidden treasures. Pluto is known for its ability to empower you to access these forces, calling you to realise your power, overcome your fears, and undertake challenges which promote daring and endurance. In fact, Pluto is the energy to call upon when you need to stop playing small and insignificant and take on your true, authentic role in life. This dark god's domain also dwells in the physical *underworld*, for under the Earth we will find precious stones, veins of gold, silver, iron, copper, tin, rare elements and minerals, and valuable oil - the very stuff that our economic structures are based upon. And our governments are set up partly to distribute but mainly to protect this economy. In this instance, Pluto can show his ruthless, cruel side. We have seen what happens when one person, leader or nation takes more than their fair share of the Earth's goodies at the expense of others. And even though money is only a medium of exchange with no intrinsic value, Pluto will counter that with, "Money is power." But it is not money itself that holds the power, it is what it represents. And the Plutonian mind understands this fully - and usually uses this underlying principle to manipulate others. What the Pluto-inspired soul really wants however, is the control that money can buy. It has been said that if you have something or someone right where you want them, it's a good idea to keep them there. Pluto knows precisely how to use money for this purpose.

To come to the point where you can reap Pluto's many rewards, you must be prepared to radically change your thinking. As Einstein so sagely put, "We can't solve our problems using the same mind that created them." Pluto can knock you for six, give you a harsh reality check, strip you bare and tear you down, but the pain associated with this dark planet, is not attributed to the planet itself - indeed, it is attributable to the pain you reinforce in your resistance to giving up the trappings of a false sense of security or comfort. If you are able to accept your suffering, to give yourself permission to mourn or grieve losses, to bring pain to the surface rather than sending it to the hidden recesses of the mind, if you can admit those dark and depressive parts of your character, you give yourself a much better chance to find redemption amid the chaos and suffering. Surrender is the key. Because Pluto wisely knows that many deaths constitute any life well lived, and for there to be a rebirth of something new and fresh, first there has to be a death.

Pluto is said to influence our creative potential, and allows us to purge and regenerate ourselves, and release our passionate self.

Pluto, the Roman ruler of the infernal regions, is the planet that tells us transformation is possible, pointing us in the direction in which we can experience regeneration and showing us how we can achieve it. It is connected with our urge for transformation, penetration, power, self-mastery, deep insights, powerful purpose, and evolutionary growth. People with a strong Pluto in their chart are attracted to mysteries and probe to get to the bottom of things, and can often be found in police work, scientific and medical research, paranormal studies and psychoanalytical work where an essential quality is the courage to face painful, disturbing or difficult truths. Pluto has a strong association with research, and those who are especially influenced by his rays are usually solitary creatures. This individual is rather distant, acutely aware, detached from worldly concerns, thrives on uncovering and extracting, and is deeply probing. Intense by nature, individuals with a prominent Pluto will tend to undertake careful, secretive planning, and are not at all daunted by doing this for long periods of time. Such a person is continually tearing down, disseminating and reassembling her psychological structure, and the drive to do so is entirely subconscious. This soul can be phenomenally powerful, as through doing this she not only develops the ability to steer the course of her own evolution, but can help bring about deep evolutionary transformations in others. Releasing blockages through conscious penetration, boring holes and diving into the deep end, Plutonian types make excellent psychiatrists, transcendental guides and psychic healers.

Pluto is associated with convicts, assassination, Hades, the devil, transformation, atomic energy, obsessions, cults, tyranny, wrecks, epidemics, mass atrocities, autopsies, cremation, monstrous, trade unions, dictators, kidnapping, evil, corruption, abattoirs, racketeers, carrion, ashes, vileness, wicked, fanatical, annihilation, power, mobs, volcanoes, bandits, underworld, gangsters, waste, phoenix, organised crime, purging, obscene, guillotine, crowds, havoc, terrorists, calamities, elimination, huge organisations, laser beams, abduction, victimisation, wreckers, black magic, compulsion, death, voodoo, defilement, bulk goods, vampires, demolition, demons, depravity, destruction, purgatory, wretched, obliteration, cesspools, fiendish, sewers, vast, maggots, vice, genocide, filth, hell, war, ambushes, horror, blowflies, pollution, mass murder, powerful cartels, vermin, control, catastrophes, clubs, lice, chasms, massacres, orgies, plagues, rats, plutonium, scorpions, septic tanks and violence. I'm sure you get the idea!

Upon Pluto-ruled Scorpios, this planet endows a sense of dynamism, mystery, power, magnetism, intensity, secretiveness, courage, perceptiveness, and yearnings to transform oneself. Too much Plutonian influence can make one suspicious, secretive, malicious, controlling, piercing, vengeful, explosive, manipulative, ruthless and power-hungry. More than any other planet, Pluto symbolises the miraculous ability of the human will to triumph over all odds, like the mythological Phoenix rising, reborn and renewed, from the ashes of the battleground. This above all else, encapsulates the essence of the Pluto-inspired Scorpio spirit. How will *you* use your phenomenally powerful Plutonian influence?

* It has been said that the distant planets are actually *more* powerful than the others as they take longer to orbit the Sun. As a result, these slower moving planets (Uranus, Neptune and Pluto) dwell in the zodiac constellations for longer periods of time, allowing them to leave a deeper and more indelible experience on the human psyche and experience than the swifter moving planets. In other words, their effect is thought to be more lingering.

YOUR HOUSE IN THE HOROSCOPE ★ THE EIGHTH HOUSE

The Eighth House is connected with shared resources, other people's values, sex, regeneration, inheritances, assorted other financial dealings such as tax, insurance and loans, and on a deeper level shows change, depth, transformation, renewal, death and rebirth and complexities, including spiritual values beyond the material world.

Analogy for the Eighth House:
"A caterpillar spends several weeks happily munching on leaves, occasionally shedding its skin as it grows into a bigger and stronger caterpillar. But eventually, it recognises the fact that it has reached its limits and can grow no more. If the caterpillar resists change, it will die, for life will be untenable in its present form.

But, paradoxically, in order to survive, it must volunteer for death. It must spin a shroud, and willingly relinquish life for the unknown. It has no idea, as its eyes close in sleep, consciousness slips away, and its bodily functions cease, whether Nature will keep faith. It only knows what must be done. It has no idea that weeks later, it will emerge into the daylight once again, reborn, metamorphosed, into a beautiful butterfly."

***Everyday Astrology: A Guide to Understanding Your Horoscope*, Jill Davies (1992)**

A house is one of the twelve sections dividing the terrestrial globe, viewed from a precise time and geographical place, into sectors from the poles to the horizon. The horoscope, or birth chart, is divided into these twelve sections called houses. Each house governs a different area or 'department' of life, such as relationships, career, leisure and even karma. The reason for this division of the Earth into houses can be understood when we consider that the Sun's rays affect us differently in the morning, at noon and at night, and also in summer and winter, and if we study the cause, we will readily observe that it is the angle at which the ray strikes us or the Earth which produces that difference in effect. Similarly, with the stellar rays, astrologers have observed that a child born at or near midday, when the Sun's rays strike the birthplace from the Tenth House, has an improved chance of public or career advancement in life than one born after sunset. By similar observations and tabulations, it has been found that the other planetary rays affect the various departments of life when their ray is projected through the other houses, and therefore each house is said to 'rule' or govern certain departments of the human life experience.

The Eighth House, ruled by Scorpio, is the house of sex, death and rebirth, shared resources, regeneration and transformation. It describes secret powers, money belonging to others, shared money, common property, investments, loss, how we deal with material loss, 'rising from the ashes', sharing, letting go, intense unions, attitudes towards growth and change, release, transcendence, elimination, our occult * tendencies, and our thoughts about the afterlife.

This house deals with the support you receive from other people, taxes, debt, gifts, insurance, legacies, joint resources (including any money you might receive from your partner), and addresses financial back-up as well as spiritual, emotional and physical support. It relates to all business transactions that involve other people's money, surgery, and anything that is hidden, such as anything within the occult realm. Strongly linked with monetary gain and of things inherited, these inheritances may be on the physical or psychic plane, including ancestral patterns and potential. As it governs death, it also deals with money connected with death, such as wills, legacies, gifts, property and estates. The Eighth House tells us about how we share and provide our finances and resources with others, allowing others access (e.g. to bank accounts, 'what's mine is yours').

As the house of sex and sexuality, it reveals intimacy, what can be gained by fusing with another, trust, the transferring of loyalties to outside of family, sharing on its deepest level, our powerlessness, helplessness and vulnerabilities, as well as opening ourselves up through being vulnerable, and where the ego dissolves and the self is surrendered. In the Eighth House we are indeed impelled to let go of our ego and abandon our separateness in order to merge with another, and to transcend our-selves. This merging almost always involves change, and change is only possible when we accept that one cycle must end before another can begin, in a new form. This house tells us that if we don't allow these 'secrets' to come to the surface and transform us for the better, they may engulf and ultimately destroy us.

Being the house of grief, it also shows us how and where we learn to love in the face of loss, e.g. through a death; love and loss are united in this house. It shows patterns of intimacy and loss, the uncovering of parts of ourselves, the entering into unions that change and transform us, where we most invest in a relationship, and at its highest level, the learning of self-mastery.

As the house of regeneration, it covers sex, birth, death, renewal, transmutation, intense emotions, legal matters, and metaphysics. Other exoteric and esoteric keywords include: Resources of others, sexuality, psychic matters, battles, the occult, and the path of discipleship. It describes your resourcefulness and resilience, as well as your abilities to develop and use your material assets and personal skills and talents in all joint ventures.

Although there is an emphasis on shared financial resources in this sphere, it also represents your capacity to become detached from material assets, and, paradoxically, what you can get from doing so. Indeed, in the Eighth House you can become detached; you no longer need to provide, and you can release your material possessions and attachments. You can transcend those nitty gritty mundane matters and connect to your innate power again; the ultimate Source. This goes some way to explaining the concept of inheritance, something this house governs. Inheritance and legacies are the things which we acquire without any effort on our part. Still, to many astrologers, many planets, difficult angles or afflictions in this house are not favourable to Earthly happiness.

The Eighth House is connected with the realm of sex and sexuality, sexual tastes and attitudes, deep interactions, secret powers, and personal magnetism. It also describes your response to death, divorce, separations and endings of any kind, capacity to rebirth and re-emerge from an ending, how easily you will surrender control or power, and how you try to manipulate others or try to avoid being controlled yourself. Planets in the Eighth House reflect the level of control and power you have over your own life.

This house discloses secrets of you or your family, gives information about legacies and inheritances, indicates the wealth of the household earner, and as a house of soul or endings, about the cause of one's death or nature of the death experience. It includes death as the relinquishing of physical forms in the process of change, and the afterlife, psychological transformation through internal processing or external work with a therapist, the worlds of the unknown and unseen, and ritual work.

The Eighth House also refers to money or property held in common with marriage or business partners, everything to do with finances and investments, discretionary money and its uses, negotiations with banks and other lending institutions, and wills and their contents.

The Eighth House is the house of sexual union and expression, the complex secrets of the Universe that are explored with the individual mind. There is a secretive aspect about this house, which is concerned with veiled wishes, power, criminal tendencies, complexes, compulsions, obsessions, secret undertakings and, from the health standpoint, the 'secret' or hidden parts of the body such as the sex organs.

If you can get in touch with these lessons, qualities and energies of the Eighth House and apply them in your own life and circumstances, you will be living in your highest expression and in the greatest alignment with your authentic self, and things should fall into place for you.

* The word 'occult' comes from the Latin *occultus*, which literally means 'the knowledge of the hidden'.

YOUR OPPOSITE SIGN ★ TAURUS
WHAT YOU CAN LEARN FROM THE BULL

If we look at the zodiac, we can see that it can be broadly divided into two hemispheres, this division being based on the natural division of the year by the two equinoxes. Astrologers often refer to the first six signs, the hemisphere in which the day predominates (the days being longer in the spring and summer months), as the Personal Sphere of Experience, and the second six signs, the hemisphere in which nights are longer, as the Social Sphere of Experience. These two halves of the zodiac perfectly balance and complement each other, and each individual 'personal' zodiac sign has something to teach its directly opposite 'social' zodiac sign.

To generalise, the signs of the personal sphere tend to experience life through a type of self-projection and self-interest which is often socially uncomplicated, unsophisticated or naïve. Their objective is to learn greater social awareness and thereby integrate themselves with the larger, more Universal human collective. On the other hand, the signs of the social sphere are prone to experience life through the use of their more developed social consciousness. In essence, the personal signs (Aries, Taurus, Gemini, Cancer, Leo, Virgo) usually provide stimulation and new energy to their environment, while the social, more Universal signs (Libra, Scorpio, Sagittarius, Capricorn, Aquarius, Pisces) provide experience, opportunities for wider expression, and give a more broad-minded approach and perspective to their surroundings.

Each sign in a pair seeks and is attracted to the qualities of its complementary opposing sign. Taurus wishes to cultivate the rejuvenated, transformative aspects of Scorpio, while Scorpio seeks the inner stability of the Bull. Taurus dwells within the realm of the collection of *personal* resources and talents, while her complementary opposite Scorpio resides in the realm of the collection of *social/shared* interactive resources and talents.

Although the word 'opposite' conjures up feelings of separateness and differences, the astrological polarities should not be seen as two signs in conflict with each other - their positive expression is to create a natural balance and equilibrium. Each sign has something to learn from its opposite, but also has a contribution to make towards the other sign's more evolved expression. The Second (Taurus) and the Eighth (Scorpio) House polarity is concerned with *personal* resources versus *shared* resources, in other words 'mine' versus 'ours'.

These two houses show personal finances, acquisitions, accumulations, possessions and the way in which you relate to other peoples' possessions. The Second House indicates simple personal values, but the much more complex Eighth House shows how these values are projected out, materially, emotionally and psychologically. In the Second House, the individual produces, becomes attached to and accumulates; in the Eighth House, she destroys, becomes detached, transcends the physical, and spreads herself. Consequently, while the Second

House is related to the instinct of survival and self-preservation, its opposite House shows obvious similarities with the death instinct and one's transcendence above physical, Earth-bound desires.

Negative and Fixed, this polarity is concerned with desire, feeling and possessions. Scorpio delves deeply into her environment and her personal experiences, while Taurus expresses herself with an enviable Earthly simplicity and refreshing lack of complexity and intensity. Scorpio's intense inner whirlpool has much to learn from the far less complex Taurus - stability, patience, experience through the senses rather than always through the feelings, natural growth, and peaceful, regular cycles.

The balance of this polarity is between the hoarder and the releaser, the holding on and the purging, the drawing in and the expelling, the creation and the elimination. Scorpio merges emotionally and sexually, shares material resources, helps others develop and use their resources, penetrates beneath the surface, is concerned with energy and its use, is interested in the occult, gains power through use of emotions and material means, has power over others, demands that others satisfy her, desires sexual release, eliminates non-essentials and enemies, experiences a kind of purging through deaths and rebirths regularly, overcomes or sublimates desires, and is passionate, complex, self-conquering, investigative, healing, regenerative, intense and self-mastering.

Taurus relates to self-worth, material possessions and personal values. Taurus has a heavy reliance on the self and consequently a wealth of inner resources which she wastes no time in manipulating and drawing forth to suit her material needs. Scorpio, who draws from her spiritual essence, could learn some more tangible, material lessons from the Bull. Scorpio thrives on the unseen, but could sometimes benefit from dabbling in what is 'real', graspable, and *seen*. Sometimes to touch something is to really feel its power, and the Scorpion will evolve more fully through more such hands-on experiences.

She can teach you how to release your obsessional tendency to be constantly transforming, transmuting and transcending the Earthly realms, bringing you back down to Earth and giving you a good, healthy dose of reality. For she knows that it's often - paradoxically - the simple things that lead to enrichment, fulfilment, and supreme personal power. Taurus, in her innately sensate wisdom, understands that there are certain things beyond our control and that the struggle to control everything is futile. She teaches the much more passionate, strung out Scorpio how to throw off the reins, enjoy the scenery, smell the roses, and swan about lazily in the fields, and this, in turn, will soothe the soul.

The Earth-bound, realistic individual, living through the physical senses and building stability through the simplicity of values (Taurus) seeks to experience the more profound world of feeling which will allow for penetration beneath the surface of things and gain an understanding of deeper realms (Scorpio). The intense and emotional individual, adept at seeing beneath the surface and caught up in the complexities of the underworld of feeling currents (Scorpio) seeks the peace and stability which stems from a realistic relationship with the world and a simplifying of values (Taurus).

Therefore, we can conclude from this, that Scorpio's main karmic goal is achieving greater stability and embracing simplicity as opposed to complexity.

Scorpio can teach Taurus the value of the deeper experience - and then indulgence, simple enjoyments and creativity can become passion. But Taurus instinctively knows that prolonged periods of unbridled passion, extreme focus and extending oneself beyond one's limits, as Scorpio is prone to do, can and *does* lead to psychological burnout, obsessions, compulsions, and breakdowns, as Scorpio is prone to experience. So although Taurus can be accused of being sedentary and lazy at times, she knows on a profound level how to relax, go with the natural flow and surrender to Divine unfoldment without question or doubt. She can indeed impart this simple wisdom to her opposite the Scorpion.

WHAT THE BULL CAN ULTIMATELY TEACH THE SCORPION

Release ★ Complexity, depth, darkness, intensity of expression, constant probing, tension, suspicion, power-grabbing, self-destruction, compulsive patterns, extreme behaviours

Embrace ★ Simplicity, trust, abundance, beauty, being rooted and grounded, luxury, enjoyment, Earthy appetites, sensuality, practicality, healthy attachments to physical and material goods, a 'comfort zone', security, indulgence for pleasure's sake, serenity, peace, a constructive life, consistency, harmony with nature

Taurus is hard-working, self-sufficient, develops her own resources, focuses upon the concrete or tangible, and is practical, productive, personally powerful, substantial, warm, devoted, grounded and easy going. She develops her own resources, focuses on the concrete and tangible, enjoys sensory pleasures, has a solid self-esteem, desires security in love, and revels in accumulating material goods.

Scorpio, so accustomed to living life with passion and intensity, is vulnerable to being prey to her own constant and obscure inner tensions, and yet her hypersensitive psyche makes her quite capable of probing the state of mind of others and perceiving instinctively the hidden meanings of everything. So, if Scorpio tries to exploit her own innate gifts in a positive and constructive manner that makes her feel comfortable and secure, she will be able to acquire a deep serenity, arising from the fact that, more than anyone else, she understands that nothing in this life - or indeed the world - lasts forever. As a result of this way of thinking, you must learn to lay your weapons down, surrender, and stop being forever on your guard on battle alert. From the Bull, you can learn how to relax, tone down your probing, abandon suspicions, release self-destructive behaviours and start enjoying the simple and good things in life. Taurus teaches you to stop and roll in the daisies, luxuriate in the warm Sun and patiently plod along knowing that everything will turn out fine, whether you try to control your own circumstances or turn it over to the Universe to do the work for you. The key word here is *trust*, and Taurus has plenty of to share with you. You must learn how to be productive, how to fulfil yourself in the material, physical world, and not be frightened of acquiring or possessing things, or of making your mark and developing your sensory powers, your impeccable tastes and your good sense.

This polarity is telling you that you need to develop slow, steady, progressive evolution and development of inner security; to develop a sense of being unshakably rooted; to sow those beautifully fertile seeds in youth so they can be harvested in their full bloom and used in later years; to transcend material possessions and dig a little deeper to find truer and deeper meaning in your life. Your overall evolutionary goals are to develop inner security and to learn the quiet, gentle kind of strength that your complementary opposite Taurus embodies.

MAGIC, DRAWING, ATTRACTION, SPELLS, RITUALS, WISHING & POWER

A Note on the Universe

Within each of us resides the merging of the Sun and the Moon, the dance of the constellations, the vibrations of the planets, and the vast microcosm and macrocosm of the entire *Universe*. Uni means 'one' and Verse means 'song'; therefore, the word Universe literally means 'One Song'. If you learn to tune yourself in, you can even hear it!

What is Magic?

Magic is a kind of special energy that is beyond description, and like most kinds of energy it has its own rules and ways of being manipulated. It remains an elusive term, and no definition has ever really found Universal acceptance. Attempts to separate it from superstition, religion and other-worldly phenomena on the one hand, and 'science' on the other, are ridden with difficulties. However slippery the term 'magic' might be, there is a general agreement that most of us wish for more of its presence in our lives and often fall short of achieving this wish.

Those performing spells, 'asking the Universe', wishing, praying, or undertaking rituals, are using this very special energy to draw things to them. Learning to manipulate energy in these ways is never hard (and shouldn't be), but it can be complex and does require knowledge, practice, creativity, patience and above all, imagination. Most of us use simple magic every day, whether by saying little prayers, making wishes, visualising, and exchanging - sending out and receiving - good, positive or hopeful vibes. When you understand that all the forces and magic you need are *within* you, and you learn to *believe* in that power, you are then able to make all manner of changes to your life and, most importantly, yourself.

Magic is an invisible force which connects and permeates everything. Every thought you have and every action you take, will affect the strength of this force, and can be influenced and directed towards a specific purpose by using certain means. The most important of these are your intentions, facing in the direction of your desired outcome, your will and your *belief* that it works. The more you want something to happen, and the clearer you can visualise the desired outcome, the stronger your will and feelings towards it will be, ensuring an avalanche of amazing people, events and circumstances will flow into your experiences, gathering speed, momentum and power as it nears your goal or dream.

The Universe (or whichever higher power you believe in) works for us and through us. Ideas are given to us but they must be carried out *through* us, in the form of asking or acting or performing a ritual or casting a specific spell. The Universe's abundance is your abundance, and it flows through your mind into manifestation. The Universe or Divine Being in which you believe, gives you the necessary ideas and clothes them with all that is needed to bring them into form when we ask *believing*.

Based on ancient human beliefs, systems and superstitions, declaring what you want and acting out your deepest desires can actually help to make things happen. Magical ideas include the notion that thought affects matter and that the trained imagination can alter the physical world, that all aspects of the Universe are interdependent and that we can discover connections and correspondences between everyday occurrences and cosmic, or Divine, energies. A miracle or a wish coming true can suggest something is going on that extends beyond the laws of nature, that something unseen has occurred; but just because we cannot see it or touch it, it doesn't mean it's not there. Magic exists, especially if you truly believe it does, but science is so far incapable of capturing its essence or the rationale behind it. Personally, I prefer to leave that task to the higher powers of the Universe.

To help your dreams come true and to use your inborn power to its full effect, you can employ boosters based on the special energies and qualities of your Sun sign. These 'boosters' are chosen to be in alignment with the purpose of a particular goal, and contain energies of their own which will enhance the strength of your spell, prayer, ritual or 'asking'. Specific magical energies can be invoked by carrying out a spell or ceremony using specific herbs or colours, or on a particular day of the week, according to either your Sun sign (to heighten the power of the asking), and/or that is in sympathy with that for which you are asking (I have included days of the week for other Sun signs and spell types).

Some materials and boosters you can use to increase the power, magic or energy in any area of your life include: candles, wish lists (written on an appropriate piece of paper written with a specially-chosen writing tool), symbols, affirmations, chants, incense, herbs and flowers, locations, colours, days of the week, elements, crystals and gemstones, animal symbols, charms, talismans, amulets, gods and goddesses, essential oils, planetary hours and your Solar totem animals. All are covered, some more briefly than others, for your very special Sun sign to radiate the energy to powerfully draw your wildest dreams towards you!

Overall, it pays to remember that the Universe (or whatever higher power/s or force/s you happen to believe in) creates *through* you that to which you give your attention. What you contemplate becomes the law of your being, and through your pure unwavering belief, is eventually brought through to manifestation on the material plane. What you think about is entirely up to you. But just be mindful that whatever you think about the most becomes your dominant thought, then your main point of attraction, and is ultimately magnified until it becomes your reality or your experience. So choose your thoughts with care. And to quote Ralph Waldo Emerson, "Be careful what you set your heart upon, for it will surely be yours." I carry a copy of this beautiful prophecy in my purse as its words resonate so strongly with me. In other words, be mindful about what you're wishing for, for you will most probably get it, whether it's good or bad - magic, after all, doesn't discriminate. Just make your dominant thoughts good ones, and you will attract everything you set your heart and intentions upon. Good luck!

ASTROLOGY & MAGIC

"Everyone practices magic, whether they realise it or not, for magic is the art of attracting particular influences, events and situations within human life. Magic is a natural phenomenon because the Universe is reflexive, responding to human thoughts, aspirations and desires …"
David Fideler, *Jesus Christ, Sun of God*

Astrology is the most sublime of the occult * sciences, while at the same time it is one of the most practical for everyday application, for it divines the human soul itself. The cosmos, particularly the patterns that formed across it at the exact moment we were born, indicates the road along which our mental and spiritual endowments are likely to impel us, therefore enabling us to prepare in advance for life's battles, pitfalls, milestones, celebrations and of course to make the utmost of opportunities. Such is the magic of the human mind, that it can 'see' into the future and relive the past without having to be physically present in either, and when combined with astrological *knowing*, particularly the knowing that springs from understanding some of the dynamics of our natal chart, however basic, our inner - and outer - magic can be lifted to phenomenal heights.

In ancient times, not only was astrology the ardent study of the most learned and powerful minds, but among the masses of ordinary people its authority and guidance was accepted and followed without question. How this powerful knowledge was used was - and still is - up to the individual, but all who used it applied it to their perceived advantage.

As primitive humans observed the skies, no doubt they gradually realised that certain stars upon which their fate depended accompanied the seasons, or certain times of the year. They may also have reasoned that if governed their fate, they also governed their bodies, and it is therefore conceivable that the skies were associated with Divine influence. Certain celestial influences were believed to emanate from the thirty-six decans of the signs, and the mysterious but apparent effect that they exercised upon humans were thought to be due to a subtle ether shed by the heavenly stars and spheres on the Earth, that affected not only people, but also other animals, plants and minerals. For the ancient mind, linking magic with astrology may have also provided a much needed sense of predictability and patterns.

Early astrologers named and made associations with the imaginary divisions of the twelve signs and the twelve houses, and people born under a certain sign were said to inherit to an extent, its properties and nature. They also believed that the influence of the planets and stars corresponded with the medicinal properties of certain plants and minerals. They therefore asserted that the influence of a star or planetary position would affect the type of medicine or healing they would offer a subject to attain the most beneficial outcome. Throughout the writings of early philosophers and theorists, there is constant reference to this unmistakable mystic connection between the seven known planets and Earthly affairs and ailments. The seven metals were connected with the seven planets, to which the seven colours and the seven transformations were added. So the alchemist came to share the astrological doctrine that each planet ruled some mineral: The Sun ruled gold, the Moon silver, Mars iron, Venus copper, Saturn lead, Jupiter tin, and Mercury quicksilver. Consequently, in alchemical symbolism the same sign came to represent the metal and its corresponding planet.

In subsequent years, astrology became closely related to alchemical knowledge and development, and the alchemist came to be regarded as an authority not only on the transmutation of metals, but also on astrology and magic. This goes some of the way to explaining how magic and divination, which had always been inseparably bound up with astrology, came to be associated with alchemy. In all the occult sciences, the supreme power was believed to be in the stars above, and from their mysterious emanations all the metals, crystals, minerals, plants and herbs derived their special properties over time. Further, as alchemy became ever more spiritual and concerned with more abstract and philosophical concepts, eventually it was considered that the transmutation of lead into gold was simply a metaphor for the transformation of base matter, in this case the human soul, into a much purer and higher state of wisdom and being.

The Sun and Moon were believed to have greater influence over the human body than all the other heavenly bodies, and to exert their influence in various ways whenever they entered a certain sign of the zodiac. And although the Moon was traditionally regarded as the most important factor of a horoscope, the Sun has come into its own in later centuries, with the result that almost everyone knows their Sun sign but only those who have delved deeper are aware of the sign their natal Moon falls in. For this reason, I have chosen to focus this book series on the twelve Sun signs, as this is what the majority of people are most familiar with.

The following pages contain methods, energies, materials and objects which may be used to increase the magic and power of your Sun sign's influence upon you. Precious stones, flowers, colours and so on, are regarded as having a potent effect upon good fortune by attuning your mind to receive harmonious vibrations from the astral forces that surround you.

Finally, a basic working knowledge of basic astronomy and astrology is an asset when working with luck, abundance, wealth and personal power. You can attract more of these things when you align yourself with the workings of the wider Universe, the movement of the Sun, stars, Moon and planets and become aware of the correlations between the outer cycles of the skies and the inner cycles within yourself. Also, for those who are knowledgeable about Moon phases, equinoxes and solstices, a world of lucky possibilities can also magically open up to you. You don't need to know about astrology's deepest complexities to understand how everything interrelates; just learning the basics will give you an edge - and hopefully the following lucky tips will provide you with at least a small glimpse into the insights gleaned from your Sun sign, which I am certain will endow upon you the potential for amazing results to manifest in your life - and maybe even a step up one further rung towards the heavens!

* The word 'occult' comes from the Latin *occultus*, which literally means 'knowledge of the hidden'.

USING COLOURS, CRYSTALS, DEITIES, PLANTS, FOODS & MATERIAL SUBSTANCES FOR INCREASING POWER & MAGNETISING MAGIC

Alchemist, reformer and mystic Henry Cornelius Agrippa, born in 1486, in his principal work, *On Occult Philosophy*, expressed his belief in the doctrines of astrology and in the theory that the spirit of the world exists in the body of the world, just as the human spirit exists in the body of man. He contended that this spirit also abounds in the celestial bodies and descends in the rays of stars, so that the things influenced by their rays become conformable to them. By this spirit every occult property is conveyed into metals, stones, herbs and animals, through the Sun, Moon and planets, and even through the stars beyond and higher than the planets. A firm believer in the efficacy of charms, he stated that they may "be worn on the body bound to any part of it or hung around the neck, changing sickness into health or health into sickness." I believe the same effect could be applied to wishing and the thinking of positive thoughts, to mean, "Changing thoughts and dreams into manifest reality." He also recommended that these charms be worn in the form of finger rings (that have been created using the materials in agreement and harmony with your Sun Sign's magical energy).

Material substances are connected with abstract purposes by a complex but highly usable and accessible system of correspondences. Use these time-honoured connections in your own spells and wishes to magnetise your desires to you. The following pages will give you some materials, energies, forces and ideas you can summon the power of in order to enhance your magic and luck.

PLANETS

The Planetary influence of the day is important when 'asking' for something. If you are wishing for luck, for example, try working with your Sun sign's inherent energies combined with the perfect day of the week for it. So a Scorpion might try using her natural instincts and shrewd powers, to ask for greater luck on a Thursday, which is Jupiter's Day and Jupiter is renowned for being a lucky planet, or better still, ask for luck on a Tuesday, which is Mar's Day, traditional planetary ruler of Scorpio, at the time of day when Jupiter's influence is at its most powerful (information about planetary hours for each day of the week can be found on the Internet or in books on the subject, and can be complex and detailed. It is an art to memorise the correct times, days and energies for the correct spells. If you are determined enough to achieve your dream or goal however, you will be determined enough to put in the research to do it properly!) Here is a very simplified list of the days of the week and their meanings:

DAYS OF THE WEEK & THEIR POWERS

MONDAY ★ Moon
Cancer

The Divine feminine, changes, intuition, emotions, secrets, dealing with women, purity, goodness, perfection, unity, psychic ability, magic, spirituality, invoking a goddess's or angel's guidance, anything that fluctuates, contracts, increases or decreases.

TUESDAY ★ Mars
Aries & Scorpio

Enthusiasm, competition, passion, energy, courage, protection, victory, anything requiring assertiveness, standing up for yourself, or a 'fighting spirit', determination, vitality, sexuality, self-confidence, men's power, men's mysteries, drive, ambition, achievement, triumph, masculinity.

WEDNESDAY ★ Mercury
Gemini & Virgo

Education, travel, exams, study, communication, making connections, thinking, dealing with siblings, writing and speaking, knowledge, learning, adaptability, charm, youth, absorbing information.

THURSDAY ★ Jupiter
Sagittarius & Pisces

Increase and expansion of anything (remember to be careful what you wish for), luck, growth, influence, worldly power, accomplishment, fulfilment, gambling, philosophy, higher education, abundance, optimism.

FRIDAY ★ Venus
Taurus & Libra

Love, luxury, the arts, indulgence, beauty, marriage, money, prosperity, fertility, women's power, women's mysteries, grace, charm, appeal, hope, pleasure, decorating, self-worth, self-esteem, personal values, business partnerships, romance, creativity, sharing, bonding.

SATURDAY ★ Saturn
Capricorn & Aquarius

Long-term goals, career, institutions, establishments, security, investments, karma, reversal, structure, protection, solitude, privacy, determination, ending, blocking, renewing, transforming, anything to do with the public.

SUNDAY ★ Sun
Leo

All-purpose, success, wishes, generosity, happiness, optimism, spirit/essence, recognition, health, vitality, material wealth, invoking a god's aid or guidance, personal empowerment, spirituality, the Divine masculine.

YOUR NATAL MOON PHASE

Although this book is aimed at enhancing your life through the energy of your Sun sign, a bit of lunar help can give your wishing a boost! As well as using the planetary days and hours system to add a bit of zest to your wish fulfilment, try combining your Sun sign's power periods with your natal Moon phase (your natal Moon phase can be calculated using a number of sources on the internet, or through an astrologer), or even studying which constellation the Moon is situated in at certain times, to increase the power of your spells and asking rituals. For example, you might like to 'ask' for a promotion at work during a New/Waxing Moon period, particularly if the Moon happens to fall under an auspicious sign for career advancement, such as Capricorn. Your natal Moon phase can also be used to similar effect, by researching when your Moon phase will coincide with a certain lunar constellation position.

In most astrological interpretations the Sun is regarded as the most important, central feature of a natal chart. But to many the Moon is equally, if not more, important than the Sun sign. Many ancient cultures considered the Moon sign to be more significant. The Moon passes through the 12 signs about every 2.5 days, usually covering the whole zodiac in around 27.3 days. The Moon symbolises our inner world, the world of feeling, emotions, habitual responses, instincts, intuition, security and the subconscious. It describes our nurturing style and needs, our emotional response to life, our attitudes and likely reactions to others, our instinctive and habitual responses, the receptive feminine side of ourselves, our experience of our mother or mother figure, and our childhood experience. It represents the soul. In relationships it symbolises how we like to be nurtured and cared for, and the potential depth of our involvement on personal intimate levels.

For many centuries, people across the world have recognised that the Moon influences the affairs of all living things on planet Earth. The waxing Moon appears to have a drawing, increasing and enhancing effect, whereas the waning Moon has a decreasing, receding and withdrawing effect. All things that come into being are stamped with the qualities of the prevailing Moon stage. It seems that people born during certain lunar phases tend to share specific attributes with other people born during this same phase. In turn, their attributes will be subtly different from those of individuals born during any of the other stages in the Moon cycle. Knowing exactly which phase of the Moon you were born under gives you all kinds of extraordinarily valuable insights into your character, emotions, behaviour and motivations in life. It can make you aware of your deepest underlying drives, the fundamental purpose that you are drawn towards in life and the contribution you can make to others and society during the course of your lifetime. This knowledge may enable you to intuit and make the most of your own personal cyclical pattern that you go through each month, and allow you to know when the most auspicious periods of time are for you and your affairs, nurture yourself and channel your energies in the most positive directions.

Because this lunar pattern repeats itself every month, you will find that you can even pace yourself on a long-term basis. This will enable you to effectively target your efforts and goals on periods of time that you know will be potentially fortunate for you. You may in fact find that your birth phase corresponds with the days of the month when you have abundant energy, feel inspired and can generate new ideas with ease. During this period, you should work towards the fruition of your efforts, bring your dreams into light and reach for the stars!

The Lunar Phases Are:

★ New Moon
★ First/Waxing Crescent
★ First Quarter
★ Waxing Gibbous Moon
★ Full Moon
★ Waning Gibbous / Disseminating Moon
★ Last Quarter
★ Waning Crescent / Balsamic Moon
★ Back to the New Moon

SPELLS, MAGIC & WISHING WITH MOON PHASES

Though the Moon has eight astronomical phases, it is the three phases corresponding to maiden, mother and crone that are the most significant in spells, ritual, wish magic and psychic work. By tuning into the physical Moon we can understand and harness these distinct energy phases in our daily lives and magical worlds. The four primary Lunar phases are the New Moon, First Quarter, Full Moon and the Last Quarter. Depending on what sort of spell you wish to perform, your spell should take place during one of these cycles or time periods. Each phase of the Moon is good for some types of magic, but not so much for others.

NEW MOON, WAXING & FIRST QUARTER

In astronomical terms, the New Moon occurs when the Moon rises and sets at the same time as the Sun. Both bodies are found in the same position compared with the Earth. Therefore, a Solar eclipse can only ever occur at the New Moon, when the two luminaries are found, for a short time, in a perfect line relative to the Earth, with the Moon positioned between the Sun and the Earth. The New Moon's sunlit face is hidden from the Earth.

In astrological terms, the New Moon occurs at a time when the Sun and the Moon are found in the same degree of the zodiac and therefore occupy the same zodiac sign, forming a conjunction, or a 'fusing' of energies.

In astronomical terms, the First Quarter occurs seven days after the New Moon. Seen from the Earth, this phase makes the Moon like a crescent, forming the shape of a capital D.

In astrological terms, it occurs when the Sun and the Moon form a ninety-degree angle, or the square aspect, inside the zodiac, the Moon always preceding the Sun.

As the New Moon marks the beginning of a new cycle, it symbolises fresh starts. This is an exceptional time to work magic and make wishes for new beginnings, and for the conception and initiation of new projects. Use this Moon phase for improving health, the gradual increase of prosperity, attracting good luck, fertility magic, finding new love, friendship or romance, job hunting, making plans for the future and increasing your general spiritual or psychic awareness.

Overall, the Waxing Crescent and First Quarter Moon phases are appropriate for spells, rituals and workings that involve growth, healing and increase. This is a period of time lasting approximately two weeks, to draw things toward you and increase things, such as love, prosperity and new opportunities. During this period is the time to bless new projects, anything that requires energy to grow, such as gardens, business ventures, new homes, or educational pursuits. Personal growth and healing are accented, as is 'attraction magic' - drawing something to you such as love, abundance, health, success or a new path - and if done well, you can expect results by the next Full Moon. Magical workings for gain, increase or bringing things to you should be initiated when the Moon is waxing (or New, going from Dark to Full). A time for divination of all kinds, spells of spiritual intention, and for any creative project you wish to see birthed, with magical and fruitful results.

While making a wish within the first forty-eight hours after the New Moon is a powerful way of helping it come to fruition, the most potent time for making wishes is actually within the first eight hours of the exact time of its position. Write down your wish list within this first eight hours on a piece of appropriately coloured paper with a special writing tool, and be sure to capture the essence of your wish by wording it in a way that charges your emotions and simply feels 'right'. Make a maximum of ten wishes (less is perfectly fine too), as making too many wishes might disperse their energy too much to be effective. After writing down your list and releasing your wishes to the Universe in whichever form you feel happy with, keep your list and check on it in a few days', weeks' or months' time to assess whether anything has shifted in the direction of your listed dreams, desires or goals. I'll bet it has - or at the very least, something even better has arrived in its place!

Although the first forty-eight hours after the New Moon is the most potent time to make a special wish, you can begin Waxing Moon magic when you can see the crescent in the sky and continue until the day before the Full Moon. The closer to the Full Moon, the more intense the energies. In fact, a personally devised ritual using any special Lunar-associated materials over three days up to and including the Full Moon is excellent for something you require urgently or within a short timeframe.

In some cultures, people turn over silver coins or jewellery three times when the crescent Moon appears in the sky and make a wish. As the Moon grows, it is believed that prosperity and good fortune will grow too.

While the New Moon is not known as a time for 'banishing' or releasing things we no longer want in our lives, I feel that if we are to ask and wish for things, we need to make room to receive them. Making room means that the Universe can slot it right into our lives where we have cleared our paths for it. Clutter, unwanted things, unhappy relationships, possessions that no longer serve us, are all things we can banish. So, to help what you are asking for come into your life quicker, the New Moon is a particularly opportune time to throw a few things out so you can make way for the new and clear up some space for that which you are wishing for. What are you waiting for? Start creating a space for your wishes today!

FULL MOON

In astronomical terms, the Full Moon occurs 14 days after the New Moon, on the day when the Moon sets at the same time the Sun rises, or conversely. The two luminaries are effectively facing each other, with the Earth in between, the Sun shining its light onto the reflective Moon, giving it the fully lit up appearance of a giant, bright, perfectly round sphere. Indeed, its entire face is bathed in sunlight. A Lunar eclipse can only occur at the Full Moon, when the Sun, Moon and Earth are all in line, and the Earth hides the lit side of the Moon to us.

In astrological terms, a Full Moon occurs at the time when the Sun and Moon are 180 degrees apart inside the zodiac, and therefore positioned in opposite signs, forming an opposition aspect.

The highest energy occurs at the Full Moon, making this is a powerful time for all manner of magical workings. Use the Full Moon phase for any immediate need, a sudden boost of power or courage, psychic protection, a change of career or location, travel, healing acute health conditions, the consummation of love or a commitment, justice, ambition and promotion of all kinds. This phase lasts approximately 3 days - 24 hours before the exact Full Moon, the day of, and 24 hours after it, according to many sources - giving us 3 full days to perform our spells. However, we are not strictly limited to a three-day period; the power of this phase can actually be accessed for seven days - three days prior to, the night of, and the three days after the Full Moon. The Full Moon period is when the Moon is at her most powerful, being the most luminous and radiant part of the cycle. Known as the 'high tide' of psychic power, the Full Moon represents culmination, climax, fulfilment and abundance. The Full Moon governs all kinds of magic, including manifestation, banishing, and is particularly good for calling forth protection and heightening your intuitive abilities. The Full Moon contains magic that calls forth personal power, fertility, spiritual development, and psychic awareness. Cleansing of ritual tools, crystals, wish lists, Tarot decks, and the like can be done during this phase. Magic worked during the Full Moon often takes one complete cycle to come to fruition. Try also reaffirming your desires during the New Moon to give them an added nudge in the right direction.

LAST QUARTER OR WANING MOON

In astronomical terms, the Last Quarter, or Waning Moon, occurs twenty-one days after the New Moon. The time difference between the rising and setting of the two luminaries is reduced to what it was at the First Quarter. Viewed from the Earth, the Moon resembles a crescent whose lit up area is decreasing in size, forming the shape of a capital C.

In astrological terms, the Waning Moon occurs when the Sun and Moon are positioned at ninety degree angles of each other in the zodiac, forming the square aspect again. However, during this phase, the Sun is instead *ahead* of the Moon.

The Waning Moon represents the lunar cycle from Full to Dark. Any spells and magic performed during this period is based purely around banishing and releasing. It could involve releasing things which no longer serve you (such as behaviours, material things, relationships and attitudes), banishing negative energies, and removing obstacles which are standing in the way of achieving your goals or dreams. The Waning Moon is the best time for cleansing, gently releasing, eliminating, expelling and completion. It is of great assistance when you are wanting to let go of something, or someone, gradually. The Dark of the Moon, the period when the Moon is no longer visible to the naked eye, until the New Moon, is the most useful time for divination of all kinds.

★ What is your natal Moon phase type? Can you think of ways you can combine it with the power of your Sun sign to effect change and bring about wonderful happenings? ★

HARNESSING YOUR PERSONAL MOON MAGIC ★ MOON IN SCORPIO

When the Moon is in your sign of Scorpio, it is a great time for working magic around: Personal power, influence, magnetism, resilience, endurance, self-discipline and anything that requires the application of passion and dedication. Suggested operations could be around rituals and spells to learn to work with inner transformation, rebirth, illumination, wisdom, depth, karma and instinct. It is also an opportune time for introspective self-exploration and strengthening your intuitive and psychic faculties. You can invoke the Lunar Scorpio for mystical powers, for a deeper sense of purpose and direction, and for overall regeneration. Spells to help you apply your power and determination to a situation which calls for it, to hone your instincts, to get to the bottom of an unwanted situation, or to end things which no longer serve you (best done during a waning Scorpio Moon), are best performed at this time. With the Moon in Scorpio, you can also call forth Divine justice (karma), cultivate greater self-discipline, and explore your interests in the occult and divination of all kinds.

THE MOON ★ WHAT IT REPRESENTS IN THE HUMAN PSYCHE & NATAL CHART

The Moon in the sky shines with the reflected light of the Sun. Although not a planet, the Moon is our nearest celestial neighbour and exerts a great influence upon us. The gravitational pull of the Moon affects our body fluids, which contribute to about 90 per cent of our biological make-up. It moves at approximately half a degree per hour and takes an average of 27.3 days to pass through all twelve zodiac signs, staying in each for around 2.5 days.

In astrology the Moon corresponds with the way in which we reflect and respond to what is going on around us. It has to do with our feelings, emotions and instincts and, in the same way the Moon influences the tides on planet Earth, it symbolises the ebb and flow of our emotional nature, our moods, fluctuations and changeability. The Moon is the archetype of the Mother, which is within us all, and represents the primary feminine principle in the natal chart. It is through the Moon that we express our parental instincts - caring, nurturing, protecting, sensitivity. The Moon has links with the past and the subconscious and it is from this almost primitive source that our natural instinctual forces flow.

The Moon is essentially a feminine principle and associates with the inner personality, receptivity, passivity and inward-oriented feelings. It can act as an inner guide to the deeper self, the unconscious self, figures half-shrouded in mystery, linking the hidden personal world of the subconscious to the clearer world of personal awareness.

The Moon is the innermost core of our being, private feelings, habitual reactions and subconscious habits. It is the caring, nurturing sustainer of life, the 'mother' of the zodiac. It tells us about how we seek security, our urge to nurture, our nurturing style, our responses and feelings and moods. The innermost core of our being, private feelings, subconscious habits. It is concerned with habits, mothering, habitual/instinctive responses and personality. It is our karma, our soul, our past.

The Moon represents our mother or mother figure, our feminine side, maternal instinct, our nurturing style and needs, our unconscious self, our emotional reactions, the subconscious, our feelings, instincts, intuition, receptivity, habits, what we need to feel secure, fluctuations, cycles, moods, and our childhood. Its position in the birth chart is very significant, because as well as revealing feminine qualities and the potential gentleness and tenderness of a being, the Moon also reveals important information about the experiences and expression of the five senses.

The Moon is essentially receptive and passive; it reflects the life experience rather than initiating it. Fluctuating and cyclical, the Moon is the planet (although technically a satellite) of the childhood experience, and instinctual reactions. It represents the mother (a child's experience and expectations of their mother), maternal instincts and the feminine principle, indicating how strongly these manifest in an individual, male or female.

As it represents what our childhood experience is likely to be, and childhood is essentially a time where our consciousness has not yet fully developed, our Moon sign traits seem to be more apparent in our younger years. We will usually show our Moon sign traits more so than our Sun sign traits during this developing period of infancy and early childhood, until we have the presence of mind to more consciously develop our ego and true core self (the Sun).

The symbol for the Moon ☽ is a representation of its crescent in its waxing phase from new to full, but it can also be seen as two half circles - these form a bowl shape, a receptacle, a feminine container that 'receives' and 'holds' anything put into it. The half circle, unlike the full circle of the Sun, is finite and incomplete, almost as if striving for wholeness.

The Moon represents our *soul*.

YOUR MOON SIGN

The Sun / Moon Polarity
Conscious & Unconscious, Night & Day, Yin & Yang

Man does, woman is.
Edward Edinger

Your Moon Sign, representing your soul, and your Sun sign, representing your spirit, work together to form the foundation of your basic personality, expression and nature. If you know what your Moon sign is, look it up below and read how it works with your Scorpio Sun to blend your mind, soul and spirit.

♈ **With the Moon in ARIES, Sun in Scorpio,** you are likely to be ★ Astute, robust, intense, self-preserving, proud, incisive, persuasive, arrogant, sharp, alert, penetrative, unable to relax, resilient, a formidable enemy, acutely aware, brash, intensely purposeful, unwilling to compromise, suspicious, motivated, powerful, sarcastic, self-protective, charismatic, torn between being light-hearted and dark, volatile, enthusiastic, eager, extreme, loyal, dedicated, adventurous, hot-tempered, courageous, magnetic, moody, intolerant, a self-starter, impatient yet circumspect, passionate, highly-sexed, assertive, unyielding, temperamental, insensitive, reckless, destructive, a powerful leader, tenacious, wilful, ambitious, self-reliant, energetic, emotionally bold, self-confident, acid-tongued, opinionated, bossy, pioneering, witty, bright, passive-aggressive, impulsive, compulsive, charismatic, charming, strategic, and a strong individualist.

Sun/Moon Harmony Rating ★ *6.5 out of 10*

♉ **With the Moon in TAURUS, Sun in Scorpio**, you are likely to be ★ Possessive, firm, stubborn, fixed, unyielding, solid, consistent, materialistic, gentle yet volatile, jealous, persevering, loyal, motivated, steady-paced but intense, tenacious, broody, deeply sensual, controlling, contained, inflexible, unmovable, vindictive, emotionally powerful, explosive, inward, devoted, stoic, faithful, capable, insightful, determined, unforgiving, in possession of a smouldering passion, shrewd, proud, committed, all-or-nothing, resourceful, dependable, peace-loving but strong-willed, persistent, and unwaveringly dedicated.

Sun/Moon Harmony Rating ★ *7.5 out of 10*

♊ **With the Moon in GEMINI, Sun in Scorpio,** you are likely to be ★ Torn between freedom and containment, cunning, changeable, an intense social presence, intensely friendly but broody, lucid, fascinating, spirited, curious, psychologically understanding, satirical, clever, socially mysterious, articulate, paradoxical, profound, sharp-witted, perceptive, clever, manipulative, likely to suffer from foot in mouth syndrome, self-serving, stimulating, able to interpret others' motives, anxious, flexible yet stubborn, curious, contradictory, emotionally destructive, experimental, vivid, passionate yet detached, insightful, penetrative, probing, gossipy, rumour-spreading, restless, nervous, creative, strongly aware, gifted, loyal, idealistic, emotionally intellectual, and always on a deep inner quest.

Sun/Moon Harmony Rating ★ *6.5 out of 10*

♋ **With the Moon in CANCER, Sun in Scorpio,** you are likely to be ★ Deeply sensitive, easily hurt, shrewd, intuitive, security- and survival-oriented, sentimental, emotional, deep, strong, compassionate, intense, hidden, tough yet tender, nurturing, demanding, imaginative, feelings-based, loyal, possessive, unable to let go of the past, satirical, dependent, secretive, nostalgic, perceptive, vengeful, insightful, passionately committed, resilient, manipulative, probing, determined, clingy, instinctive, resourceful, fanatical, sincere, supportive, attentive, intensely guarded, poetic, moody and broody, devoted to family, self-protective, needy, suspicious, past-dwelling, jealous, smothering, occasionally moved to emotional volatility, and in possession of deep reservoirs of emotional strength.

Sun/Moon Harmony Rating ★ *7 out of 10* **

♌ **With the Moon in LEO, Sun in Scorpio,** you are likely to be ★ Fearless, courageous, all-or-nothing, vain, intolerant, broody, ambitious, prone to tantrums, sulky, whole-hearted, forthright, proud, egocentric, individualistic, feisty on the surface with a great strength within, prone to emotional outbursts, ardent, wilful, ruthless, dramatic, driven by sex, money and power, a prima donna, flamboyant, extreme, charismatic, passionate, magnetic, pompous, enthusiastic, inflated, uncompromising, determined, pursuing of excellence, dictatorial, powerful, romantic, highly-charged, intense, bossy, powerful, extroverted, bold, driven, fiercely loyal, anarchistic, direct, vain, stubborn, strong, upfront yet secretive, tense, inspiring, purposeful, controlling, emotionally expressive, theatrical, deeply aware of social nuances, ambitious, despotic, self-centred, self-reliant, deeply creative, affectionate and demonstrative.

Sun/Moon Harmony Rating ★ *7.5 out of 10*

♍ **With the Moon in VIRGO, Sun in Scorpio,** you are likely to be ★ Robust, fussy, discriminating, efficient, puritanical, intelligent, judgemental, highly critical, shrewd, an emotional extremist, methodical, calculating, a devoted researcher, helpful, cool, serious, intense, brooding, prone to self-criticism, intense, agile, mentally alert, rigid, compulsive, a worrier, reserved, conventional, uptight, tense, fearful, motivated, hard-working, clear-thinking, quietly dedicated, conscientious, pedantic, difficult, organised, a relentless perfectionist, analytical, witty, forceful yet modest, self-effacing, anxious, logical, cautious, cutting, accurate, healing, 'entitled', narrow-minded, strategic, principled, productive, obsessive, self-controlled and in possession of an excellent intellect.

Sun/Moon Harmony Rating ★ *6.5 out of 10*

♎ **With the Moon in LIBRA, Sun in Scorpio,** you are likely to be ★ Introverted but sociable, instinctively compromising, vivid, expressive, keen, refined, paradoxical, affectionate, perceptive, charming, sensual, a commanding presence, powerful, a hider of feelings, charming, magnetically sociable, innately just, distanced from your true emotional power, hedonistic, incisive, romantic, passionate, cooperative yet demanding, acutely observant, naughty but nice, eloquent, co-dependent, honourable, engaging, suave, able to perceive feelings, probing of others, relationship-oriented, witty, humorous, able to see the darker side of human nature, intense and delightful at the same time, persuasive, artistically sensitive, abstract, conflicted, and in possession of expensive tastes.

Sun/Moon Harmony Rating ★ *8.5 out of 10*

♏ **With the Moon in SCORPIO, Sun in Scorpio,** you are likely to be ★ Intense, compelling, loyal, emotional, powerful, self-possessed, devoted, enduring, wary, driven, self-motivated, deep, black and white, shrewd, forceful, highly charged, obsessive, sarcastic, relentless, introspective, controlled, focused, channelled, dictatorial, extreme, possessive, cynical, keenly insightful, investigative, unbending, strong-willed, passionate, unyielding, resourceful, vengeful, resilient, controlling, stubborn, persevering, unapologetic, thorough, psychologically penetrative, secretive, courageous, perceptive, self-reliant, dogmatic, stern, exacting, ruthless, compulsive, manipulative, and emotionally powerful.

Sun/Moon Harmony Rating ★ *6 out of 10*

♐ **With the Moon in SAGITTARIUS, Sun in Scorpio,** you are likely to be ★ Passionate, keen, a stern judge, uncompromising, emotionally reckless, eager, adventurous, fascinating, self-sufficient, intuitive, impatient, restless, dictatorial and preaching, forceful, dramatic, focused, unshakable, persuasive, investigative, generous, commanding, intellectually discerning, ardent, outspoken, unaware of the subtleties of social intercourse, intensely inquisitive, feisty, extreme, compulsive, unbreakable, expansive, a passionate crusader, fixated, vital, excessive, spirited, probing, questing, powerful, witty, far-sighted, deeply philosophical, brooding yet optimistic, self-preserving, a voracious student, inspiring, outrageous, aspiring, socially intense, articulate, sharp, in possession of strong moral integrity, and often torn between reason and emotion.

Sun/Moon Harmony Rating ★ *7.5 out of 10*

♑ **With the Moon in CAPRICORN, Sun in Scorpio,** you are likely to be ★ Cautious, mistrustful, dependable, steadfast, resourceful, effective, tough, tenacious, self-demanding, judgemental, enigmatic, cynical, quietly powerful, calculating, painstaking, committed, unbending, ambitious, robust, critical, driven to succeed, self-righteous, persevering, defensive, unyielding, determined, withdrawn, all-or-nothing, broody, cool, resilient, courageous, efficient, tight-fisted, deeply wise, dry-witted, harsh, bitter, resentful, disciplined, earnest, sombre, authoritative, aware, shrewd, organised, loyal, darkly intense, direct, strong-willed, down-to-Earth, satirical, penetrative, complex, serious, introverted, personally honourable, ruthless, overly-strict on self and others, hard-working, inflexible, fearless, uptight, socially rigid, self-contained.

Sun/Moon Harmony Rating ★ 7.5 out of 10

♒ **With the Moon in AQUARIUS, Sun in Scorpio,** you are likely to be ★ Stubborn, independent, complex, intense, eccentric, passionately dispassionate, exacting, powerfully intellectual, broody, contrary, unruly, frustrated, extreme, difficult, proud, unconventional, tenacious, cool, sharp, aloof, paradoxical, imaginative, scrutinising, original, hard to reach, rebellious, hot and cold, indifferent yet interested, controlled, insistent on the truth, articulate, fussy, discerning, clear-headed, focused, highly observant, radical, wilful, principled but intolerant, self-reflecting, magnetic, acutely aware of the human experience, progressive, scientifically investigative, living an unusual lifestyle in some way, open to the unusual and darker aspects of life, interested in occult matters, enigmatic, isolated, emotionally intense, over-identifying with causes, unorthodox, idealistic, loyal, strongly humanitarian, courageous and committed to your ideals, a law unto yourself, and in possession of deep sense of belief in human potential.

Sun/Moon Harmony Rating ★ 6 out of 10

♓ **With the Moon in PISCES, Sun in Scorpio,** you are likely to be ★ Highly imaginative, mystical, interested in occult subjects, intuitive, reflective, secretive, lacking boundaries, complex yet naïve, intriguing, a natural healer, emotionally intense, lurid, self-indulgent, insightful, telepathic, lacking in objectivity, sensitive, psychic, sharply perceptive, conflicted between trust and mistrust, prone to addictions or self-destruction, emotional, ruled by your feelings, prone to despair, deeply sentimental, an escapist, yearning, understanding, elusive, acutely aware of others' suffering, vulnerable, a poet, altruistic, psychologically insightful, receptive, creative, devoted to loved ones, mysterious, empathetic, impressionable yet strong, impractical, evasive, and acutely aware of the needs of others.

Sun/Moon Harmony Rating ★ *8 out of 10* **

** If your Moon is in Cancer or Pisces, your Sun and Moon will form what is known in astrology as a trine aspect. This aspect is the easiest, most flowing and harmonious astrological aspect, ensuring that your Sun and Moon, or spirit and soul, are well integrated. With both luminaries in Water signs, this gives them the best possible degree of complementary energy - a blending of the elements suggests a balanced expression of personality. One drawback of the trine aspect lies in the fact that its easy flow can be *too* harmonious; if our path is too smooth and difficulties don't arise to challenge us from time to time, we can often become lazy and complacent, stunting our growth and spiritual evolution. As Water signs, you share the art of sensitivity, creativity, intrigue, compassion, a nurturing instinct, poetry, understanding, spirituality, a deep need for connection and merging with others, but may be overly sensitive, illogical, clingy, impractical, too emotional, irrational, dependent, manipulative and elusive.

YOUR BODY & HEALTH

> "A physician without a knowledge of astrology has no right to call himself a physician."
> **Hippocrates (born c. 460 BC)**

Hippocrates, the fifth century BC Greek physician and 'father of medicine' and supposed author of the Hippocratic Oath, maintained that no one should be allowed to practise medicine who had not first studied astrology. Another Greek physician, Claudius Galen, brought together a huge range of knowledge and ideas in the second century AD which dominated medical practice until the 17th century. Among his teachings was a diagnostic technique which assumed that illnesses and their treatments were affected by and governed by the phases of the Moon. For centuries, astrology was a compulsory component of medical training (and still is in some natural medicine degrees), albeit only one aspect of diagnosis and treatment.

Medical or health astrology concerns particular ways of determining and interpreting an individual's horoscope with particular reference to health issues - diagnosis of current dis-eases, identification of areas of bodily weaknesses, and the prescription of natural cures and remedies. In ancient times, and still even today, the movement of the stars and planets was believed to affect bodily functions, and to cause ailments, or cure them.

During the Middle Ages, many drawings of the 'zodiac man' were made, which showed which signs of the zodiac were related to each part of the body, providing information as to the best times of the year to undertake cures for ailments affecting the corresponding body parts.

Health astrology persists today in many forms and among astrologers themselves, from whom clients seek counsel on health-related issues, and while it certainly cannot be used diagnose a condition or dis-ease, one's Sun sign, along with other factors of the natal chart, can definitely indicate potential problem areas of weakness or possible troubles. This branch of astrology has been found to be surprisingly accurate in most cases. While mostly accurate, none of the following information should ever be used as a substitute for professional medical advice should you be personally concerned about any of the conditions or afflictions listed for your Sun sign.

SCORPION HEALTH

Scorpio is associated with the Reproductive Systems, Pelvis, Colon, Excretory System, Organs of Elimination, Immune System, Bladder, Prostate Gland, Rectum, the Nose, Orifices and Hormones. It also governs the Pubic and Nasal Bones, Sigmoid Flexure, Sweat Glands, the Sphenoid Area of the Brain, and Haemoglobin.

Just as Scorpio energy must be evenly spent and controlled, so the physical system needs a regular, controlled diet. This may not be easy, as Scorpio being a sign of extremes, has a tendency towards self-indulgence in food and drink (although at the other end, is your extraordinary self-control, which you use to great effect when necessary), which often provokes stomach upsets and eliminatory complaints, such as constipation. Moderation doesn't come easily to you but you must cultivate it, both in diet and exercise. The martial arts may interest you, not just for the physical aspect, but for their spiritual and esoteric qualities; the mind and spirit discipline these call for are appealing to you.

Scorpio represents the energy of survival and purification. Scorpio's nature is watery, cold and magnetic. Principal rulerships include functions and organs necessary for the survival of the species, for example reproduction, genetic coding, DNA, hormones, ovaries and testes, as well as the purification and eliminatory systems of the body.

Whatever ails Scorpio, their extraordinary willpower and resilience will see them bounce back quickly. The phoenix symbolises Scorpio, and your amazing dynamism and fortitude will usually see you rise from the metaphoric ashes of ill-health and fly again with transformed wings. Many Scorpios, due to their passion, simmering emotions, intensity and never doing things by halves (largely fuelled by the Mars element inherent in your character), are prone to accidents. Hernias, haemorrhoids, poor toxin elimination, hormone problems, and prostate, bladder and reproductive system complaints, are the most common ailments to afflict Scorpios. Additionally, uro-genital problems and blockages may manifest.

Pluto, being the modern ruler of Scorpio, is linked, like Mars your traditional ruler, with the gonads. Pluto is connected with all Excretory Functions, Genitalia, Anus, Rectum, Bladder,

Urethra, Sweat Glands, Sinus Cavities, Pituitary Gland, Reproductive System, Mastoid Cavity, and the Immune System. Plutonian ailments may afflict you - conditions associated with the immune system, transformative and genetic functions, and the endocrine system. Other complaints may include venereal dis-ease, genital problems, sex drive issues, obsessions, compulsions, stress, mucus and sinus congestion, hernias, uterine and prostate ailments, and infections and epidemics of all natures.

Excessive drinking can be a problem for Scorpio souls. You can hold your alcohol better than most, and outdistance most of your associates in the liquor arena. There is a strong self-destructive streak to your character, and although you don't deliberately set out to destroy yourself, you refuse to acknowledge any limits as you wish to experience all there is in life - which often includes the good, the bad, the ugly and the downright dangerous. Often this search for sensation and knowledge leads to perilous experimentation with drugs. Occult phenomena, with their self-charging emotional energies and strange rites of invocation, are likely to draw you in too. The changes in perception that emotional stimulus and narcotics induce can be fascinating - but utterly perilous - to a psyche of your nature. And sexual excess is another area you may find difficult to resist. But you can just as easily exercise your tremendous self-control and give up a bad habit if it is detrimental to your health. Your inner resources are stronger - and thus more pronounced and accessible - than any other zodiac sign, and stand you in good stead through any health storm.

One of your most vulnerable areas is the stomach. Various disturbances are likely in the digestive system, especially as a result of the excesses and extremes already mentioned. It can be difficult for you to overcome internal toxic effects, for once a poison is in your body it is hard to eradicate a build-up of any type, so toxic experience and substances are to be avoided at all costs. This is why it is so important that you prevent the build-up of emotional corrosives that weaken the organs and attack the stomach, causing ulcers and the like. Brooding, worry and depression should always be watched by Scorpions.

Scorpio individuals are the stuff that heroes and heroines are made of. You are disdainful of personal danger when your strong principles and fixed convictions are involved; you will suffer without complaint for what you believe in, and are willing to die for a highly valued cause or person.

Generally speaking, your constitution is robust, rugged and healthy. No other Sun sign has at its disposal such a great reserve of sheer tenacious energy. But there is always a danger that you will push yourself beyond physical endurance once you've resolved to accomplish something. You are such a demon for sustained, devoted effort that you can ignore the normal limitations and wind up with a breakdown of some sort. Therefore, you should remain ever conscious of the fact that your will is far stronger than your body. You have a strong constitution provided you also keep your elimination channels open for good health and take care not to push your body beyond its reserves. If you are a typical Scorpion, your attitude is the chief factor determining the state of your health. So strong is your willpower that you can actually will yourself to recovery; on the other hand, so pernicious is your power to resent, seethe and hate, that you can poison yourself with your own emotions. When unwell, Scorpios need a secluded, even hidden environment, in order to process and rebalance their minds, bodies and spirits.

Keeping yourself in excellent health overall, with a special awareness of Scorpio's vulnerable points, is key to achieving all you set out to do, and getting the most out of your life!

THE CELL SALTS ★ ASTROLOGICAL TONICS

Homeopathy and astrology have colluded to provide a wonderful list of astrological tonics, one particularly suited to each of the twelve signs. These are called 'homeopathic cell salts', 'tissue salts' or 'biochemic cell salts', and are available in most health food stores, are inexpensive and easy to take. They are considered to be gentle, effective and safe, even for children, people in fragile health states, and the elderly. Although the full picture, drawn from a full natal horoscope, gives a fuller, more accurate idea of an individual's unique constitution, even simply working with one's date of birth can be enough for the medical astrologer to suggest the use of a cell salt based upon the correlation with an individual's Sun sign.

As well as the cell salts having a significant effect upon physical ailments, they can also profoundly influence the subtle energy bodies, including the mental, emotional, etheric and spiritual. Although the most common use of these salts is based upon each salt's correspondence with a Sun sign, use of the cell salt related to one's Moon sign can assist with addressing deeper underlying emotional issues, such as anxiety, depression, panic and fear. Use of the cell salt relating to your Moon sign will therefore help to restore your sense of safety, balance, security and emotional resilience. In the first seven years of life, when the Moon is the most influential sphere in our lives, Lunar cell salts are the most appropriate choice as a remedy or tonic.

For specific health problems, take both the salt of your Sun or Moon sign, *and* the salt that pertains to the specific condition. The same principle applies to the Ascendant sign, as the First House represents one's physical health, and especially if the Sun or Moon is a rising planet, which means rulership of the whole chart. For the purposes of this book, however, the cell salt that correlates with your Sun sign only is outlined.

TISSUE SALT FOR SCORPIO ★ CALC SULPH.

Calcarea Sulfurica, or Calc Sulph. (Calcium sulphate) is the cell salt for Scorpio. Calc Sulph. is found in bile, mucous membranes and tissues, and promotes continual blood cleansing. An excellent blood purifier, it also has a potent detoxifying effect on the liver. Calc Sulph. can be used for cellular regeneration, and as a purifying agent is essential to all healing processes. Along with the cell salt Silica, this is the salt most commonly used for wound-healing. Present in connective tissue and liver cells, it helps the blood clot and builds tissue. Calc Sulph. provides a coating to all the bodily areas associated with Scorpio, such as the colon, internal sexual organs, large intestine, prostate gland, and eliminative channels and outlets. When a deficiency occurs, toxic build-up can result, manifesting in respiratory clogging, skin disorders, chronic constipation, abscesses, styes, fistulas, pus infections, liver disturbances, slow healing, boils and ulcerations. Another manifestation of Calc Sulph. lack is impotence and infertility, as it renders the body incapable of providing an adequate protective coating for egg and sperm. Overall, this tissue salt is effective in preventing general ill health and infections of all kinds. Foods naturally containing this tissue salt are onions, garlic, blackberries, asparagus, leeks, watercress, gooseberries, mustard greens, radishes, figs, cauliflower and prunes.

WATER SIGN SCORPIO & THE PHLEGMATIC HUMOR

Greek physician Hippocrates (460 - 370 BC) theorised that certain human behaviours were caused by body fluids, called 'humours'. Later, Galen of Pergamon (AD 131 - 200), a Greek physician, developed the first typology of temperaments to encompass many facets of the human psyche and physiology. These also related to the classical elements of Fire, Earth, Air and Water - as choleric, melancholic, sanguine and phlegmatic respectively. According to the Greeks who developed the temperament theory (the word stems from the Latin word *temperamentum*, meaning mixture), temperament is the 'mixture' of qualities that combine to form elements in physics and humours in medicine. The Greeks sought equilibrium in the four qualities of hot, cold, wet (moist), and dry, the elements of Earth, Air, Fire and Water, and the four humours of choler or yellow bile, melancholer or black bile, blood and phlegm. If balance was achieved, the person was said to be well- or even-tempered, and the importance of determining the temperament allowed for imbalances to be treated.

In ancient times, each of the four types of humours corresponded to a different personality type, which were associated with a domination of various biological functions. It was suggested that the temperaments came to clearest manifestation in childhood, between around the ages of six and fourteen of age, after which they become subordinate, but still influential, factors in our personality. It is important to note that your temperament is not your personality. However, your personality can incorporate parts of the temperament in its expression. Personality is shaped by both external and internal factors, whereas the temperament is innate, an inborn, inherent part of each individual.

For Water, the humour is phlegmatic, and it is characterised by a longer response-delay, but short-lived response. Generally low in drive and motivation, phlegmatic natives seek to preserve low energy stores. Phlegmatic types usually give the impression of being calm, naïve and simple, longing for peace in the soul.

Generally inward, people with this temperament tend to be private, reasonable, patient, caring, thoughtful, passive, sluggish, content, tolerant, have a rich inner life, and seek quiet, peaceful environments. Being impressionable, phlegmatic types are often 'awakened' by others' interests in a subject. Steadfast, placid, controlled, reliable, even-tempered, consistent in their habits, they make steady and loyal friends. Your speech may be slow or hesitant, and you may appear clumsy or ponderous. On a physical level, the home of this humour is in the veins and lymphatics, and this humour nourishes the body on a deep and fundamental level.

A phlegmatic disposition represents a slow, even temperament. Its taste is sweet, its nature alkaline, its indication phlegm. The phlegmatic humour is connected with the *liquid* ^ body, and is traditionally associated with cold and wet conditions.

Additionally, the ethereal (or vital) body, comprises four ethers or subtle fluids, which are governed by the four Fixed signs of the zodiac: Taurus, Leo, Scorpio and Aquarius. Scorpio corresponds to the *vital ether*, which governs the physical body's functions concerning reproduction, procreation and gestation.

^ A couple of thousand years ago, the Mesopotamians, Chinese and Egyptians, and more recently the Arabs, practised a medicine called 'of three bodies'. According to the doctors of the ancient world (who often practised as astrologers as well), a human being had three bodies: the physical body, the ethereal (or vital) body and the astral body, imparting a holistic approach to health. In modern medicine, usually only the physical body is focused upon fully. According to tradition, this physical body comprises three principles or states corresponding to three primordial elements: *solid* (Earth), *liquid* (Water) and *gas* (Air). This is the material body, the physical outer cover of muscles, nerves and organs held together by the skeleton. The Fire element corresponds with the *astral* body, which sits outside the physical body in one's auric field.

MONEY ATTRIBUTES

Colour for Increased Earning Power ★ Dark Red

The following plants can be used by all zodiac signs to assist in attracting money ★ Ginger, Allspice, Clover, Orange, Marjoram, Cinnamon, Sassafras, Woodruff, Bergamot, Tonka Beans, Heliotrope, Alfalfa, Coltsfoot, Thyme, Mace, Irish Moss, Clove, Almond, Corn, Honeysuckle, Sesame, Nutmeg, Vetiver, Poppy, Jasmine, Dill and Elder Flower. To attract luck and success, try using any of the above, combined with any of the following: Alfalfa Seeds, Basil, Mustard Seeds, Vervain Leaves, Poppy Seeds, Rosemary, Lemon, Anise and Holly.

Striving for financial gain and abundance with a healthy inner moral compass is, in my view, one of the most noble goals we can set for ourselves. When we have more money, we are better placed to help ourselves and of course others; after all, as Abraham Maslow's Hierarchy of Needs model (1943) attests, once our primary and base survival needs have been satisfied, we can then advance higher towards loftier achievements, such as self-confidence, creativity and self-actualisation. Prosperity allows us to turn our attention to these more transcendental matters - to reach for lives not just of material comfort and luxuries, but of meaning, generosity, balance, harmony, fulfilment and joy. Our Sun sign can offer clues as to how we go about acquiring, earning, saving, maintaining, and allowing the overall flow of giving and receiving money. What's *your* money style?

Love, sex, birth, and life, as well as death, are nature's most potent transformative mediums, and Scorpios are interested in all of these. Money is a transforming energy too, and a Scorpio is interested in money for that reason if nothing else. To Scorpio, money is power, money causes change, and money can control. Even the word 'plutocrat' comes from Pluto, your ruling planet, and refers in large part to a wealthy group of individuals who combine to form a reigning financial superpower. Scorpios are competent in making money shrewdly and creatively with a great deal of common sense. Being mistrustful of others and secretive in all their affairs, Scorpio rarely loses money, but when you do lose money it is usually due to a betrayal of some kind. You are passionate about money and can use it to control others. Money comes and goes for you, but sometimes stays fixed for long periods of time. In essence, it goes through many births and deaths and exerts a regenerative influence over your life.

You strive patiently and passionately to achieve long-term financial prospects, thinking and planning ahead. Like everything else in life, you apply yourself to your finances intensely. You possess a resilient quality that sees you sorting out your financial situation, no matter how dire, time and time again. Your main source of income comes from - or should come from - investments, legacies and inheritances.

Intuitive and shrewd, you are often in the right place at the right time to make opportunistic contacts and be presented with the right opportunities. Always in control of your finances, you have an attitude of 'what's mine is mine', although you are not necessarily mean. You have an instinct for self-preservation and secrecy, which shows itself in well-ordered finances aimed primarily at conserving wealth and often, keeping it private. You can also be a lavish spender and enjoy making risky investments, intuitively knowing the outcomes will always be beneficial.

COLOURS

Chromatomancy, or divination by colour, is a form of energy therapy that has been used for thousands of years by many different cultures. It works on the principle that we make both instinctive and rational choices or preferences based on circumstances which are already present in ourselves; colour also has an effect on the energy in an environment, and we in turn respond consciously or subconsciously to our surroundings. If we look at the causes, and try to understand the reasons, as to why we are so receptive to one particular colour over another, we will see that there is a subtle link between certain hues and our emotional and instinctive individual reactions. The colour which we give to things results from a combination of three elements:

1. The light or the vibration of a body;

2. The context in which it is found and the interaction between its own light and that of its environment;

3. The sensitivity of the eye's retina which sees the body in question. Because of this, a colour can vary, depending on the individual's perceptions, namely, his sensitivity, his mood, and his view of reality. For a long time, people have understood that their vision of reality depends a lot on their moods, feelings and emotions. Chromatotherapy, or colour healing,

stems from this body of evidence, and its main application is the use of colours for healing purposes. Colours are generally associated with characteristics, feelings, stones, metals, plants and flowers, planets and even the zodiac signs. In varying cultures, they play a significant role in ceremonies and regalia.

We vibrate to the frequency of colour, shown through its continual movement and change in our aura ^. One of the most beautiful examples of colour is the rainbow. This architect of colour is caused by the refraction and internal reflection of light in raindrops. Colour can be perceived as either a pigment, or as illumination. The colour spectrum can be divided into eight main colours: red, orange, yellow, green, turquoise, blue, violet and magenta. Each colour has a wavelength and frequency that carry different therapeutic qualities which have indirect effects upon our health and bodily systems, and because of this, coupled with the fact that we as living energy centres emanate colour, colour can be a great medium in healing, calming, energising, increasing and attracting.

Aristotle, in the fourth century BCE, considered blue and yellow to be the true primary colours and related them to life's polarities: Sun and Moon, male and female, stimulation and sedation, in and out, expansion and contraction. He also associated colours with the four elements of Fire, Earth, Air and Water. Hippocrates, the father of medicine, used colour extensively in medicinal healing and recognised that the therapeutic effects of a white violet differed from those of a purple one. In the fifteenth century, Paracelsus placed particular importance on the role of colour in healing.

Each Sun sign and planetary body has a specific colour or colours which when used in combination with wishing rituals, can enhance their power immensely. Coloured candles can be used to good effect, as the fire energy of the flame/s increases the power of any wish, and flames are also a useful aid to meditating on, focusing upon or clarifying what you want. Coloured candles help to focus the energy for whatever purpose the colour is in sympathy with (e.g. green for money, pink for romance, orange for joy, etc.)

With all this in mind, wearing or using your Sun sign or ruling planet's magical colour/s on a regular basis will undoubtedly bring great benefits.

^ The aura is defined as an energy field, which interpenetrates with, and radiates beyond, the physical body. Clairvoyantly seen, the aura is full of light, colour and shade. The trained healer or seer sees or senses indications within the aura as to the spiritual, physical and emotional state of the individual. Much of the auric colour and energy emanates from the chakras.

YOUR LUCKY COLOURS

For Scorpio ★ Black, Burgundy, Russet Brown, Maroon, all deep shades of Red and Red-Brown

For Mars and Pluto ★ Red, Cerise, Burgundy, Beetroot, Plum, Brown, Black, Grey, Infra-red, Dark Purple

Scorpios have a strong presence and great sexual magnetism, hence the dark, blood red associated with your sign. You also instinctively gravitate towards black and like to accessorise with red.

Each of the eight colours of the rainbow spectrum also has a complementary colour to which it is matched. Red is complementary to turquoise, orange to blue, yellow to violet, and green to magenta. If these colour pairs enhance each other's most spellbinding qualities and energies, perhaps you could try wearing your Sun sign's lucky colour with its matching complementary colour in order to produce extra magical results! Your lucky Scorpio colours are black, and red, which complements turquoise. Now you know your colours, you can dress for success!

FEATURE COLOURS ★ BLACK & RED

★ BLACK ★

Planetary Associations ★ Saturn, Pluto

Healing Qualities ★ Power, Domination, Protection, Elegance, Sophistication, Status, Control, Protection, Willpower, Banishing and Absorbing Negativity

Keywords ★ Mystery, Power, Authority, Luxury, Sexy, Confidence, Dedication, Self-Importance, Protective, Wealth, Outer Space, the Universe

Technically speaking, black is not a colour but rather the absence of colour that occurs when light is totally absorbed by a surface. This means that none of the light hitting a black is reflected back into your eyes, which is how you usually perceive colour, giving black a number of useful properties, such as: if you are feeling cold it's better to wear darker shades such as dark grey or black, as these will retain heat, making you feel warmer (in summer, however, white is the most effective colour for helping you keep your cool). Also, because black is the colour you arrive at when all colours are 'absorbed', it is ideal for soaking up negativity, thereby possessing protective qualities.

A powerful and thought-provoking colour, black is the colour of Saturn and of the element of Spirit. Black is symbolic of the beginning and the end, the abyss, the culmination of things, the completion of a cycle, the void, termination, and the unknown. All colours are included in black, the Universal colour, which used to be considered evil, darkness and bad luck. According to Native American tradition each of the Four Winds has its own colour. Black is the colour of the West Wind and this usually augured ill fortune. Because when living matter breaks down it darkens and blackens, indicating that it no longer contains the vital life force, we associate this colour with decay, endings and mortality. Instinctively, we have an aversion to these concepts and naturally view them with suspicion. We also use phrases such as 'black magic', 'dark mood', the 'black death' (referring to the 14th century European plague pandemic during which millions perished), and 'blacklisted', which further contaminate our feelings around this mysterious and oft-maligned colour.

Although it has a bad reputation, being associated with death, fear and mortality, it can be used for positive ends - that is, through absorbing negativity, binding, dealing with depression and grief, divination and for bringing things to a conclusion. Because it is associated with grief and endings, black is a useful colour to use for binding in spell and ritual work; and in crystal therapies, black stones can be used for overall divination, connecting one to the Earth (through grounding), to protect and even to treat depression or helplessness. It is the colour of power and domination but has important spiritual overtones, as can be seen in the yin-yang symbol.

Black is also a colour of elegance and luxury that can suggest power and authority. It is a sophisticated colour, signifying status and achievement, as shown by those reaching the highest levels in martial arts being awarded a 'black belt'. Black can encourage introspection and is useful for situations where you want to feel in control. Black, being the colour of mysteries and secrets, can provide answers when we gaze, for example, at the 'black spaces' between the stars above, or indeed, into a black surface or sphere (black crystal balls can be used for 'scrying' or crystal-gazing in order to conjure images, illuminations or visions that can enlighten and guide our life's journey). Being connected to the Earth element, black can also help to ground you when you are feeling disconnected, 'floaty' and dislocated from the world. Due to its tendency to make things look smaller, in crystal work this could be applied to problems that you wish to diminish. Also seen as the colour of unrealised potential, of ideas yet to be manifested, it can be used in magical rituals to harness and take control of your inner powers so that you may attain your desires. Black overall can enhance self-confidence, feelings of self-control and authority, grounding and all-round connectedness.

★ RED ★

Planetary Association ★ Mars

Complementary Colour ★ Turquoise

Healing Qualities ★ Passion, Energy, Confidence, Courage, Sensuality, Security, Power, Inspiration, Activity, Motivation, Dynamism

Keywords ★ Fire, Passion, Aggression, Danger, Power, Desire, Lust, Stop (sign), Strength, Sexual Energy, Courage, Success, Willpower, War, Warning

Red is the colour with the slowest rate of vibration and the longest wavelength. Known to be able to raise blood pressure, red can strengthen and stimulate the body. Red is associated with the planet Mars and the element of Fire, and also with love, desire, motivation, power, arousal, inspiration, activity, war and success. It is a warm to hot colour which is symbolic of life, strength and vitality. Red is a powerful energiser and stimulant and has the ability to contract energy. It is the colour of passion, intensity and sexuality, conjuring up feelings of excitement and danger. Psychologically red can help make us feel warm and activated.

Red is connected with the Root or Base Chakra, located at the base of the spine, which is associated with security and survival and grounds you to the physical reality of your life. It will revitalise your whole energy system, alleviate exhaustion, boost energy and promote boldness; red is the great revitaliser, restorer and replenisher. Red is also associated with emotional outbursts, erotism, anger and stimulation. Frustration and resentment can ferment and then explode as anger or violence if too much red is in your environment. On a more subdued level, these can fester into restlessness, impatience and irritation. Red has good and bad connotations; 'red letter days', Dorothy's ruby slippers, 'rolling out the red carpet', Little Red Riding Hood's cape, and 'painting the town red' imply richness, adventure and vitality, but holding a 'red rag to a bull', red herrings, 'seeing red' and being 'in the red' aren't such positive connections. Additionally, red is recognised as the colour of both Cupid and the Devil. It can also burn out or scorch you with its heat. However, red is often given bad press and dismissed as being 'unspiritual' because it is connected to our primitive instincts and desires and governs our fight-or-flight adrenal glands, linking one to all things material and to the Earth itself. But these are all an integral part of your journey, and when the path gets too wearing and dispiriting, red can re-endow you with motivation, confidence, energy and joie de vivre!

Red and turquoise, its complementary rainbow spectrum colour, as well as black, are Scorpio's special LUCKY colours! The three can be worn or otherwise used together to dazzling and mesmerising effect.

SCORPIO'S CHAKRA CORRESPONDENCE
★ SACRAL

The word 'chakra' comes from the Sanskrit and means 'wheel', disc' or 'circle'. Chakras are vitally important to your physical health, emotional wellbeing and spiritual growth, and are regarded as a complete integrated system that works holistically. The chakras are funnel-shaped spinning energy vortexes of multi-coloured light. These swirling vortexes of energy absorb and distribute life-force, the subtle energy known as *prana*. The seven master chakras - Root, Sacral, Solar Plexus, Heart, Throat, Third Eye and Crown - lie in the centre line of the body, with the first five embedded within the spinal column. Each chakra vibrates at a different vibrational frequency and on a different note, and responds to specific life issues or 'thought forms'.

The lower body chakras deal with physical issues. As we move up the body, the chakras correspond to increasingly spiritual concerns. As a consequence, each chakra's energy vibrates at a different rate, depending on whether they govern earthbound or ethereal issues. The lower chakras have slower and denser vibrations, while the higher chakras spin at faster speeds with higher vibrations.

Because the chakras have no physical manifestation and cannot be located using any scientific instrument, they have tended to be viewed with scepticism by many Western medical professionals, a distinction they share with energy points in acupuncture and the notion of meridians. Instead, they are believed to have been sensed intuitively by many people over many centuries, and indeed people in yoga positions and in deep meditation have reported experiencing the sensation of a surge of energy rising from the base of the spine and emerging through the top of the head. Some people have even said they have seen points of blue light when their *kundalini* energy has risen from the lowest chakra to the highest, as well as experiencing a profound sense of happiness and ecstasy.

In summary, the Universal Life Force enters the body through the Crown chakra at the top of the head. As it works its way through the body, it flows through the other centres. As it spreads to the Base chakra, it is said to arouse the kundalini energy, which yogis believe sleeps in a coiled serpentine form.

The chakra associated with Scorpio is the second, or Sacral chakra, which governs sexual, physical, material and creative desires and expressions.

SACRAL CHAKRA

Location ★ Below the Navel
Colour ★ Orange

Concerned with ★ Physical, Sexual, Creative & Material Desires
Gland ★ Cells of Leydig *
Essential Oils ★ Carrot Seed, Dill, Geranium, Jasmine, Hyssop, Neroli, Marjoram, Sandalwood, Rose
Animals ★ Sea Creatures
Shape ★ Light Blue Crescent
Element ★ Water
Planets ★ Moon, Pluto
Zodiac Signs ★ Cancer, Scorpio
Flower ★ Six-petalled Lotus
Energy State ★ Liquid
Mantra ★ VAM

* The Sacral chakra regulates what are called the 'cells of Leydig', which are testicular or ovarian cells that produce and secrete testosterone.

Positive Expression ★ Balanced, creative, personally vital

Negative Expression (Blockage) ★ Imbalanced, over- or undersexed, inflexible, emotionally cold, low energy, low libido, inhibiting, difficulty changing, difficulty experiencing joy, hyper-emotional, overly focused on physical pleasures

The Sacral chakra is located around the sexual organ region. Its Sanskrit name is *svadhisthana*, and its symbol is a six-petalled orange lotus flower containing a second lotus flower and an upward-pointing crescent Moon in a white circle. Balance in this chakra is expressed as originality, creativity and vitality. It corresponds to the sex glands and the sacral nerve plexus. Crystals that can be used to cleanse and balance this chakra are mostly orange stones, including: Carnelian, Amber, Orange Calcite, Citrine, Golden Labradorite (Orange Sunstone), Topaz, Tangerine Quartz and Thulite.

LUCKY CAREER TIPS & PATHS THAT WILL MAKE YOUR BANK BALANCE & SPIRITUAL SELF SOAR

The branch of astrology known as 'vocational astrology' encompasses the areas of one's calling, career path, or ideal profession. Careers, jobs, professions and occupations can all mean different things to different people, but to simplify the definition, I refer to a vocation as one's true calling, one's authentic path, and a dynamic way of life which pays an income in some form and leads to a deep fulfilment of personal and spiritual needs. An ideal vocation will provide self-fulfilment, ego satisfaction, and feed one's inner drive to achieve what they ultimately wish to achieve, whether that be to gain recognition, wealth or approval, to travel, to learn and fulfil an inner need for knowledge, an urge to serve others in some way, or an urge to improve personal, societal or Universal conditions.

In order to gain ultimate fulfilment and self-esteem, we all need a purpose in life. Many people gain this through their work, providing the job or career they choose suits their temperament, talents and aspirations. If our professional life is unsatisfactory or disharmonious in any way, frustration, unhappiness and even despair can result. Although your whole horoscope would need to be drawn up and interpreted in order to gain more substantial, deeper insights into your ideal career and purpose, you can begin by being guided by your Sun sign, which can give you many pointers to a suitable, and therefore successful, career path. You just never know, something in the following might jump out at you and make your soul dance immediately - and hopefully all the way to the bank!

With your Sun in Scorpio, you are powerful, intense, controlling, disciplined, resilient and put your heart and soul into everything you undertake. In fact, one description of Scorpio states, "You put a great deal of intensity into everything you do, whether it is working, playing, or loving." In terms of vocation, this indicates there is nothing the Scorpion cannot achieve once you set your mind to it.

Of all the signs, yours is the most determined, the one who will never give up, give out or give in. You frequently put yourself to the test, push yourself to the limits, and are always demanding as much from others as you do from yourself.

With your penetrating perception you pick up things that other people miss and you perceive the environment - and others - with astonishing accuracy and insight. These can be excellent business skills. As a typical Scorpio, you are a natural sleuth and somewhat psychic, making you ideal for the investigative and detective fields. You excel at ferreting out hidden facts and secret information, and this type of ability makes you efficient in such fields as Archaeology, Industrial Chemistry, Clairvoyance, Surveillance, Private Investigation, Astronomy, Forensics, Psychoanalysis, Undercover 'Gossip', Crime Reporting/Writing, Astrology, Botany, Geology, Government or Industrial Espionage, Psychic Mediumship, Surgery, Criminal Psychology,

Psychiatry, Undercover Work, Exploration, Science, and any other occupations which involve the unravelling or unveiling of hidden, secret, deep or unknown facts and mysteries.

Scorpios take life very seriously, and are quite happy to expose errors and fight for their beliefs. Your ideal vocation uses your sharp perceptions and your ability to transform and influence other people, and also provides you with sufficient challenges, of which you are also a supreme master. Any work demanding determined effort, a passionate temperament or intense concentration is your ideal path.

Scorpio, being specifically connected with the realm of sex, is suitable for work or fields which deal with the exploitation of sex, either overtly, covertly or symbolically. You, more than anyone, can capitalise on the well-coined phrase that 'sex sells'.

Scorpio is also connected with death, and knows instinctively that everything that has a beginning also has an end - and it is the end which you are most concerned with, and to some this may even be an obsession. Abattoir Workers, Butchers, Coroners, Waste Disposal, Livestock Farmers, Undertakers, Death Doulas, Transition Aides (helping people to 'pass over'), Cemetery Workers, Mediumship, Ghost Hunting/Ghost Tours, Exorcism, Fishing Industry Workers, Coffin Makers, and Funeral Directors are all occupations related to Scorpio. However, with death also comes rebirth, and Scorpios are also suited to the transformational or healing professions, such as Trance Work, Art Therapies, Meditation, Past Life Therapy, Psychiatry, Psychology, and Counselling.

Being a Water sign, and a secretive one at that, any profession dealing with Plumbing, Drainage, Dam Building and Maintenance, or working underground in Mines, Caves, Lakes, Rivers or the Ocean in any capacity are suitable career fields.

On the other end of the scale, there are some Scorpios who operate on the deviant side of the law, such as Drug Smugglers, Gangsters, Illegal 'Sport' Operators, Underground and Underworld Activities, and many more, expressing many a Scorpio's clandestine leanings. This may stem from a simmering resentment of society at large, and more specifically of people occupying positions of power, wealth, status or privilege to which the Scorpio herself feels entitled; or it may stem from the Scorpio's single-minded need for power and control over others.

Whichever career you decide to undertake, you are ever ambitious and devoted to making money. Your sense of purpose and incisive mind make you an excellent business person, a successful researcher, a masterful detective, and second to none at reaching the bottom of things and solving complex puzzles. Nothing fazes or baffles you, and no job is ever too big for you. Your resourcefulness, accomplishment of the seemingly impossible, and ability to outwit others makes you good at sealing nearly every deal you make. Invisible and unconquerable, you strive courageously to reach the heights of any vocation. Ultimately, your shrewd mind and intuition often help to place you in the right place at the right time, and to make the right contacts.

LUCKY PLACES WHERE YOUR ENERGY IS HEIGHTENED

As the Water element and phlegmatic humour corresponds with cold and moist conditions, cool, damp, rainy places suit your constitution, disposition and temperament. The following nations, countries and cities are also places whose vibrations are closely allied with the sign of Scorpio: Cuba, Norway, The Seychelles, Antiqua and Barbuda, Puerto Rico, Micronesia, Lebanon, Korea, Liverpool (England), Dominican Republic, Martinique, Algeria, Morocco, Angola, Queensland, Uruguay, Queensland, South Africa, Syria, Tibet and North America (Cincinnati, Washington DC). Finland, Bavaria, the Transvaal, Mexico, Panama, Hungary, St Vincent and the Grenadines, Zambia, Turkey and Chad are also in tune with the Scorpion energy, as are desert islands, anywhere which boasts dark cobble-stoned alleys, cities whose dwellings have basements and cellars, and places where vermin and reptiles breed. A guided tour to any place whose history is steeped in the occult, underworld criminality, inquisitions, genocide, tragic figures, or ghosts, a visit to Scotland Yard or the American FBI Headquarters, or any other place which allows you to probe into the dark corners of its bygone past or investigate the underbelly of a city, a walk through a famous cemetery, gothic architecture-spotting, and visiting otherwise creepy and profoundly interesting places in which you can undertake your own investigative detective work and take self-guided strolls at midnight, could very well be your ticket to Scorpion heaven!

GEMS & CRYSTALS

"People love stones, and apparently stones love people. Like the angels they may be, they seem endlessly willing to serve the wellbeing of humans and to help us achieve our desires ...Unlike people of the ancient past, we now have access to virtually the entire mineral kingdom. We have the opportunity to work like modern alchemists, combining and arranging the stones and their currents, looking for combinations and patterns that can help us enhance our inner and outer lives."

Robert Simmons, *Stones of the New Consciousness*

Each crystal and mineral of the Earth embodies different qualities, patterns or potential expressions of the Divine language, the silent whispers of the Universe. If we can accept the fact that the human body is a sophisticated, multi-faceted antenna system comprised of a crystalline matrix that is constantly transmitting and receiving all manner of energies, it could then be assumed that energy and body workers who use quartz, shells and stones, which are also crystalline materials, have the power to promote resonant interactions with the liquid 'crystal' structures found in human tissues. It could even be said that we are all made of essentially the same substances and structures, and that crystals and gemstones vibrate at varying energetic levels which can connect with our own in order to 'buzz' and dance together to make a harmonious Uni-verse both within and without.

All crystals work through vibrational balancing and by channelling energy. The magic of crystals is in their colour, which is determined by the rate at which their atoms vibrate; these vibrations can be matched to the energy given by your own body's aura. And just as light can be focused and refracted through gemstones, so too can all kinds of psychic energy, from healing energies to Divine communications.

Gemstones can help us attune to higher vibrations and bring them into our own experience and being. This theory of crystal resonance suggests that the characteristic energy patterns emanated by any stone can be transferred into the 'liquid crystal medium' of our bodies through resonance. Our bodies, being composed of these tuneable liquids, can mimic and mirror any consistent vibrational pattern with which we come into contact; we can therefore resonate with the healthful qualities of various crystals and minerals.

Crystals and precious stones have been valued throughout world cultures over many centuries for their healing virtues and capacities to imbue courage, strength, invulnerability, clairvoyance, love and numerous other qualities. Wearing gemstones is one of the simplest and most effective self-healing practices you can undertake, and wearing or carrying those stones whose vibrations correspond with the qualities you wish to embody brings their energetic currents into engagement with your body.

Over time the phenomenon of energetic integration, may be felt tangibly and your own vibrational field may internalise the stone's currents and adjust to them and effectively 'store' them, making them, eventually, a part of your own vibrational make-up. And we seem to know from the resonances we feel within our bodies when in contact with these gemstones, that crystals emanate tangible, if oft immeasurable, currents.

Crystals act as transmitters and amplifiers of your will or intentions - as long as your will or intentions are in sympathy with the crystal's energy. The mineral kingdom refers to stones, minerals and crystals and the associations and vibrations they carry. When working with stones, we are working with several different layers of spiritual energies, and although they can be regarded as inanimate 'psychic batteries', they are actually moving, vibrating masses of energy which transmit potential and power into our lives. Some crystals and stones even have receptive powers, which means they can absorb energy and retain it within until cleansed or re-programmed.

Although it is untrue that the only stones you can usefully wear are the ones astrologically matched with your Sun sign or ruling planet, those which align with your Sun sign or ruling planet are your most fortuitous and therefore strongest 'attractors' and 'amplifiers'.

Twelve oracular gemstones were described in the Bible, as the author of *Exodus* (28-15 and 17-21) knew them. Yahweh spoke to Moses about the breastplate he would have to wear to train for priesthood, and described it to him in these words: "And thou shalt make the breastplate of judgement with cunning work; ... And thou shalt set in it settings of stones, even four rows of stones; the first row shall be a sardius, a topaz, and a carbuncle. And the second row shall be an emerald, a sapphire and a diamond. And the third row an opal, an agate and an amethyst. And the fourth row a beryl, and an onyx, and a jasper; they shall be set in hold in their inclosings. And the stones shall be with the children ... (all) twelve (of them)." Given that the compilers of the Bible lived during a time when astrological belief was prevalent in Babylon, it seems valid to assert that these previously named gemstones would have some astrological basis. Further, since these ancient people supposedly made correlations between each of the twelve precious stones, and one of the twelve zodiac signs, there are seven crystalline systems set down in crystallography (or the science of the laws which influence the formation, structure and geometric, physical and chemical properties of crystallised matter) as analogous with the seven traditional ruling planets of the zodiac.

However, nobody is under the rule of one planet alone. We are all in essence a complex mixture of every planet, many elements and varying aspects, depending on their positions, placements and prominence in our birth chart. Everything that goes on in the skies above us affects what is going on here on Earth, and also *within* us. Your lucky stones are to assist you to tune into your Sun sign's energy and planetary influences, but you are by no means limited to the ones listed for your sign alone. Above all, let your stones, whichever ones you choose, work for you and allow them to transport your very own unique and magical energy into the wider Universe.

> "Beautiful and strong is the material of stones, but more beautiful and much more powerful is the mystery that emanates from them."
> **Chinese Poet & Alchemist, Li Po, 8th Century A.D.**

★ CLEAR QUARTZ ★

The Master Healer ★ *For All Zodiac Signs*

A common, well-known and popular gem, clear quartz (sometimes known as rock crystal) is an all-purpose 'jack-of-all-trades' stone. It amplifies the magic of any work you do or wishes you make. It is connected with all the chakras and increases the power of all other crystals. Clear quartz is a deep soul cleanser, which unblocks and regulates energy and emotions on all levels. It is balancing and harmonising. In various cultures, quartz crystal is reputed to be the most powerful crystal, the 'grandfather crystal', and the 'chief of the Stone People'. Clear quartz is also considered to be the only gemstone that is modifiable to suit your needs *, as other crystals automatically contain and retain their own specific resonance or natural signature. In essence, clear quartz is the most easily programmable and the most overall healing and readily accessible crystals of the mineral kingdom, holding a unique importance in the Universe of gems. And because of its all-encompassing nature and wide-ranging healing abilities, it has zodiacal affinities with all the signs.

* To program your clear quartz crystal, simply hold it on your Third Eye chakra (between and just above the

physical eyes) and concentrate on the purpose for which you wish to use it. Be positive and receptive while you allow your crystal to fill with this energy. If you wish, you could also state the intention of the programming out loud, for example, 'I program this crystal for love / healing / meditation / abundance / protection or (insert your own word here)'. You could also run your clear quartz crystal under running water, allow it to dry naturally, then hold the stone with both hands, bring it up to your mouth and blow into it sharply three times in order to impregnate it with your own breath. Then, hold it firmly in one hand and silently invite and welcome it into your life as a friend, helper and guide.

SCORPION & PLUTONIAN LUCKY CRYSTALS, STONES & GEMS

Scorpio birth stones ★ Topaz, Malachite, Peridot

October birth stones ★ Opal, Aquamarine, Tourmaline

November birth stones ★ Topaz, Citrine, Pearl

Topaz, Malachite, Peridot (your three primary birthstones), Opal, Aquamarine, Tourmaline, Citrine, Pearl (October and November birthstones), and Red Coral (Mars) are your luckiest stones, and one or more of these gems should be worn about your person to ensure good luck and increase your overall magnetism. Labradorite, Hematite, Carnelian, Moonstone, Turquoise, Magnetite, Ruby, Beryl, Red Spinel, Rhodochrosite, Emerald, Apache Tear,

Obsidian, Hiddenite, Stibnite, Tibetan Quartz, Titanium Quartz, Variscite, Boji Stone, Flint, Shiva Lingam, Dioptase, Green Tourmaline, True Jasper, Yellow Calcite, Iron Tiger's Eye, Red Jasper, Jacinth, Sunstone, Red Amber, Garnet, Kunzite and Herkimer Diamond also align with Scorpio's energy. Additionally, all scarlet and dark red stones are especially beneficial attractors for Scorpios.

CRYSTALS & THE PLANETS

All the Vedic texts agree in relating gems to planets. This verse from the *Jatax Parijat* links each gem to a planet:

'The ruby is the gem of the Lord of the Day (the Sun),
The shining pearl is the gem of the cold Moon,
Red coral is the gem of Mars,
The emerald is the gem of noble Mercury,
Yellow sapphire is the gem of Jupiter, instructor of gods,
Diamond is the gem of Venus, instructor of demons,
Blue sapphire is the gem of Saturn.'

Each planet influences its gem, and their curative power varies according to the position of its planet in the zodiac. Ayurvedic medicine has always paid attention to these details in their healing practices, often advising people to wear their corresponding zodiacal stone as a ring or a talisman.

CRYSTALS & THE ELEMENTS

Crystals are inextricably linked to the four elements, from their original creation to their potency and use in magical rituals and healing. Formed by the combination, in varying conditions, of different physical elements, such as metals, non-metals and gases, some stones require the enormous heat generated by volcanoes or deep thermal currents to bond their molecular makeup, while others may require pressure or water sources. The effects of the four elements of Fire, Earth, Air and Water is evident in these formation processes. The heat generated by Fire, pressure from the Earth, and the chemical reactions involved in absorbing elements from the Air and Water, all demonstrate the four elements in action to produce the correct conditions and ingredients necessary for the creation of crystals, lending them each their unique qualities.

CRYSTALS & THE WATER ELEMENT

The depositing or the evaporation of Water is a component in the formation of many crystals, including stalagmites and stalactites. Water also finds its balance by assuming its appropriate state as a gas, liquid or solid (ice). Therefore, Water-inspired gemstones help to balance your emotions and influence your dreams by shifting notions between the conscious and unconscious mind.

Some Watery crystals are ★ Pearl, Beryl, Moonstone, Aquamarine, Selenite, Tourmaline and Amethyst.

THE CRYSTALLINE SYSTEM OF YOUR TRADITIONAL RULING PLANET MARS

Associated with your ruling planet Mars, are Amethyst, Magnetite, Cornelian, Barite, Garnet, Ruby, Topaz and Bloodstone. This is the third crystalline system, known as orthorhombic, that is having a rectangular parallelepiped. The stone which perhaps represents this system best is Topaz, which was famous for the good fortune it brought to those who wore it, but also for its therapeutic properties in treating and even healing eye-related conditions.

MARS'S GEMSTONE ASSOCIATION

★ **RED CORAL** ★ Coral is among the most ancient of gem materials and was first used for adornment in prehistoric times. The name comes from a Greek word that means 'nymph of the sea'. Long regarded as a powerful talisman that was able to stop bleeding, give protection from evil spirits and even ward off hurricanes, red coral is renowned for its strength and energy. The wearing of coral was reputed to cure or prevent many ailments, and as an amulet it banished nightmares, protected children and warded off demons of the darkness, so in this sense it could be used as a protective gem. The coral used in jewellery is the hard skeleton formed by certain polyps of the corallium nobile family and occurs in red, blue, golden, black, white and pink. These polyps are minute living creatures that live in vast colonies. When they die, their skeletal remains - mostly calcium carbonate - build up to form massive coral reefs. Red coral is considered the best colour for protective charms and is called 'Witch Stone' in Italy. It was thought to absorb emotional negativity and was used against the Evil Eye. Coral, particularly red coral, encourages one to have more determination and courage. As an ocean dweller, coral's astrological correspondence is with the Moon, which also befits its watery genesis. When sourcing your coral, however, you should bear in mind that coral reefs are among the world's most vital yet fragile ecosystems and materials taken from them should only be purchased from a sustainable marine operator.

SCORPIO'S FEATURE CRYSTAL ★ MALACHITE *

'The Transformation and Power Stone'

Malachite is a striking, rich-green layered opaque stone of intense energy. Its dramatic patterns echo its versatile and vast healing qualities. It is so named because its layers resemble the soft green of the marshmallow plant, derived from the Greek word for the plant's colouring - *malache*. It is connected with the Solar Plexus, Throat and Heart chakras, and although powerful and probing, it will increase courage and determination, dissolving fear and anxiety, and help you break free from limitations. Malachite is a copper-rich crystal which can be used diagnostically to get to the heart of a problem. It is a stone of balance that soothes, but also strengthens, the nervous system. A resolute stone that draws insights out from deep within the subconscious mind and facilitates the regeneration of the self, with dedicated use, this intense stone can balance and bring harmony to the body and psyche. Malachite is an exceptionally evolving ** stone that is perfect for all self-transformational explorations, and the more you work with it, the more expansive its influence becomes. It illuminates the darker corners of the mind, and in doing so demands that you examine the deep-rooted causes of any physical or mental issues. This is also a stone of alignment and is excellent to use in self-exploration journeys.

Working with malachite ultimately helps you confront whatever it is that is blocking your spiritual unfolding and wellbeing. It also has a detoxifying effect, cleansing the body of both physical and emotional impurities. Assisting in the release of outworn or restrictive patterns of thought or behaviour, it is both physically and psychologically vitalising. It also facilitates release and letting go, enabling you to move forward. Used in combination with other similarly acting crystals, malachite can heal grief, ease heartache, draw out toxic emotions, break unwanted ties, root out psychosomatic causes of bodily dis-ease, and teach you how to take responsibility for your thoughts, actions and feelings. Malachite is known as the 'sleep stone' because it has the effect of inducing drowsiness if gazed at for long enough. Indeed, it can ease insomnia, improve quality of sleep and dreaming, and offer protection from nightmares. Malachite is used for its protective properties as well. It absorbs pollutants and negative energies, picking them up from the atmosphere, the physical body and the aura. It guards against radiation of all kinds and soaks up plutonium pollution. It also clears electromagnetic pollution and heals Earth energies.

Malachite can be used for scrying - journeying through its convoluted patterns can stimulate pictures, and assist in receiving insights or messages from the future. It is regarded as "the mirror of the soul" and so some crystal experts may advise against wearing malachite as it may prove too powerful and confronting for some. Essentially, it is a true empowerment crystal, which helps you reclaim your power by bringing to the surface any hidden issues, toxic thoughts or repressed feelings that are holding you back. If this stone had an expression, it would be, "I Am." It will help those who are brave enough to work with it, to step into your true power. As a stone of transformation and change, life is lived more intensely and adventurously under the influence of this vivid gem. It will enhance spiritual rebirth and growth, and when placed on the Solar Plexus it will facilitate deep emotional healing, allowing one's deepest self to shift in a new, positive direction. This profound crystal will surprise you with its merciless spotlight on what has held you back for so long - and will further astound with the depth of transmutation that you can achieve with it.

* Malachite will lose its sheen if cleansed in salt water - smudging this crystal with sandalwood or sage incense is preferable. It should be cleansed before and after use by placing it on a quartz cluster in the Sun. Also, malachite needs to be handled with caution and is best used under the supervision of a qualified crystal therapist. Always use malachite in its polished form, and wash your hands after use.

** It is believed by some people that malachite is still evolving and will be one of the most important healing stones in years to come.

SCORPION POWER CRYSTALS

Around six thousand years ago, in ancient Mesopotamia, the Sumerians started studying precious stones and minerals, as well as the stars, with a view of improving their lives in many ways by probing the secrets and mysteries of the Universe. Their esoteric interests and knowledge were such that they began to grasp the general connections between the Earth and the heavens, or the Solar system as they knew it, and the functions of stones and minerals as a link between the two. Their method of making these connections was by colour (for example the Sun was allocated all yellow stones), as well as other spiritual links. The gemstones listed for the portion of your zodiac sign are given their status as your 'power crystals' due to the links that can be made between your primary planetary ruler/s and your mutable planetary ruler (listed last), and each stone's particular colour, chemical and mineral compositions, healing properties, and the number they are given (based on the Mohs scale of hardness: for example, diamond scores a perfect 10 out of 10), all of which combine to align with your planetary rulers. Working mindfully with your planet's special crystals is one way you can increase the flow of power and magic into your life.

POWER CRYSTALS FOR FIRST HALF SCORPIONS ★ (23 October - 6 November)

Influenced by Pluto, Mars and Neptune
Ruby, Benitoite, Blue John, Stibnite, Crocoite

★ **RUBY** ★ Ruby derives its name from the Latin *rubens* or *rubeus*, meaning 'red'. A variety of the mineral corundum, it has a hardness of 9, corresponding to the planet Mars's number. Because it symbolised happiness and brightness, and was believed to be the most beautiful of gems, it came to be associated with the sign of Leo. This association was also made because of its power in bringing success, wealth and joy, and because its symbolic virtues included courage, nobility, spirit and loyalty. The ancients considered ruby to be the stone of the Sun and believed it represented the life force and fire. The gem of northern summer, ruby burns with a captivating fire. Ruby has long been regarded as a symbol of love, beauty, passion, success, strength, protection and power. It aids in strengthening and refining the natural abilities you were born with. It is a stone of immense power and vitality, and can be worn to stimulate pure life force energy. Its spirit is a great ally to those who wish to work magic in their lives. Imparting vigour to your journey, it energises and balances but may sometimes overstimulate more delicate or irritable types. Ruby encourages the setting of realistic goals, improves motivation and stimulates passion for living. It stimulates the Heart chakra and enlivens the heart, encouraging you to 'follow your bliss'. It is also a powerful energiser for the Base chakra. Ruby signifies and arouses lust, and governs the sexual and reproductive organs. It can be used to release any energy blockages deep within the self, and to activate, vitalise, intensify and increase desire. It utilises infrared, the slowest vibration of the colour spectrum, giving a new boost to processes that have been sluggish or stagnant. Ruby is one of the stones of abundance and aids in retaining wealth and a healthy, driven passion. Ruby brings up anger or negative energy, transmutes them, and removes anything unfavourable from your path. Promoting lively leadership and confidence, ruby brings about a positive and courageous state of mind. Essentially, ruby is a dynamic stone which charges up passion, banishes sadness, warns of danger or imminent misfortune (by darkening in colour), attracts sexual activity, fires up enthusiasm, and helps one overcome exhaustion, apathy and lethargy by imparting potency and vigour. It can stop outside forces from draining your energy. Ruby renews one's passion for life, truth, courage, wisdom and perseverance, emitting an abundance of cheerfulness.

★ **STIBNITE** ★ Stibnite is expressed in straight radiating needles or flat rods, sometimes with criss-cross lines which are usually grouped in parallel. It is an attractive stone occasionally exhibiting surface iridescence. In magical use, stibnite is regarded as a shaman's stone: facilitating shape-shifting and creating a powerful shield around the body while it is spiritually journeying. When used as a wand, stibnite separates the pure from the dross and reveals the inner gold in your centre.

POWER CRYSTALS FOR SECOND HALF SCORPIONS ★ (7 - 21 November)

Influenced by Pluto, Mars and the Moon
Rhodochrosite, Alexandrite, Amethyst, Okenite, Prehnite, Quartz

★ **RHODOCROSITE** ★ Otherwise known as 'Inca Rose', rhodochrosite was only discovered about sixty years ago, so like its cousin rhodonite, is new in holistic terms. Rhodochrosite is found in two varieties: the sunset-coloured stone of gem quality, and the white-lined, rosy or baby-pink semi-precious gemstone. Tests have shown that both have beneficial properties, emitting light vibrations which cheer the depressed, preserve youth, and help to coax back the life-force into sickly subjects. On a spiritual level, rhodochrosite represents selfless love and compassion. It expands the consciousness and integrates the spiritual with the material. Encouraging a dynamic and positive attitude, rhodochrosite is an excellent stone for the heart and relationships, particularly for people who feel unloved or unlovable. It is a stone which improves self-worth, lifts depression and soothes emotional stress. Mentally enlivening, it promotes the spontaneous expression of feelings, including passionate and erotic urges. Because it prompts spontaneity, it is ideal for those who find it difficult to express their emotions. Rhodochrosite also enhances dream states, creativity and lightness of being and feeling. Although rhodochrosite has a charming reputation for having the ability to attract one's soul mate, this may not be the blissful experience hoped for, as a soul mate may be someone who appears in our life to teach us important, though not always pleasant, lessons for our higher good. This stone works on the Solar Plexus and Base chakras, gently bringing painful and repressed feelings to the surface, allowing them to be acknowledged in order to then be dissipated and released. Rhodochrosite is believed to be an effective stone for helping to heal the effects of sexual abuse. It also teaches the heart to assimilate hurtful feelings without shutting down. It is a stone which removes denial and insists that you face the truth about yourselves and others with loving awareness rather than evasion. Rhodochrosite is a perfect companion with rose quartz when working on the Heart chakra. It is an emotional balancer, trauma-soother and resonates with the subtle bodies, swiftly clearing the Sacral, Solar Plexus and Heart chakras of traumatic events and feelings by bringing repressed emotions to the surface to be healed. Overall, rhodochrosite holds the higher octave of love that can dissolve emotional wounds, and is a powerful heart-healer and psychological tonic.

★ **ALEXANDRITE** ★ Alexandrite is a variety of chrysoberyl, a beryllium aluminium oxide with a hardness of 8.5. One of the hardest gemstones, second only to diamond and corundum, its crystal pattern is orthorhombic. Alexandrite is a crystal of contrasts. It opens the intuition and metaphysical abilities, and creates a strong will and personal magnetism. One of the world's rarest gemstones, the finest specimens of alexandrite are costlier than diamonds - and its price understandably reflects its rarity. Discovered in the Ural Mountains of Russia in around 1830 on the birthday of Czar Alexander II and named after him, its key words are joy, wisdom and release of sorrow. A notable feature of this crystal is its stunning optical property of colour change - it is light red or red-purple in incandescent artificial light, and green (often an intense grass-green) or blue-green in daylight. Since green is the colour of new growth and pink the shade of impartial love, the Russian name for Alexandrite, 'Stone of Good Omen', could not be more apt. This stone has a positive electrical charge which stays for hours after rubbing, and an energy factor which changes with its colour. But potent though this stone looks, it radiates sensitivity. In physical healing, it bypasses the actual condition and goes directly to the root of it and balances any disharmonies out. It is a regenerative stone, aiding the tissues of the body to renew after dis-ease - both internally and externally. It has even been used to treat leukaemia and cancer. These regenerative properties also extend to spiritual transformation and growth, enhancing your ability to find joy in life and aiding psychic protection when undertaking such work. It also carries the beneficial qualities of making one's head feel 'roomier', improving the memory, clearing the eyesight, and relieving any physical tensions. In its colour change, it signifies a spiritual metamorphosis and embodies an inner pattern of flexibility, adaptability and willingness to shift its expression in the presence of varying conditions; it can teach us this very quality in ourselves. Since its discovery, alexandrite was believed to be a stone of good fortune in its native country. It carries a very joyful vibration and is a powerful agent of inner transformation and spiritual evolution. Primarily stimulating the Crown chakra, it embodies both the heart energy (green) and the higher mind energy (purple). It can stimulate a harmonic opening of the Heart, Third Eye and Crown chakras, during which the three can operate as an integrated whole. Alexandrite's emotional tone is one of exuberant joy. It calls forth the heart's natural state of delighted engagement and teaches us that the spiritual qualities of the celestial realms are also simultaneously here at every moment, encouraging us to take on all the energies that come to us and to do this with a pure commitment to joy. Overall, it centres, reinforces and realigns the mental, emotional and spiritual bodies, enhancing manifestation in all its forms. This precious, rare gem transmits inner peace by developing magnanimity of heart and should be valued and used extensively.

★ **AMETHYST** ★ An extremely well-known, common, easy-to-source and popular stone, this is the stone of spiritual power and psychic energy. Its colour varies from pale lilac to an intense purple, depending on its iron content. The Ancient Egyptians consecrated this stone to the god of wisdom, Thoth, while in Ancient Greece it was associated with Mercury. It has a high ethereal vibration and is an extremely powerful, healing and protective stone. Its name is derived from the Greek word *amethystos*, literally meaning "not intoxicated." Its violet colour is created by the presence of iron oxide impurities in its crystals. This charming stone awakens and activates our higher awareness and psychic abilities, and has been used since biblical times; it is mentioned in Exodus as one of the 12 sacred stones worn on the High Priest Aaron's breastplate. Amethyst has strong cleansing and healing powers, and its serenity assists with enhancing meditation and the reaching of higher states of consciousness. It fights against inferiority complexes, insecurities and fears, through calming states of stress. Connected with the Crown and Third Eye chakras, amethyst offers protection, wisdom, focus, power, access to divine understanding, ethereal awareness, and increases psychic abilities, healing and inner peace. Its best known use is for heightening and enhancing one's spiritual connections and insights; it can even open doors to other dimensions, planes and realities. Many spiritualists believe that it can also bring the divine into the mundane parts of your life, heighten your receptivity to all manner of things, and generally enhance *all* healing. The radiation of violet light issuing from amethyst has been placed on record as providing a calming influence upon the nerves, making it balancing and comforting to the wearer, and is said to be instrumental in slowing rapid and agitated bodily movements, and helpful in easing neuralgia, headaches, gout and stress-related insomnia. Amethyst can be worn on parts of the upper body to encourage conversations with your higher self, and is especially beneficial when worn over the throat or heart. Encouraging selflessness, intuition, spiritual wisdom and divine visualisation, amethyst can transmute earthly energies to the higher vibrations of etheric realms. As a stone of tranquillity and contentment, it can also dispel anger, irritability, mood swings, fear and negativity. Amethyst can act as a compassionate anchor and ensures that you are emanating your energy from a place of peace and understanding.

★ **OKENITE** ★ Okenite is a white 'new age' stone with a soft and furry energy. By linking one to one's higher self, it supports the conscious manifestation of its energies on the Earth plane. Okenite identifies karmic debts and opportunities that will help you to grow. Psychologically, okenite encourages profound self-forgiveness. It facilitates deep vibrational healing on all levels by bringing to your attention the reasons for your current experiences, and promotes the completion of cycles, going back into the past to forgive yourself for your mistakes and easing karmic guilt. A stone of mystical grace, it teaches that everything is part of the cycle of learning the soul's lessons and, emanating from that knowledge, that nothing has to be endured forever. It imparts the wisdom that when you have done all you can in a situation, you can step out of it without incurring further karmic debt. Okenite purifies the chakras and the physical and subtle bodies, uniting their energies, and facilitates changing your mental set, releasing old belief patterns and ushering in new, more appropriate ones.

★ **PREHNITE** ★ Prehnite has an ethereal quality to it when tumbled, cut and polished, and often has a pearly lustre. Though not always easy to find, it is well worth searching for. The serene prehnite is a stone of unconditional love. This is an ideal stone to 'heal the healer' and when meditating with this stone, you are put in touch with the Universe's energy grid. The higher self may be contacted through this gem, and it is said to help one connect with angels and spiritual and extra-terrestrial realms. Prehnite enhances inner knowing, precognition and attuning to divine energies. It can bring about prophecy and light the way forward for your spiritual growth. Prehnite can enable one to trust in the Universe again and restore the soul's belief in divine manifestation. Prehnite is a protective stone, sealing the aura in a shield of energy, calming the environment and surrounding you with peace and protection. It aligns with the Solar Plexus and Heart chakras, enhancing and balancing the flow of energy along all the chakra points. Prehnite is an excellent stone to use for relaxation, clarity of thought, and bonding within personal relationships.

★ **QUARTZ** ★ Otherwise known as rock quartz or clear quartz, this is truly the master healer of the crystal world, the perfect all-rounder with wide-ranging healing applications. The word crystal comes from the Greek word *krystallos*, meaning ice. Clear quartz is thought to be the only crystal that is modifiable or 'programmable' to suit your needs *, as other crystals automatically contain their own specific resonance or natural signature. In ancient times quartz was thought of as a permanent form of ice, its clarity and purity having magical similarities to water and glass. A common, well-known and popular gem, rock crystal is an all-purpose 'jack-of-all-trades' stone because it contains the full spectrum of the visible white light - a broad spectrum healing energy which clears dis-ease from all levels. Clear quartz stabilises, focuses and amplifies the vital life-force, and its resonance will swiftly go to any area/s in need of healing or restructuring. It also activates, amplifies and channels the magic of any work you do or wishes you make, by receiving, storing, transforming, transmitting and magnifying all energy and thought forms. It is connected with all the chakras and increases the power of all other crystals. Kirlian photography ** has revealed that when a quartz crystal is held in the hand, the strength of the bio magnetic energy field is at least doubled. It therefore follows that placing one on any part of the body will increase the energy in that area. Its vibrations, which begin at about room temperature, giving this mineral an important role in all holistic practice, and whether held in the hand, placed on a person, or positioned in close proximity to any living thing, clear quartz enlarges the aura of everything near it, even increasing the healing powers of other minerals. Many healers find they obtain swifter results when the patient holds a piece of clear quartz. It was, and still is, the stone most favoured for crystal gazing or scrying, for its lustre quickly 'freezes' the optic nerve, with the result that outside impressions are suppressed and the eye is 'released' to gaze into its depths. This is a deep soul cleanser, which unblocks and regulates energy and emotions. It is balancing and harmonising, and can attune you to your spiritual purpose. Rock crystal is believed to strengthen the link between Earth and the heavens, enabling its user to see into other times and places, so it is a useful aid for psychic travelling and dream journeys. In various cultures, quartz crystal is reputed to be the most powerful crystal, the 'grandfather crystal', and the 'chief of the Stone People'. In essence, clear quartz is the most easily programmable and the most overall healing of crystals, and holds a unique importance in the Universe of gems. It has zodiacal affinities with all the signs, and a special connection with second-half Scorpios.

* To program your clear quartz crystal, simply hold it on your Third Eye chakra (between and just above the physical eyes) and concentrate on the purpose for which you wish to use it. Be positive and receptive while you allow your crystal to fill with this energy. If you wish, you could also state the intention of the programming out loud, for example, 'I program this crystal for love', healing, meditation, abundance, protection or (insert your own word here)'.

** Kirlian photography is a technique of photography that captures the electrical field that radiates from organic matter and the biomagnetic sheath or aura surrounding the body.

YOUR LUCKY NUMBERS

Your lucky numbers are ★ 5 for Scorpio ^ & 9 for Mars (your traditional ruler) (also, see 'Lucky Magic Square of Mars')

LUCKY MAGIC SQUARE OF MARS

In Western occult tradition, each planet has traditionally been associated with a series of numbers and particular arrangements of those numbers. One such method of numerological organisation is the magic square. Magic squares date back to ancient times, appearing in China about 3,000 years ago. The first Chinese square is seen in the scroll of the river Lo - the Lo-Shu, a scroll believed to have been created by Fuh-Hi, the mythical founder of Chinese civilisation. Certain squares came to be linked with the planets; these associations came from the Babylonians. Each *kamea*, or magic square, is linked with a particular planet, and each of the squares has a *seal*, which is the geometric pattern created by following the numbers in order of their value. This pattern touches upon all the numbers of the square and the seal is used to represent the entire square. An intelligence and a spirit are also associated with each kamea, derived from the key numbers contained within it, using a Hebrew form of numerology. This intelligence is viewed as an inspiring, guiding and informing entity.

The 'Magic Square of Mars' is divided into 25 cells, or squares, five across and five down. The sum of the numbers in the vertical, horizontal and diagonal lines is a constant of 65. The total of these numbers is 325. Therefore, the numbers 5, 25, 65 and 325 are also assigned to Mars.

YOUR NUMEROLOGY NUMBER & LUCKY SUN SIGN NUMBERS

"Everything that exists has a vibration. The vibration of sound, music, colour, matter, even our words, thoughts, and names show form. All vibration is measurable. To measure we need numbers. Numbers are the basis of all. Numbers are the key to all mysteries."
Shirley Blackwell Lawrence, *Behind Numerology*

Numerology is essentially the metaphysical * 'science' of numbers. The use of numbers in magic is its cornerstone of power. The ancient Greek philosopher and mathematician Pythagoras, born around 590 BC, embarked on a thirty-year spiritual quest studying with important religious and esoteric teachers and healers to find the mystery of 'The Hidden Light', and came to see mankind as living in three worlds: the natural, the human and the Divine. He asserted that all things can be expressed in numerical terms, because they are ultimately reducible to numbers. Pythagoras stated that "Numbers are the first things of all of Nature" and followed the theory that "Nothing can exist without numbers."

Many believe that numbers have an arcane, mystical relationship with words, and with inanimate and animate objects; the interpretations that arose from these relationships date back to a time when the dawning intelligence of primitive man first visualised the meaning of numbers and associated it with spiritual significance. Numerology is the science of the exploration of this relationship in order to discover hidden meanings, forecast the future or interpret the character of a person. In its more modern applications, a series of figures which correspond to an individual's name and date of birth are calculated, and practitioners believe one's prospects, fortune and character can be deciphered from the results ^.

So what is numerology and how does one use it? Everything in the Universe has a vibrational frequency, an energy, a force, all vibrating at various rates, and we as humans are no exception, the difference between one person and another is their rate of vibration. This force or energy is constantly in motion and changing, and we can even 'tune into' and feel our vibrations if we are still for long enough.

Along with letters, sounds, colours, crystals, and many other things, it is believed that numbers also have vibrations, and when we are able to familiarise ourselves with our own numerical frequencies, we can use this familiarity to add power and magic to our lives. The numbers of our birth date, the letters of our names, and the numbers of our Sun sign and ruling planets, all have a unique vibrational frequency, and herein lies the key to understanding our self and our journey through life. Numerology refers to the knowledge contained within the numbers of our birth date and our name, and this is our own personal magic which can greatly assist us through life.

* Metaphysics is the study of those sciences that extend beyond the physical or tangible

HOW TO FIND YOUR NUMEROLOGY NUMBER

^ Your Sun sign's number was added up according to the principle of corresponding a number with a letter, for example 1=A, 2=B, 3=C and so on in sequence and up to 9=I, then beginning again at number 1 for the next letter J and following this same sequence. Following this system, the sum of the letters in Scorpio vibrates to the number 5.

Your personal numerology number is determined by adding up all the numbers in your birth date until they reach a two-digit figure. The two resulting numbers are then added together again to form a single digit, which is your personal numerology number. For example, someone born on 3 February 1983, would add the digits 3 + 2 + 1 + 9 + 8 + 3 = 26 = (reduced to two digits) 8. So that person's personal numerology birth number is 8.

Each primary number or birth number from 1 to 9 has a specific meaning and is governed by a planetary force. The principle of numerology reduces all numbers down to the following: 1 to 9, and 10, 11, 13 and 22 *. The last four numbers only apply to people specially concerned with the occult and spiritualism - and can be studied at greater length through other sources if so desired - and can in any case be reduced further to a single digit if preferred.

Your birth number contains a unique power, and therein lie your strengths, shortcomings and opportunities. It is beyond the scope of this book to outline your individual numerology number possibilities, so for the purposes of astrological applications, I have only included your Sun sign and ruling planet's special numbers.

* The numbers 10 and 13, and the master numbers 11 and 22, can be further reduced to one digit if so desired; however, they can be interpreted as they are without further reduction. The choice is personal.

BASIC MEANINGS & KEYWORDS

1 ★ Sun. Masculine influence, beginnings, independence, inventiveness, originality, leadership, exploration, innovation, ambition

2 ★ Moon. Feminine influence, cooperation, partnership, tact, diplomacy, harmony, unity, emotions, imagination, adaptability

3 ★ Jupiter. Communication, expression, youthfulness, self-confidence, creativity, inspiration, optimism, curiosity

4 ★ Uranus. Order, form, security, stability, patience, restriction, work, values, practicality

5 ★ Mercury. Freedom, inconsistency, change, variety, travel, activity, learned

6 ★ Venus. Love, home, family, sense of duty, responsibility, marriage, justice, nurturing, balance, gentleness, peace, friendship

7 ★ Neptune. Analysis, wisdom, mystical, spiritual, solitude, precision, research, integrity, mystery, psychic perceptions

8 ★ Saturn. Money, power, success, organisation, hard work, business, health, purpose, control, authority, mastery

9 ★ Mars. Completion, endings, Universal, service, humanity, philanthropy, loyalty

10 ★ Fortunate, creative, vibrant, stable, optimistic, original, successful, determined, individualistic

11 ★ Master number. Prophecies, inspiration, moral courage, missionary, long-suffering, foolhardiness, enlightenment, invention

13 ★ Misunderstood, fearful, changeable, interested in the occult, fatalistic, flexible, sacred, beguiling

22 ★ Master number. Powerful, successful, idealistic, attracted to the occult, creative, wise, successful, masterful, spiritually understanding

★ THE NUMBER 9 - FOR MARS ★

Names ★ Novena, Ninth, Ennead, Enneagon, Nonagon

Arithmomantic connections with the letters of the alphabet ★ I and R

Ruled by Mars, 9 is a multiple of the lucky 3, so 9 is also a lucky number. The number 9 is usually regarded as second in significance only to number 3 among the odd numbers, primarily because it is the product of 3 by 3. It is sometimes considered the ultimate number, with special and even sacred significance. The Nonagon, the number 9, or the Ennead was known to many ancient cultures as Perfection and Concord, and as being unbounded. Magicians of former times would draw a magic circle 9 feet in diameter, in which to practice their magic. It is the number of the Universe and of vision, representing spiritual ideals, philosophy and perfection. Nine is the number of completion, bringing together all the creative forces to reach a conclusion. It is almost the most indestructible of the odd numbers in the sense that all its multiples reduce to nine if we add together the digits of which they are composed. Consequently, it is considered the number of ultimate achievement and without interruption, and along with the number 8, as the symbol of eternal life. Cats are thought to have nine lives and are often connected to witchcraft and other magical doctrines. Number 9 is a tolerant, impractical and sympathetic vibration.

Character ★ Number 9 symbolises the planet Mars, and its people are often fighters - active and determined, they usually succeed after a struggle, but they are also prone to accidents and injury, and may be quarrelsome. It signifies a jack-of-all-trades, generosity and heartiness on the one hand, but self-centeredness, arrogance, self-pity, fickleness, financial carelessness, moodiness, discontentment, restlessness, sullenness, mental instability and emotional volatility on the other. They are helpful, compassionate, active, determined, tolerant, emotional, sophisticated, generous, charitable, humanitarian, romantic, cooperative, creative, proud, self-sufficient and self-sacrificing. Carrying the Martian vibe, those under its influence love all forms of art, drama and entertainment as well as being drawn to a deep interest in philosophy. These souls' doors are always open and there is always a pot of something boiling away on the stove. Perfect for artistic and philanthropic types, it is not so ideal for those who are more retiring. Number 9s are life's drama queens, there being rarely a dull moment around them, but they also stand for unconditional love, forgiveness and completion. With a great love of stage, food, movies and travel, they adore and immerse themselves in anything that resembles the broader canvas of life. The conception of perfection, concord and boundlessness, when applied to the human character, must necessarily be modified if you were born under this influence, for none of these traits, in their fullest sense, is human - they are all Divine. Number 9 types will show great intelligence and a power of understanding and discretion. You will know how to use your knowledge effectively, however your chief interests will lie not so much in practical matters as in affairs of the intellect, in logic, philosophy and an appreciation of the fine arts. Success by sheer hard work or slogging is not for you; you become outstanding among your peers because of natural intellect and sheer inspiration. You make a good friend and never take advantage of others; you are always willing to help other people succeed, and make an excellent advisor because of your naturally sympathetic understanding. Like number 6, 9 inspires a lofty sense of morals, its subjects being strictly honest in all their thoughts and actions. Frequently the number 9 is the number of the genius. Issues which may handicap or hinder your development are similar to those present in the number 6. Excessive dreaminess and too much value set on knowledge itself, apart from its application, may tend to cause lethargy and lack of progress. You should learn the value of hard work and concentration, otherwise there is a danger you may degenerate into a clever dabbler, without achieving outstanding success in any particular field. You are fortunate enough to be blessed with natural gifts, and should do all in your power to put these to the best purpose for benefiting both yourself and the world at large. At its best, number 9 will influence the highest qualities of courage, humanity, service and brotherhood. Number 9 people should try to carry out their plans on a Tuesday, the day governed by their planet, Mars.

Alchemy ★ Nine is a significant and magical number. It equals three times three, and in mythology, we often find an original trio who have expanded to nine. Each point of the triangle can generate another triangle. In this sense, nine has an essentially expansive, lively form of energy, that can include detail and diversity expanded from the basic three. Representations of nine usually combine the three triangles in some way. It represents completion - life flows in cycles of 9 - 9 years, 9 months, 9 days - and throughout life our major changes tend to happen with our personal 9 year. Numbers 1 to 9 are the basic vibrations and represent our 9 basic experiences of life. These experiences relate to our inner world and also to our outer world, and with a deeper understanding of the correlations between our experiences and the identifying numbers 1 to 9, we have an excellent reference for all aspects of our self and our journey through life.

LUCKY 'MAGIC HOURS' OR 'TIME UNITS'

One rule of magic, luck and power, as already outlined elsewhere in this book, can be found within the well-known phrase, "As above, so below." From the most ancient times, the planets were said to rule Earthly destinies and powers. Days of the week were named after the seven planets which were the only ones then known: Sun Day, Moon Day, Mars Day (French: Mardi), Mercury Day (French: Mercredi), Jove Day (French: Jeudi), Venus Day (French: Vendredi) and Saturn Day.

The planetary hours are based on an ancient astrological system, the Chaldean order of the planets. The Chaldean order indicates the relative orbital velocity of the planets, and from a heliocentric (helios = The Sun) perspective, this sequence also indicates the relative distance of the planets from the Sun (the Sun switching places with the Earth in this sequence), and the distance of the Moon from the Earth.

Before an action is taken in daily life, or a transaction undertaken, for instance, it is possible to choose the appropriate day and hour that will provide the greatest chances of success. By studying the planetary hours system, you will discover which actions are propitious to which of the seven planets or 'star-gods' and at what time it would be advisable to undertake them.

The planetary hours system uses this Chaldean order to divide time, and each planetary hour of the planetary day is ruled by a different planet. The order is repeated, starting with the slowest: Saturn - then, Jupiter, Mars, Sun, Venus, Mercury, Moon, then back to Saturn, Jupiter, Mars, etc., ad infinitum. The planet that rules the first hour of the day is also the ruler of that whole day and gives the day its name. So the first hour of Saturday is ruled by Saturn, the first hour of Sunday by the Sun, and so on. It is important, for the purposes of using specific planetary energies for our magic and wishes, to note that planetary hours are not considered the same length as our normal time-keeping slots of sixty minutes. Each day is split into time periods, day time and night time, beginning at around sunrise and sunset respectively. These two time periods are each divided into twelve equal-length hours, which are the planetary hours. So the planetary hours of the day and the planetary hours of the night will be of different lengths, except during the equinoxes when light and darkness are balanced.

In sequence, the Sun, Moon and the five visible planets each exerts its own special influence over a twenty-four-hour period. I like to call your planet's special day and hour the 'Magic Hour'.

Magic rituals to draw luck and love to you should be conducted at astrologically correct times and with the appropriate instruments, tools, cards, herbs, flowers, oils and plants which are linked with the ruling planet. For example, a love ritual, spell or potion demands a concoction of any or all of the above ruled by Venus. Do not underestimate rulerships, for they wield an unseen power that can help make our dreams, big and small, come true.

Further, as specific hours of each day are ruled by certain planets, if you are really serious about attracting some power, luck or magic into your life, it is imperative that you wish, pray or ask at the most opportune times for your Sun sign. There are two methods you can use for fine tuning your magical workings. The first method is to perform your spell, ritual or wishing on the day your Sun sign's ruling planet during the planetary hour that signifies the essence of what you are asking for (e.g. A Scorpion who is looking for love might perform a love-seeking ritual on a Tuesday, during a Venus-ruled planetary hour). Alternatively, if you wish to summon the power of your Sun sign's own ruling planet, then that same Scorpion might perform their love-seeking ritual on a Friday (ruled by Venus) during Mars's planetary hour.

The nature of that which you are asking for, such as love, travel opportunities, money, career guidance, protection or friendship for example, should always be considered when choosing the day or hour during which your magic will be heightened.

The answer to the question why are there seven days in a week, is a very important one to know in unravelling the secret of your Magic Hours. Ancient people recognised the supreme importance of the seven heavenly spheres, which comprised those which could be seen by the naked eye: The Sun, Moon, Mercury, Venus, Mars, Jupiter and Saturn. They then named each of the seven days of the week after one of those spheres and assigned that planetary 'ruler' to one day of the week. As viewed from Earth, these seven spheres appear to move at varying speeds, and the ancients used this factor to arrange them in order of varying speed. If you intend to use your Magic Hours to attract wonderful things, you must memorise that sequence because it is what forms the basis of the whole system.

Whenever you intend to use your Magic Hours or, perhaps more accurately, Magic *Time Units*, it is important to find out the exact time of sunrise for the area in which you live, as sunrise marks the time when your planet's magic is at its most powerful on its specific day. So, at sunrise on Sunday, the Sun rules the hour following the sunrise, the Moon rules the first hour following sunrise on a Monday, and through the week the pattern is repeated, with each day's ruling planet beginning the cycle in that first hour after dawn. It is logical then, that the rest of the planets, in sequence, follow on with one planet per hour for that day thereafter for the rest of the 24-hour cycle, creating a Magic Hour or Time Unit for each planet throughout the day and night, depending on which planet rules that particular day and is therefore the first in line.

If you wish to explore the idea in more depth, it is worth noting first and foremost that each day contains twenty-four hours, but, depending on the season, day and night will be of varying lengths. In summer, daylight is longer than darkness, whereas the reverse applies in winter. During autumn and spring, day and night are usually about equal. Therefore, although a complete day always contains twenty-four hours, there are not always twelve hours between sunrise and sunset and another twelve hours between sundown and the following sunrise. So, depending on the season (and location), a time unit may be shorter than one hour, longer than one hour, or equal to one hour. So whenever you intend to use your Magic Time Units, it is important to find out the exact time of sunrise and sunset for the area in which you live. The next step is to divide the amount of day time (if day if when you wish to work your 'magic', otherwise the same following theory applies to night time) into twelve equal sections by calculating the number of hours and minutes between sunrise and sunset and divide by twelve. An example is if the Sun rises at 6.27 a.m. and sets at 5.49 p.m., the amount of time contained in this day is eleven hours and twenty-two minutes. Convert this total into minutes (682) and then divide that figure by twelve (57). Therefore, each of the twelve daylight time units will be 57 minutes on that day.

Although this wonderful method of using astrology is very ancient, it may be completely new to you. You are in for a pleasant surprise though, because if you are willing to delve into a little research and put the system to the test, rich rewards are in store for you!

YOUR LUCKY DAY ★ TUESDAY

Planet ★ Mars
Basic Energy ★ Action
Basic Magic ★ Combat, Courage, Vitality, Willpower
Element ★ Fire
Colour ★ Red
Energy Keywords ★ Assertion, Force, Combat, Frankness, Will, Passion, Expression, Leadership, Construction, Courage, Strength, Defiance, Destruction, Dynamism, Audacity, Energy, Self-reliance, Fearlessness, Heroics, Impulsivity, Spontaneity

Tuesday is the day of Mars, your traditional ruler. In commonly used calendars, Tuesday is the third day of the week, though in others it is the second. The English name is derived from Old English *Tiwesdaeg*, and Middle English *Tewesday*, meaning 'Tiw's Day', the Day of Tiw or Tyr, the god of victory, war, combat and heroic glory in Norse mythology. Tiw was equated with Mars. Shrove Tuesday, which precedes the first day of Lent in the Western Christian calendar, and Black Tuesday, referring to Tuesday 29 October 1929, part of the Great Stock Market Crash of that year, are two famous days with which Mars's day is associated.

In the folk rhyme 'Monday's Child', ' Tuesday's child is full of grace'. Tuesday offers Mars energy to end conflicts, to overcome inertia or to deal with those matters that may metaphorically need to be kick-started, or have physical energy applied to them. It can be a day of passionate feelings, strong motivations and determined efforts that bring desired results.

Tuesday is a day of Enthusiasm, Competition, Passion, Energy, Courage, Protection, Strength, Victory, Anything Requiring Assertiveness, Masculinity (Yang Energy), Standing up for Yourself, a 'Fighting Spirit', Determination, Vitality, Sexuality, Virility, Self-confidence, Men's Power, Men's Mysteries, Drive, Ambition, Achievement, Triumph and Potency.

MARS'S MAGIC TIME UNITS
(BASED ON THE PLANETARY HOURS)
FOR EACH DAY OF THE WEEK

SATURDAY ★ Third and Tenth time units after sunrise
SUNDAY ★ Seventh time unit after sunrise
MONDAY ★ Fourth and Eleventh time units after sunrise
TUESDAY ★ First and Eighth time units after sunrise
WEDNESDAY ★ Fifth and Twelfth time units after sunrise
THURSDAY ★ Second and Ninth time units after sunrise
FRIDAY ★ Sixth time unit after sunrise **

Choose the Hour/s of Mars for any transaction, activity, exchange, initiative or venture which involves sport, winning, overcoming enemies, conquering, overthrowing enemies, self-mastery, bravery, combating, calling one into battle, gaining courage, resolving quarrels, being more decisive, and taking action in any given situation.

** Please note that for the purposes of simplification, the information regarding 'Mars's Magic Time Units' is a very diluted and simplified version of using magical times to your advantage. These hours cover only daylight hours, or the first twelve hours after sunrise, and do not take into account magical times after sunset or throughout the night. 'Hours' is also a deceptive term, as most 'time periods' used in this system are less than an hour, but for the purposes of simplifying the technique, I refer to them as Magic Hours (to keep with the tradition of the term 'planetary hours') rather than magic 'time units', which is what they really are. Should you wish to do further research on your ruling planet's most powerful time units, or require further information about the planet/s from which you are seeking 'energy' from in order to assist your wish-making, other sources may provide you with more comprehensive and detailed information.

A LITTLE NEW MOON / MAGICAL TIME UNIT WISH RITUAL

Step 1 ~ Choose the Magical Hour and/or day that matches your intentions. The first dawn hour of Sunday, ruled by the Sun, is a great time for all-purpose magic, success, joy, abundance, prosperity, bliss, personal power & all-round expansion.

Step 2 ~ Write out a little wish list with the appropriate coloured pen on the colour paper which corresponds to your desire.

Step 3 ~ Choose a small stone of your choosing that is connected to your wish (or a number of stones, that are perhaps linked with your planetary ruler's number, for example 9 for Mars).

Step 4 ~ Find a nice patch of soil in your garden or any special place to you, dig into it, affirm your wish in your mind, place the crystal/s and piece of paper in the hole, then place a plant on top of the crystal/s and wish list.

Step 5 ~ Fill the soil back in over the roots of the plant and feed it with a little water out of a magical vessel (a small genie bottle would be ideal).

Step 6 ~ Thank the Earth, the Universe and the Sun (or whatever planet you are summoning the power from) for bringing forth your desires.

Step 7 ~ Repeat all day long: "Thank You, Thank You, Thank You!"

Step 8 ~ Watch your plant - and your wish - grow bigger and bigger as time goes on!

YOUR LUCKY CHARM/TALISMANS

The following are three 'materials' or talismanic symbols from which to make your lucky charms, and the planetary energy under which to do it, corresponding with your Sun sign:

SCORPIO ★ Topaz, Tau, Iron, Mars

"When any star ascends fortunately, take a stone and herb that are under that star, make a ring of the metal that is congruous therewith, and in that fix the stone with the herb under it."
Henry Cornelius Agrippa, *On Occult Philosophy*

Charms, talismans and amulets are among the oldest forms of magic. A charm or talisman is a symbol, often used to communicate a thought, prayer or wish to, or to make a connection with the Divine. It is usually in the form of an object, which has been imbued with mysterious and magical powers. A charm may be as simple as a stone, a flower or a feather, or it might be a parchment bearing writing; the meaning and significance that you attribute to the symbol is what is important. It can be created by yourself (to best effect) or by someone else, and works as a tool to activate our subconscious mind.

You can use general charms such as a cross, or a universally lucky symbol such as a horseshoe, but you will exude and therefore attract more potency and protection if you make and wear the appropriate charms with the matching gemstone, set in the right metal and created under the corresponding planetary influence. While most people wear silver or gold, cheaper tin or copper may be more appropriate and indeed beneficial for your Sun sign. An amulet (for protection) or a talisman or charm (for luck), must also be made, ordered, designed or purchased on the appropriate day of the week for its power to be most effective. Your day, as previously described, is Tuesday.

You can even go further and create or buy your amulet or charm at one of the hours and/or days when your planet is exerting its most powerful influence. It may sound complicated and requiring of forethought and effort, but if you are going to summon magic and are superstitious enough to truly *believe* that you can do this (and remember pure belief in something is the starting point of all manifestation), you should be scrupulous enough to do it properly. For your planet's day and time, please consult the information under the previous headings 'Your Lucky Day' and 'Mars's Magic Time Units'.

GODS, GODDESSES, ANIMAL TOTEMS & OTHER 'GUIDES'

Gods, goddesses and guides can be summoned to help you live your life to its optimal best. Some are connected with your Sun sign, while others may be of your own personal choosing, ones you may feel particularly drawn towards. Those which align with your ruling planet and your Sun sign, give a good indication of those who will shine a guiding light along your desired path, but you can choose your own too, based upon exploration, observations, research, meditation or simple intuition - I believe choosing your own, based on your inner *knowing* or guidance system, is a very powerful magical tool. However, to get you started, following are some animal spirit guide ideas for your contemplation. Good luck!

YOUR LUCKY ANIMALS & BIRDS

Scorpion, Dove, Eagle, Wolf, Panther, Leopard, Owl, Wild Boar, Dragon, Scarab Beetle, Invertebrates, Tiger, Fox, Lizard, Falcon, Griffin, Phoenix, Dog, Spider, Vulture, Snake

★

"Somewhere beyond the walls of our awareness ... the wilderness side, the hunter side, the seeking side of ourselves is waiting to return."
Laurens van der Post, *The Heart of the Hunter*

"(People) everywhere are being made acutely aware of the fact that something essentially to life and wellbeing is flickering very low in the human species and threatening to go out entirely. This 'something' has to do with such values as love, unselfishness, sincerity, loyalty to one's best friend, honesty, enthusiasm, humility, goodness, happiness ... fun. Practically every animal has these assets in abundance and is eager to share them, given the opportunity and the encouragement."
Jay Allen Boone, *Kinship with All Life*

Some astrological systems, such as Shamanistic or Native American Astrology, tell us that the Sun sign we were born under has a corresponding animal totem, which informs us about our characteristics and act as a kind of spiritual guide or mentor throughout our life's journey. These totems are described as Solar totems, because many of them share similarities with the Solar system and the sign the Sun was passing through at the time of our birth, and therefore relate to animals and animal behaviours which also correspond to environmental conditions and seasonal changes. These animals encompass many aspects of the Solar system, from seasonal relationships, to creature instincts, to reciprocal links with the planetary vibrations, and 'clans' within nature that you are inherently closely connected with through your date of birth.

Carl Jung, a master of dream analysis and interpretation, proposed that animals symbolise our natural instincts, operating through our dreams. He theorised that certain dream symbols, among them animals, represent core emotions and concepts, archetypes that will hold true for all of us the world over, regardless of so-called 'divisions' such as sex, customs, age or culture. In *Man and His Symbols*, Jung states that primitive societies believed that each person had a bush soul and a human soul. The bush soul incarnates as a tree or animal - a totem - and when the bush soul is harmed or injured, the human soul is considered injured as well.

Some of the most important and powerful spirit guides are those belonging to the animal kingdom. Both in ancient times and in some traditional modern tribal systems, people consult with animals for their wisdom and personal power. Even though most societies today have drifted away from this connection, it has never really left us, and different creatures continue to communicate with us on both the physical and spiritual planes in an attempt to speak to our souls and spirits.

As part of the teaching world, animals can bring us wisdom and survival skills, while others show us how to adapt, transcend or morph. Others still can remind us the importance of play and humour, and guide us around how to overcome life's challenges. Many are known for their loyalty and ability to love unconditionally and without judgement, while some have a grounded and healthy detachment, remaining true to themselves rather than pleasing others, an important lesson in itself. Whatever the qualities of the unique animal guides for your Sun sign, all have some enlightening soul-awakening traits that can teach us much about our own true inner selves. Ultimately, your animal spirit guides, and in particular your Solar totem animal, endow you with qualities that will enhance your life and help to activate your creativity, wisdom and intuition, helping to heal the broken or return the lost pieces of your soul and reconnect you to the natural world.

Your Solar totem animal (listed last on your lucky birds and animals list) is not the same as an animal spirit guide, which is based on metaphysical principles and is also based on your soul's mission in this embodiment - however, you can definitely make your birth Solar totem animal your spiritual guide if you wish, as you may find that its qualities, traits, symbolism and messages strongly reflect and define your own nature - or what you aspire to become, manifest or draw towards you. Your birth totem power animal comes from a place of trust and innocence, and represents the essence of your creative inner child. If you spend some time meditating on your Solar totem animal, asking what lessons it can teach, and reflect deeply on its character, life and habits, you may find it connects with you on a deep spiritual level and you can make the necessary changes to your life to draw in more magic and power.

Overall, if your life is stagnant or in need of healing or an energy boost, you can request your animal spirit or spirits to come and help you change your vibration, awaken your truth and arouse your inner forces. If you are aware of your animal spirit's presence in your life every day, you can use its particular energies to support, guide and teach you. And above all, pay attention to any signs and expressions of its lessons, and remember to thank your chosen animal guide for helping you.

* Shamanism is a traditional spiritual practice of the Native American culture. A shaman, one who practices this age-old art, is an intermediary between the human world and the world of the spirits. He inherits his magical powers at birth, but spends many years as an apprentice, so that he is usually much older in age before he is able to practice and call upon his skills. People ask for a shaman's help when there is a crisis on either a personal or wider spread scale, such as famine, drought, war or illness. The shaman makes contact with the spirits by going into a trance. First, he may perform a series of rituals, which usually include drumming, singing and chanting, and when these have brought on the right conditions, he leaves his body behind to travel to the other world. There he meets with the spirits of his ancestors, who inform him what must be done to relieve the suffering of his people. If the shaman is asked to cure someone of a dis-ease, then the spirits may accompany him to find the correct medicinal herbs or treatments for his patient.

YOUR FEATURE ANIMAL ★ SNAKE

The Snake's Message ★ Shed your old skin to make way for the new
Brings the totem gift of ★ Creativity, acceptance, imagination, healing
Shares the power energies of ★ Rebirth, transformation, ability to change, influence, power
Brings forth and teaches the magic of ★
Emergence of new self, expression of inner intuition

Certain animals have attained an historic symbolism that far transcends their biological reality; they are animals of myth, legend and stature. They become metaphors for qualities we despise or desire, and our perception of these animals can extend and expand well beyond the realm of the physical. We tend to imbue certain animals with often fantastical notions, depending upon our experience, and cultural and personal perceptions of them. As symbols, there are many examples of animals who represent both good and evil, for example. Depending on the community, society, culture, or one's religious or political beliefs, a certain animal may be considered friend or foe. Such is the case with the much-feared and much-revered Snake. For example, in Judeo-Christian belief systems, snakes represent the ultimate demise of Adam and Eve and are therefore considered evil and destructive. However, among many Native American tribes, the Snake embodies the powers of transmutation and creation.

Representing fire, passion and energy, the Snake teaches us to welcome change as an opportunity for growth, and to let go of the past. The Snake has been a powerful luck-bringing symbol since the dawn of time. Ancient people believed that snakes had unusually long lives because of their ability to shed and regrow their skins. Perhaps for the same reason, they associated snakes with old age and the wisdom that maturity brought. As a lucky charm, a snake with its tail in its mouth, forming a circle, was a symbol of eternity and ensured a long life. Snakes are symbols of transformation, renewal and morphosis, as they shed their old skin to reveal the new one beneath. They are also associated with water, Scorpio's element. The Snake is powerful, unseen, and working at ground level. Snakes have been linked to magic in every spiritual tradition. Serpents make strong healing allies, helping us to shed the fears and negative beliefs that may trigger mental and physical illnesses.

The Snake is a natural at all things spiritual, and most shamans are born under this Solar animal totem. Easily attuned to the ethereal realm, the Snake makes a wonderful and influential spiritual guide or leader. As well as being highly regarded as a potent healer, the Snake also excels at medical professions. They can, however, be seen as mysterious and even frightening by others, due to their preoccupation with intangible matters and unseen dimensions. The Snake can indeed be secretive and dark, and prone to despondence and abnormal mood swings, but in a nurturing supportive environment, will be passionate, helpful, sensitive, caring and inspiring, if a little cool.

SPIRITUAL KEEPER ★ BEAR

Your spiritual keeper guides your spiritual growth and brings illumination. Your spiritual keeper is determined by the season in which you were born. Regarded as the 'keepers' or 'caretakers' of the Universe, the four Directions or alignments were also referred to by the Native Americans as the Four Winds because their presence was *felt* rather than seen. The Direction to which your birth time belongs influences the nature of your inner senses. The West Direction's totem is the Bear. The Bear is a symbol of transformation, introspection, conservation, and strength drawn from within. The Bear has played a prominent role in many Native cultures, and because of its significance, a constellation, Ursus Major, was named for it.

Bears can be amazingly fast and even climb trees, and many tribal people have regarded it as too powerful a medicine, fearing that the Bear would even hunt them and kill them if it was feeling threatened or starving. Despite its ferocity and the fear it can invoke, the Bear is considered to be a highly desired ally and spiritual keeper because of its fearless and instinctively protective powers. In many ways it is the epitome of the Great Protector, the protective mother. The Bear holds the teachings and wisdom of introspection. Unlike other animals who are active during a specific time of day or night, the Bear is active *both* day and night, symbolising its connection with Solar energy, that of strength and power, and Lunar energy, that of intuition and the inner life. It enhances and teaches those born under this totem to develop both within themselves. Sometimes quick to anger and too sure of its own power, the Bear can throw caution to the wind and forget - to its detriment - that being unaware of its limits in certain situations can be disastrous.

Bears, through their well-known hibernation periods during which they do not need to eat or drink for months at a time, teach us how to go within and find the resources necessary for our personal survival. People with Bear as their totem may find their own symbolic periods of Winter hibernation are opportune times to reflect, restore, and give birth to new ideas or projects which will take root and sprout in the springtime. This time of withdrawal or retreat represents the need to tap into our hidden strengths and teaches us to look inward in order to awaken the power of the subconscious in order to truly know oneself. Your animal keeper the Bear is, above all, a potent symbol of fearlessness, introspection and protectiveness.

CLAN ★ FROG

Your clan animal comes from a place of inner knowing and intuition, helping you to discover the essence and magic of your true self. The Frog, a Totem of the Water clan, represents the song that calls the rain to Earth, and cleansing, teaching us the opportune times to purify, refresh and replenish our reserves. A charm or amulet in the shape of a frog is said to attract true friends and to help you find long-lasting love. To the Ancient Egyptians, Romans and Greeks, frogs symbolised inspiration, fertility, good luck and speedy recovery from illness, beliefs that carry over into some cultures today. People of the Frog clan have deep, easily flowing feelings, which enable them to have empathy for others and to heal. They have natural gifts for healing, sensitivity, creativity, and a deep appreciation for rain and being around water. Frog clan people are blessed with an abundance of emotions, feelings, perception, insights, and the ability to pick up on the innermost feelings of others. They are also able to delve into the incredible depths of the Soul. As the Moon is so strongly associated with emotional and watery realms, Frog clan people can connect with this deep Lunar magic by studying the cycles, patterns and energies of the Moon, the ruling celestial sphere of their clan animal, the Frog.

THE SCARAB BEETLE & SCORPIO

This ancient Egyptian talisman, derived from a beetle common in Egypt, was the symbol of Khepri *, a form of the Sun god, and was therefore a symbol of creation and resurrection. As a talisman the scarab was worn to attract good fortune in general, but especially to instil masculine qualities into the wearer, such as health and strength, both physical and mental. Not only was this sacred beetle considered to protect the living, but an image of it was placed in the bandages of mummies, and sometimes in the heart of a dead person, as a protection from evil influences during the journey to the other world. Perhaps the best-known example is the dung beetle, whose binomial name is *scarabidae*, revered in ancient Egypt, where in hieroglyphs it was the symbol of the Solar deity. The beetle rolls pieces of dung into balls in which it lays its eggs. The ball-rolling was thought to symbolise the movement of the Sun. Another connection they have with the cosmos is that dung beetles are currently the only known animal to orient and navigate themselves using the Milky Way. The legend of the sacred scarab beetle in Ancient Egypt endures, and modern interpretations of the hieroglyphic image of the beetle, assert that its trilateral phonetic translates as 'to come into being', 'to become' or 'to transform'.

* The Ancient Egyptians believed that Khepri, the god of the rising Sun, renewed the Sun every day before rolling it above the horizon, then carried it through the other world after Sunset, only to renew it again the next day.

THE PHOENIX & SCORPIO

The legendary and fabulous Arabian bird said to sing, set fire to itself and rise anew from the ashes every 500 years.

"Pluto's symbol is the triumphant phoenix, rising from its own smouldering ashes, and Scorpio personifies the resurrection from the grave ... without ever revealing the secret of their sorcery. No use to ask - Scorpio will never tell. But he knows the eternal truth of the circle contained in the symbolic zero."
Linda Goodman

★ Keywords ★
Renewal, Transformation, Regeneration,
Metamorphosis, Rebirth, Healing, Beneficial Change

A mythical creature of glorious colours and living flame, the Phoenix can live for a thousand years (or as many as 12,000 years) before submitting to its legacy of death and rebirth. It is one of the most ancient mystical animals, sacred to the Sun, and the most beautiful and inspiring of all the birds. Its crimson, gold, blue and purple plumage is the colour of the rising Sun and, although its head and beak resemble those of the heron or the eagle, its size varies enormously over its life cycle - and it can grow to gigantic proportions. Only one Phoenix can exist at any time, but each bird can live from 500 to over 1,000 years before it is consumed by its own flames in order for a new bird to be reborn from its ashes. The Phoenix is a firebird and it is believed it has the ability to turn its body into flame and fly through outer space, sometimes causing a Solar eclipse. This mythical bird was linked with Heliopolis, the ancient centre of Egyptian Sun worship. Throughout history the legendary Phoenix has been closely related to this worship and mysticism of the rising Sun and has become an enduring symbol of resurrection, immortality, transformation and life after death. When the Phoenix was about to die, legend tells it that it built itself a nest from scented twigs and incense, then flapped its wings with such vigour that it set the nest on fire and burned itself to a pile of ashes, and from the ashes the beautiful bird rose once again. The Phoenix and its connection to the Sun appear in the mythology of a number of ancient cultures, its message, story and meanings being surprisingly constant within each.

Legend of the Phoenix

The legend of how the Phoenix came into being tells of a bird with magnificent plumage that laid no eggs, had no young and was already in existence when the world began. The Sun granted this magnificent creature the gift of immortality and, in return, the Phoenix promised to sing only for the Sun. The Phoenix then flew to a faraway desert in the East and praised the Sun with its songs for 500 years. But the beautiful bird grew old over time and, eventually, it wanted nothing more than to be young and strong again. So the Phoenix returned to the home it had left behind and, having crafted itself a nest out of cinnamon bark and an egg out of myrrh, it sat upon a tall palm tree and asked the Sun to bless it with the vitality of youth once more. The Sun looked kindly on its old friend and responded to its request by shining down with the full force of its Solar power. The other animals hid from the Sun's strong rays, but the Phoenix remained in the nest it had built and was consumed by flames until nothing was left but ashes. From its remains rose a new, younger bird, and this wondrous cycle has continued ever since.

THE EAGLE & SCORPIO

★ Keywords ★
Victory, Courage, Power, Freedom, Success, Influence, Will, Abundance, Lucidity, Clear-sightedness, Happiness

"He can imitate the nocturnal Scorpion, who will string others and even sting himself to death for the pure pleasure of stinging - or he can imitate the glorious, soaring path of his symbolic Eagle, who rises above Earthly limitations, and uses his strength wisely and justly."
Linda Goodman

The eagle is the 'sacred messenger', flying high to deliver our prayers to the Great Spirit and returning with gifts of illumination and clearer vision. The eagle is an amazingly powerful and significant symbol for many different cultures. It is such a large and dominant bird, that it has always been associated with supremacy, triumph and majesty. Believed to be all-seeing, hence its link with superiority, it is the only bird capable of looking into the Sun. In the animal kingdom, it reigns supreme as the undisputed ruler of the skies, the fastest and most powerful bird of all. In Greek mythology, the eagle is often associated with Zeus, often depicted flying towards the Sun, believed to be transporting the souls of the dead to heaven. The Native Americans regarded this much revered bird as an important symbol and its feathers are used for tribal and religious occasions, as well as for head-dresses worn by the bravest tribe's people. For the

Cherokees, obtaining an eagle feather is a significant ceremonial rite. The eagle is a mighty spirit guide bringing the qualities of fortitude, courage and clarity into your life. Able to soar higher than other birds, the eagle teaches us to see the bigger picture and to develop our powers of objectivity. A skilled hunter, he teaches strength in patience. The eagle will also help you achieve your ambitions, no matter how difficult they may seem to be to achieve. In essence, this majestic bird helps us to see the bigger picture, to recognise what really matters in life, and ultimately to rise above our Earthly concerns and into a higher realm.

THE GRIFFIN & SCORPIO

The griffin is a mythological creature common in the Middle East. It has the head and wings of an eagle, the body of a lion and sometimes a serpent's tail. Because it has the head of an eagle and the body of a lion it is said to represent both land and air. Considered Divinely powerful and imperial, it is a Solar symbol and as such it symbolises the power of the Sun - and of Leo, another Fixed sign. Altogether the griffin is a very powerful symbol, whose roles have been, among many, of treasure protection and gold guardianship. To many cultures, it is regarded as the King of birds and Lord of the Air. It is associated with Scorpio by virtue of its eagle head.

YOUR CORRESPONDING CHINESE ASTROLOGY ANIMAL

The Chinese Zodiac, known as Sheng Xiao (literally meaning 'birth likeness'), is based on a twelve-year cycle, each year in that cycle related to a particular animal. These animals are: Rat, Ox, Tiger, Rabbit, Dragon, Snake, Horse, Sheep, Monkey, Rooster, Dog and Pig. The selection and order of the animals that so influence people's lives, particularly in East Asian cultures, originated in the Han Dynasty (202 BC - 220 AD) and was based upon each animal's traits, characteristics, tendencies and living habits. Further, ancient people observed that there were twelve Full Moons in a year, and that, among other similarly related celestial observations, suggests its origins are also based on astronomical concepts.

The legend of the Chinese zodiac's story usually begins with the Jade Emperor, or Buddha (depending on who is telling the tale), summoning all the animals of the Universe for a race or a banquet. The twelve animals of the zodiac all appeared at the palace, and the order in which they arrived determined the order of the Chinese zodiac.

Each oriental animal corresponds with a Western astrology sign. For Scorpio, it is the Pig, or Boar.

> "Of all God's children
> I have the purest heart.
> With innocence and faith,
> I walk in Love's protective light.

> By giving of myself freely
> I am richer and twice blest.
> Bonded to all mankind by
> common fellowship,
> My goodwill is Universal
> And knows no bounds.
> *I am the Boar."*
> **Theodora Lau**

Chinese name for the Boar ★ ZHU
Ranking Order ★ Twelfth
Hours ruled by the Boar ★ 9 p.m. to 11 p.m.
Direction ★ North - Northwest
Season and principle month ★ Autumn - November
Corresponds to the Western sign ★ Scorpio

★ **BOAR** ★ *Fixed Element Water*

★ **Keywords** ★
Chivalrous, gallant, loyal, reliable, intellectual, shrewd but sometimes naïve, sincere, tolerant, honest, generous, indulgent, light-hearted, lucky, easily provoked

The Boar, or Pig, is the twelfth and last sign of the Chinese zodiac. Associated with children, welfare and comfort, the Pig type has a great capacity for transforming environments, looking after those in need, and working hard to accumulate wealth, usually all at once. Traditionally a yin animal sign, Pigs are chivalrous, gallant, loyal, charming and romantic. In relationships, the Pig offers sensitivity and pure love.

A powerhouse in all the caring and giving you do, you are sincere and honest in your approach; dishonesty makes you nervous. You can be a little taciturn and tend to withdraw into yourself rather than socialise with other people, which makes you best suited to natural and quiet environments, where you can build, create and improve to your heart's content.

YOUR METALS

Scorpion power metals are Iron, Steel and Plutonium.

Although the magic power of crystals is widely recognised and applied, the influence radiating from metals is often overlooked. Metal, too, emits a powerful energy and in fact, in Chinese philosophy, metal is considered so essential and powerful that it is classified as one of the elements, alongside Air, Fire, Earth and Water.

As already mentioned earlier in the book, throughout the writings of early philosophers and theorists, there are countless references to the unmistakable mystic connection between the seven known planets of the time, and Earthly affairs, ailments and objects. Seven metals were connected with the seven planets, to which seven colours and the seven 'transformations' were added. So the ancient alchemist came to share the astrological doctrine that each planet ruled a mineral: The Sun ruled gold, the Moon silver, Mars iron, Venus copper, Saturn lead, Jupiter tin, and Mercury quicksilver. Consequently, in alchemical symbolism the same sign came to represent the nominated metal and its corresponding planet.

IRON

Iron is a chemical element with symbol Fe (from Latin *ferrum*). By mass it is the most common element on Earth, forming much of our planet's inner and outer core. The symbol for Mars, your secondary ruler, has been used since antiquity to represent the element iron.

Iron is the metal most associated with magic. Although not glistening or beautiful like silver or gold, at times in history iron's value was considered superior. Because iron is not found in its pure state except as a meteorite, it was known as the 'Metal of Heaven'. Iron's celestial origins were recognised early in human history and meteorites were perceived as supreme conduits to the spiritual realm. Iron is known for its protective and healing capacities; iron boxes serve to safeguard their contents, keeping their powers intact, and an iron bed is thought to be psychically protective, enhance one's dreaming processes and even promotes physical healing. These protective qualities are well-known and iron amulets are said to also guard and protect children and newborns. As well, because iron is connected with virility and fertility, an iron bed and iron jewellery are considered auspicious for romance and conception.

The metal iron has been used since ancient times, and is relatively soft but significantly hardened and strengthened by impurities, particularly carbon (a certain proportion of present carbon will produce steel, which can be up to a thousand times harder than pure iron). The first production of iron began in the Middle Bronze Age, but it was several centuries before iron displaced bronze. Iron of meteoric origin was highly regarded due to its origins in the heavens, and was often used to forge weapons and tools, having a distinct advantage over bronze in warfare instruments, as it is much harder and more durable than bronze (albeit more susceptible to rust).

In more modern times, steels and iron alloys are the most common metals used in industry, due to their vast range of desirable properties and Earth's widespread abundance of iron-bearing rock. It is the most widely used of all the metals, accounting for over 90 per cent of worldwide metal production. Its low cost and high strength make it invaluable in many engineering applications, such as the construction of machinery, mechanical tools, the hulls of large ships, automobiles and the structural components of buildings. And since it is in its pure state quite soft, it is the most commonly combined with alloying metals to create steel. This industrial iron production begins with iron ores, principally hematite and magnetite, two of your 'lucky stones'.

Iron also plays a vital role in biology - iron proteins are found in all living organisms - forming complexes with molecular oxygen in haemoglobin and myoglobin, and in the functioning of various enzymes, cellular respiration, and oxidation and reduction in animals and plants.

The word iron, when used metaphorically, refers to certain traits of the metal. Used as an adjective and sometimes as a noun, it can refer to something that is sturdy, unyielding, stern, unbreakable, harsh, strong, formidable and robust. The 'Iron Lady' Margaret Thatcher was so named because of her 'iron-fisted' style of rulership.

Iron may be etched with hydraulic acid, or engraved. Iron is primarily used for healing when you feel under attack, and is believed to increase physical strength. Steel is sometimes used as an alternative.

Overall, iron has a number of good and not-so-good associations. The earliest specimens of iron were found in meteorites and it was highly prized among the Aztecs who regarded it as a metal sent from the gods. However, at the beginning of the Iron Age, smelted iron had evil connotations, and it was considered inferior to the other metals such as gold, copper and bronze. Although it is a metal usually linked with brute strength and masculinity, it has been adopted as a symbol of fertility; in folklore, wearing a bracelet made of iron is said to help with conceiving a child. In some countries, people would touch iron to bring them good luck. It certainly couldn't hurt to try.

PLUTONIUM

Plutonium is a transuranic radioactive chemical element with the symbol Pu and is named after your ruling planet Pluto, following from the two previous elements uranium and neptunium (also named after planets). Like most metals, plutonium has a bright silvery appearance at first, but when exposed to air it tarnishes and oxidises very quickly to a dull grey. When exposed to moist air, plutonium forms oxides and hydrides that expand up to 70 per cent in volume, which in turn can flake off as a powder that can spontaneously ignite. These properties, combined with it being radioactive and accumulative in human tissue such as bones, make the handling of plutonium dangerous.

Mostly a by-product of nuclear reactions, plutonium was produced in useful quantities for the first time as a major part of the Manhattan Project during World War II, which developed the first atomic bombs. The Fat Man bombs used in the bombing of Nagasaki in 1945, had plutonium cores.

As well as being used in the first few atomic bombs, plutonium is still used in nuclear weapons, and is also a key material in the development of nuclear power, and as a source energy on space missions.

There are two aspects to the harmful effects of plutonium: its radioactivity and its heavy metal toxic effects. Metallic plutonium can become pyrophoric under the right conditions, meaning that it poses an extreme fire and explosive hazard. More dangerous when inhaled than ingested, it has been linked to cancer, radiation sickness, genetic damage and death. Overall, plutonium is a dangerous element, much like the Scorpionic character itself, with the power to destruct and perhaps even worse, to self-combust.

PLANTS, HERBS, SPICES, TREES, SHRUBS, FLOWERS, SCENTS & INCENSE

Plants have long been associated with magic, medicinal properties, superstition, nutrition and even astrology. In ancient times, some were endowed with magical properties based upon beliefs of the time, but also upon anecdotal evidence that some herbal concoctions, flowers or essences helped alleviate and even cure uncomfortable, painful or dis-eased physical or mental states. Whether these were based upon 'old wives' tales' or beliefs in supernatural forces matters little, for in modern times we can prove and indeed *have* proven through scientific research and controlled experiments, that plants have their place in our health and medicine cabinets. Some 'magical' plants have aphrodisiac or narcotic properties, while others have formidable toxic effects, but all are considered in some way to affect the human system on physical, spiritual and psychological levels. Plants such as cocoa, tobacco and coffee, which have accompanied humans over the course of millennia, are still, more than ever, an integral part of our daily lives. They still incite the same pleasures, the same fascinations, and the same dangers, and some still carry the same taboos. It is interesting to note that more than 80 per cent of chemical medicines in existence today, and found in pharmacists' dispensaries, are made from plants.

In modern astrology herbs are often associated with the zodiac signs and have evolved from an old system where a specific planet rules each herb. The planet that governs a herb is chosen according to its appearance, scent and where it grows; herbs are additionally categorised as hot or cold, and dry or moist. In this way you can see how the nature of the herb corresponds to the nature of the planet. If you are familiar with your ruling planets' basic associations, you will find it easy to match it to herbs. Although you can simply buy whatever herbs you wish to use for your magic, the optimum effect will be obtained if you can gather them at a favourable astrological time. Once you are armed with astrological knowledge, you can choose a time when the planet that rules your chosen herb is in a position of strength. Keep in mind that each planet rules a substantial amount of plants, so if one isn't easily obtained, it should be simply to find another one to use for the same purpose.

There sometimes seems to be a wide variance in the list of herbs associated with a specific astrological influence. This is because the different parts of the plant have different rulerships and uses. For example, whichever planet rules it, a plant that bears fruit is naturally related to Jupiter, its flowers relate to Venus, seed or bark to Mercury, leaves to the Moon, wood to Mars, and roots to Saturn. So, as well as the planet that traditionally rules the plant, it can be regarded as having a secondary ruler according to the part of the plant being used. Although you don't need to work with a highly complex system of deciding which herb will suit your purposes, you can make your magical workings more powerful by paying attention to some of these nuances.

Essentially, different scents, herbs, flowers and plants have their own specific vibrations. Their essences should be worn on your skin (you can make up your own combinations using essential oils or flower waters), burned in an oil burner, inhaled from a cloth, diffused in a bath or bowl of steam, or burned as incense sticks. Many plants, herbs and spices, however used, contain gentle yet effective energies which will affect not only your wishing ceremonies, but also your moods, associations and emotions, which can assist in carrying your wonderful Self in the direction of your dreams. Lifted up on incense smoke, for example, your wish is carried out to the wider Universe. Try making your own, out of any or all of your power plants, woods, flowers, shrubs, trees or herbs!

Thirty-three magical, mythical plants are: Cocoa, rosemary, tobacco, thyme, wheat, coffee, sugar cane, cinnamon, hemp, tea, pumpkin, foxglove, incense, amanita (a mushroom), tarragon, pepper, rice, belladonna, reed, ginseng, clove, ginger, sage, maize, mistletoe, lily, mandrake, St John's Wort, poppy, peyote, cinchona, verbena and the vine *. How many of your Scorpion 'lucky plants' (listed under the next sub-category, 'Your Lucky Plants, Herbs, Spices', etc.) can be found on this Magical 33 List?

YOUR LUCKY PLANTS, HERBS, SPICES, TREES, SHRUBS, FLOWERS, SCENTS, OILS & INCENSE

Gentian, Rue, Chilli, Tamarind, Sweet Basil, Pepper, Ginger, Garlic, Mustard, Tarragon, Chives,

Chrysanthemum, Catmint, Sarsaparilla, Orchid, Poppy, Rhododendron, Geranium, Red Honeysuckle, Holy, Periwinkle, Water Horehound, Blackthorn, Milk Thistle, Aconite, Squaw Vine, False Unicorn, Witchhazel, Thorn Apple, Horseradish, Dong Quai, Pennyroyal, Raspberry Leaf, Senna, Carnation, Blessed Thistle, Eupatorium, Aloe Vera, Charlock, Bramble, Birch, Gorse, Lily, Blackberry Leaves, Cramp Bark, Ginseng, Saw Palmetto, Wormwood, Heather, Nasturtium, Black and Blue Cohosh, Broom, Nettle, bushy trees, and all dark and deep red flowers. *

For Mars ★ Onion, Garlic, Nettle, Mustard, Cayenne, Holly. Mars is the planet of assertiveness, and plants associated with it are often red in colour and have thorns. Barberry Berries, Hawthorn & Sarsparilla are connected with Mars *

* Some plant products can be poisonous, toxic, hallucinogenic or even fatal if consumed. Always research first.

YOUR SPECIAL POWER FLOWERS

SCORPIO IN GENERAL ★ Chrysanthemum

OTHER BIRTH FLOWERS ★ Geranium, Rhododendron, Basil & Purple Heather

OCTOBER BORN ★ Calendula or Marigold ★ Those gifted with marigold, follower of the Sun, as their birth flower are spirited lovers of nature, radiating happiness to all around them. The marigold was associated with Apollo, the Greek god of the Sun. In Greek mythology, Nereid Clytie was spurned by Apollo and turned into a marigold - ever since then, marigolds have turned to face the Sun. The seeds of the marigold were often worn as an amulet to protect the wearer from theft, and they are frequently used in love charms and in wedding decorations. As a result, marigolds came to symbolise faithfulness and long-lasting unions.

NOVEMBER BORN ★ Chrysanthemum ★ Japan's national flower is considered a symbol of perfection of the human spirit. For thousands of years it has been the emblem of the emperor; warriors in Japan would wear this flower into battle to bring courage - and these emperor's men always won the war. In this country it is on the official seal of the imperial family; this is because its petals look like the rays of the Sun. The chrysanthemum is a universal symbol of autumn. In the East, it symbolises good fortune, happiness, longevity and wealth. In Feng Shui the chrysanthemum is one of the five beneficial flowers, representing joy and laughter. The chrysanthemum symbolises perfection which is often expressed as the well-balanced philosophies of life practised by those who call it their birth flowers.

YOUR FOODS

Passion, depth, intensity! In other words, don't serve Scorpio a peanut butter sandwich. The recipes must be ancient, the intention must be concentrated, and the flavour has to be as deep and dark as a winding cave. Your ruling planet Mars rules the colour red and is associated with heat and Fire. Being instinctive and primal, Scorpios enjoy dense, rich, sustaining pleasures of the flesh - both in the bedroom *and* on the dinner table. Being naturally hot-blooded and brooding, you prefer spicy and pungent foods and have the patience to wait; slow-cooked and deeply-flavoured suits you fine. Complex flavours and intricate combinations appeal too. As you like sharp and extreme varieties of everything in life, eating exotic, bloody and outrageous foods, such as Scottish haggis, tripe, black pudding, fried tarantulas, Dragon in the Flame of Desire (a.k.a. yaks' penis) and anything eye-poppingly hot and zesty or otherwise intense is a likely and regular indulgence; the more adventurous and madcap the dish, the more appealing you will find it! It is a rare Scorpio who will knock back an outright dangerous dish such as fugu, or what the Japanese call some species of blowfish or puffer fish - unless prepared correctly, it can be deadly as it contains a powerful toxin that can kill victims within hours; however, Scorpio is usually up for the challenge and lives to tell the tale to shocked but utterly fascinated listeners. Culinary Scorpio types will also gravitate towards underground and grown-in-soil foods, such as all root vegetables and on the upper end of the scale, truffles. Fermented foods and all fungus will also catch and usually sustain your interest. Overall, bland, simple, every day or tedious are definitely not on the menu for Scorpio. To you, character and depth are everything.

SCORPIO POWER FOODS

"Let food be your medicine; let medicine be your food."
Hippocrates

Pungent, spicy, fermented, mould-based or curdled foods appeal to the Scorpio palate. Scorpio is associated with aquatic foods such as Frogs and Snails. Foods that dwell in the 'underworld' such as Truffles and aged, 'brewed' foods, from Blue Cheese to Fish Sauce, are also attractive to the Scorpion appetite, as are 'hot' Mars plants which come from hot climates, such as Capsicums, Nettles, Onions, Garlic, Radish, Leeks, Eggplants, Goat, Spiky-Skinned Fruits (Pineapple, Lychees, Tart Rhubarb), and all red foods in general. Cherries, Citrus Fruits, Cabbage, Kale and Liver are also Scorpio foods. Your power beverages are Cellared Wines, Black Tea, Stout Beer and Dark Ales, Ruby Red Grapefruit Juice, Dark Red Drinks, Black Coffee, Berry Juices, and Fortified Wines. *

* Caution: Always use essential oils, alcohol and/or herbs with caution and research each one prior to use, as not all are safe for use by certain people, or under certain conditions such as pregnancy, intoxication or illness. Some

herbs and oils may be hallucinogenic, toxic in high doses, or produce other undesirable effects, and may be considered potentially harmful or hazardous if used or consumed before operating machinery, driving, or combined with alcohol or other drugs. Always consult a qualified practitioner or undertake thorough research from reliable sources before use or consumption of any of the listed essential oils, herbs or foods.

YOUR LUCKY WOOD ★ MAHOGANY
(Great to make a magic wand out of!)

Native Americans referred to trees as 'Standing People' because they stand firm, obtaining strength from their connection with the Earth. They therefore teach us the importance of being grounded, while at the same time listening to, and reaching towards, our higher aspirations. In Norse mythology, Yggdrasil, the tree of life, is a cosmic map that represents all life. The tree has its roots in the Underworld, is linked to the Earth through its trunk and its branches reach into the air of the Otherworld of spirit. The dryad, or tree's spirit, needs to be respected and asked when 'taking' from a tree for the purposes of magic. The essence of tree magic lies in understanding the qualities of each type. These can be drawn on for such things as healing and spell-casting. For example, the rowan tree grows high up the sides of mountains, often in hard-to-reach places, so if you need to develop tenacity or access to difficult spiritual spaces, you can call on this tree; the oak tree is durable and strong, so if you are needing fortification or firmness, you can gain power from this tree. When respected as living, breathing beings, trees can provide insights into the workings of Nature, cycles, and our own inner essence. Each birth time is associated with a particular kind of tree, the basic qualities of which complement the nature of those born during that time. Appreciate the beauty of your affinity tree and study its nature carefully, for it has a connection with your own nature and lessons to impart.

MAHOGANY ★ Mahogany is a commercially important lumber prized for its colour, beauty and durability. Its reddish-brown colour darkens over time, and displays a reddish sheen when polished. Popular as a body wood for electric guitars, mahogany's primary magical functions are spiritual growth and guidance, and fertility. While most woods have a range of differing uses and applications, mahogany is very specialised, focusing mainly on these areas. Additionally, but perhaps not an entirely unrelated feature, is this wood's possessing of a powerful bond with the Earth element; it is particularly useful for channelling Earth energy. Aside from fertility and growth, this wood does have some other uses: those of enhancing intuition, strengthening kinship bonds, and exploring and clarifying goals. An excellent wood for emotional and spiritual healing, mahogany can be used to provide guidance in these areas.

YOUR SACRED CELTIC CALENDAR TREES
★ IVY (MOON) OR REED (MOON)

IVY MOON ★ (30 September - 27 October)
REED MOON ★ (28 October - 24 November)

The Celts and other ancient peoples had many beliefs and traditions based around the magical lore of trees. The system of Celtic tree astrology was developed out of a natural connection with the

Druids' knowledge of Earth cycles and their reverence for the sacred knowledge they believed was held by trees. The Druids had a profound connection with trees and regarded them as vessels of infinite wisdom. Their calendar, being based on a Lunar year of thirteen months, contains a tree for each of these Lunar months, corresponding with (but not exactly) each of the twelve western astrology zodiac signs, which are based on the Solar calendar. Because there are some crossovers, I have included two possible trees for your zodiacal birth period.

IVY MOON ★ Three of the 13 Celtic Moon months are governed by plants other than trees. Your birthday, if it falls between 30 September and 27 October, is ruled by the Ivy Moon, which is an opportune time to cast a little magic to boost your health. A spiralling symbol of immortality and magic, the ivy provides the key to the other worlds and the kingdom of the fairies. In the Celtic lore, fairy folk, the Sidhe, were said to have once walked the Earth in the realm of mortals. Since their retreat to the fairy kingdom in the Otherworld, they are now only seen as butterflies. This insect was assigned to the ivy by the Druids, because the spiralling plant was thought to open an entrance to the world of the Sidhe. The short lifespan of the butterfly (about one month) also associates this elegant creature - and fairies - with the phases of the Moon.

Ironically, although ivy was chosen as a ruler of one of the Celtic Moon months, this plant actually destroys the health of trees by growing all over them, effectively choking them, and stealing their nourishment from surrounding soil. In effect, it is a parasite that clings to trees and walls by tiny 'adhesive' roots that grow out from its stem, and its tenacious nature means that it is difficult to eradicate or discourage. It is a persistent, hardy and long-lived evergreen plant that can adapt to a huge range of environments. Due to its strength and longevity, it has become associated with the enduring immortality of the spirit. Growing in a spiral formation towards the sky, it can be found just as easily on derelict buildings and dying trees - it is indeed a symbol of resurrection.

Ivy types are most noted for their sharp intellects and their ability to overcome all odds. Compassionate and loyal, you have a giving nature, but being born during the time of a waning Sun, you can encounter more challenges in life than most. You do, however, endure these troubling times with a soulful grace and silent perseverance. Although you are softly spoken, you have a keen wit, charm and charisma that holds you in good stead in social settings.

REED MOON ★ Your birthday, if it falls between 28 October and 24 November, is ruled by the Reed Moon, which is a time to stay inside, hibernate, reflect and recuperate. The haunting sound of reeds in the wind has inspired much of the reed's legend and folklore, closely associating it with the spirit realm. The family of reed organ instruments includes the harmonica, clarinet, panpipes and accordion, which work upon the principle of a thin strip of metal, or reed, held in a slit, which vibrates and produces an enchanting sound as air blows past it. Early reed organs actually used real reed stalks held in pipes.

Reed is a name given to a family of hardy, large grasses that occur globally and can be found along lakes, riversides, marshes and other shallow bodies of water; the strong, fibrous roots need moisture to survive. It is a resilient, fast-growing and integral part of many habitats and landscapes, earning it the reverence and respect of Celts. The dense roots push through and bind the saturated Earth, which is thought to link the reed with the Underworld, the realm of the dead and the hidden. The Druids celebrated Samhain during the Reed Moon, a time when the doors between worlds opened, reinforcing this plant's link to the spirit world.

Reed types are the inquisitors and the secret keepers of the Celtic tree system. You have an amazing knack of getting to the core of any matter, and have a way of subtly probing and manipulating people to coax them into revealing their deeper inner yearnings. However, this is coupled with a strong sense of truth and honour and so most of your scheming is harmless.

ESPECIALLY FOR AUSTRALIANS (OF ALL ZODIAC SIGNS)

If you live in Australia, here are two Australian-based magical woods, for those who prefer to source their woods closer to home and nature. Australia has a less documented history than many European civilisations, but still has no less mythology and legends swirling in its mists of time.

EUCALYPTUS ★ Eucalyptus is very plentiful and has a wonderfully intoxicating, distinctive, clean aroma which is reminiscent of the continent's vast areas of bushland, and has played an important ceremonial and medicinal role in the culture of Australian Aborigines, who have inhabited the nation for 40,000 to 50,000 years. Eucalyptus is a wood of feminine energy whose elemental association is Earth and main origin is Australia. One of the strongest healing woods known, eucalyptus wood has been used for centuries for medicinal as well as ritualistic purposes. Heady and Earthy, the energy of this wood is clean and pure. Eucalyptus is recommended for the promotion of good, robust health, and is also related to luck, especially if regarding knowledge. An excellent tool in divination, particularly when worn as a charm to invoke luck, it brings the wearer or user good fortune when used in rituals seeking positive results.

LEOPARDWOOD (or LACEWOOD) ★ Leopardwood or the Leopard Tree, so named because of its spotted wood, carries the energies of both the masculine and the feminine, Mars (Aries, Scorpio) and Venus (Taurus, Libra), and its main affinity is with the Water element (Cancer, Scorpio, Pisces). Leopardwood is a very useful tool for divination and is associated with positive luck, earning it the label 'gambler's wood'. Overall, its energy is very positive, making it an ideal wood for use in almost any ritual or spell, especially those concerning luck, magic and divination.

THE POWER OF LOVE

Each Sun sign exudes their own love and romance style. This style is an energy unique to that sign, and has the power to magnetise to that person their true, soulful match. Unhappy or unsuccessful relationships are often the result of incompatible Sun signs, personal values, goals, hopes, viewpoints or expectations. I believe everyone has a perfect soul partner (or three!) who is especially for them, and just knowing that special person or persons are out there can illuminate your life's romantic path. In this lifetime, we may not find that person or persons, but can still experience the joys and wonders of many other significant relationships which enrich and add tremendous meaning to our lives. Some partnerships are only fleeting, but the feelings they give us can last a lifetime, while others are more enduring, and the rewards they give us and lessons they teach us can last a lifetime too. Small gestures of love on a frequent basis, consistent nurturing and communication, and making the effort to understand each other, are just four ways to keep the fires of passion and romance burning long after the initially roaring fire has diminished into glowing embers.

Your whole natal chart would need to be examined to form an overall picture of your romantic nature, and although the Sun is a fantastic starting point, it is not the sole consideration. Regarding these other planets, in Carl Jung's studies on psychological astrology, and in traditional synastry (the comparing of two people's natal charts to determine overall compatibility), the harmonious link between the Sun in one person's chart and the Moon in the other's (usually the man's Sun and the woman's Moon) is considered the best indication for a happy and enduring relationship. More specifically, the sextile aspect, an angle of 60 degrees, appeared most frequently between the Sun of one and the Moon of the other in fulfilling relationships. Other positive planetary contacts, such as one person's Moon to another's Venus, or the Mars to the Moon (again, traditional indications of attraction and harmony) also occurred frequently.

The feminine personal planets in a male's chart (Moon and Venus), and the masculine personal planets in a female's chart (Sun and Mars) tell a lot about the inner self and how this is projected onto relationships. However helpful chart analysis is in telling a story about your relationship style and approach, it all depends not on your chart, but on what you do with the resources at your disposal, which your chart can indeed tell you a lot about. Relationships and marriages involving harmonious planetary and zodiacal energies between the two people tend to last longer because they are simply more 'flowing' and easier.

The signs in which the four personal and 'relationship' planets - the Sun, the Moon, Venus and Mars - are placed, coupled with the aspects they make with the other planets in the chart, give important clues into understanding the often unconscious drives within you that shape your relating style, tastes, mannerisms and patterns.

Expanding upon the other planetary considerations is beyond the scope of this book, but it is useful to know, particularly if you are interested in examining the dynamics of a current relationship a bit deeper, or are wishing to attract a new one into your life. But for now, your Sun sign is a wonderful place to start! Your Solar sign is regarded as being at the core of the complex - and very fun - study of relationships! So for now, we will begin this study of love with your essence, your core self, the brightest light shining from within - your Sun sign!

SOME LUCKY-IN-LOVE TIPS
GENERAL HINTS

★ To attract and retain love, the Heart chakra (an energy centre within the body) needs to be balanced and clear from blockages. The Heart chakra is located in the region of the physical heart. Its Sanskrit name is *anahata*, and its symbol is a twelve-petal green lotus flower whose centre contains a green circle and two intersecting triangles making up a six-pointed star representing balance (and also could be said to symbolise six as the number of Venus). Its element is Air and its colour is green. Balance in this chakra is expressed as unconditional love for ourselves and others. Crystals that can be used to cleanse and balance this chakra are mostly green and pink stones.

★ Pink candles (two, representing a couple, or six, representing Venus, is preferable) can be used in love spells.

★ Any 'love-attracting' wishing rituals should be done on a Friday (ruled by Venus) night around the time of the New Moon (signifying the principle of increase and growth).

★ Basil, otherwise known as witch's herb or St Joseph's wort, is said to be the most potent lover herb of all. Basil vibrates to the energy of Mars, which is all about lust and sexual energy, and it is used prolifically in all sorts of love potions and rituals throughout the world.

★ Ginger has a reputation as a potent sexual tonic and aphrodisiac *. Arousing and warm, it can increase sensual vitality, particularly in men. Being warming and spicy, its vibration aligns with Mars. Saffron is also regarded as a potent, albeit expensive, aphrodisiac!

★ Wear red and pink (associated with Mars and Venus respectively), as these colours in all their shades are said to incite passion, lust and romance. Green is also connected with the heart by virtue of its association with the Heart chakra and the planet Venus, and its links with fertility, nature, abundance of all kinds, and new growth.

★ Call upon some higher spiritual help. When working your 'love magic', some planetary influences, goddesses and gods that you can call upon are: Aphrodite, Venus and Eros/Cupid, and other lesser known deities such as Juno Lucina, Demeter, Freya, Ishtar, Circe and Hathor.

★ The planet Venus has developed a rich culture of gods and goddesses associated with her varying levels of love and passion. These include the virgin - Brighid; the fertile woman - Aphrodite, (the Greek goddess); and of course Venus (the Roman equivalent); the mother and provider - Demeter; and desirous or physical love - Eros/Cupid (Venus's son).

★ The pine tree is sacred to Adonis (Venus's lover) and is said to balance the male and female energies. Pine is cleansing and protective and, as an evergreen, symbolises life. Its cones represent fertility.

★ Cardamom is said to have aphrodisiac qualities

★ The three almost universally recognised symbols of love are the goddesses Venus and Aphrodite, and the Cupid. Venus is the patroness of flowers and vegetation, and represents the regenerative cycle of creation, as well as beauty, herbs and physical love. She can be called upon for general love wishes and rituals. The dove, roses, rings, copper, apples, rosemary and the ankh are some of her sacred symbols. Aphrodite is a Greek goddess who has the ability to brings lovers together. Her names mean 'of the sea' as she is believed to have been born of the foam of the ocean. She can be called upon in ceremonies and spells for affection, love, marriage and partnership. Some of her associated symbols are the Flower of Aphrodite, swans, dolphins, frankincense and myrrh. Cupid, the cherubic winged boy with a bow and arrow, is the Roman name, and Eros is the Greek name for the same deity. The son of Venus/Aphrodite, he is an aspect that represents lustful love and desire.

★ Heartsease, another name for the wild pansy, Latin viola tricolour, was one of the most popular additives to the love potions of the ancient Romans and Greeks.

★ In centuries past, when people were more in tune with nature and its cycles, ceremonies, rituals and festivals were held on certain dates or times of year. The following are some examples, and you can reawaken their powers through craft and ceremony: February 2 is Bridhid's Day, or Bride's Day, and represents the white goddess; February 14 is Valentine's Day, traditionally the greatest and most well-known love 'celebration' of the year; March 1 is one of the festival days of Juno Lucina, the light bearer and goddess of women and marriage; the month of April is especially linked to the love goddess Aphrodite; the Summer solstice which falls on or around June 21 is an important time for reconnecting with the spirit of love, fertility and marriage; August 1 is the first of three harvest festivals in the Celtic calendar: The Harvest Festival honours Demeter, the goddess of love, as bountiful mother and faithful wife; the Festival of Lights, Diwali, in October, is sacred to Lakshmi, the Hindu goddess of happiness, love, and good fortune; the Winter solstice which falls on or around December 21, marks the turning point from long dark nights to lengthening days, and is the time of the wheel of love when virgin goddesses gave birth to their children - it is also fittingly symbolised by evergreens such as pine, ivy and holly; in Mexico, December 31, the last night of the year, is traditionally 'wishing night' and is an opportune time to make a wish for a lover in the coming year, using evergreen branches to enhance your request.

* The term 'aphrodisiac' is derived from Aphrodite, the Greek goddess of love, beauty, lust and sensuality

★ GEMSTONES ★

When it comes to calling love into your life using crystals, the general rule is that any of the pink or green stones are closely aligned with matters of the heart and can therefore help you to entice the affections you seek. Although your Sun sign has its very own special gemstones, outlined elsewhere in the book, the following stones can be used by all the signs (except for the first point, which are your own sign's feature stones), as their energies and qualities contain the power to attract and create love in all its forms, from self-love to deeper soulful connections with another, or to increase states of being which open the heart, thus enhancing your abilities to magnetise love.

★ Topaz, Malachite and Peridot ★ Using your Scorpion luckiest crystals is a fabulous start to working on heightening your romantic zest, and making your sensual energy more potent. Red Coral is also useful in raising your attracting powers.

★ Rose Quartz is the ultimate love stone. It invites love into your life by helping to open your heart to receive love, and gently reminding you that you are worthy of love. Connected with the Heart chakra, it is the stone of unconditional love, enhancing all forms of it and opening up the heart. It is excellent for increasing self-worth and acceptance. The colour of rose quartz is pink, the colour of Venus, the amorous planet of desire and nurturance. Balancing and calming, it helps to heal emotional pain. Wear this stone, keep some beside your bed, or sleep with some under your pillow to remind you that love it coming your way - and that you whole*heart*edly deserve it!

★ Green Aventurine is considered the 'opportunity and luck stone'. Connected with the Heart chakra, it helps us to recognise opportunities and is said to place us exactly where we need to be for good things to transpire, as energetically it opens our mind and heart to increased perception to recognise lucky elements. It also promotes new growth, optimism, and is an overall attractor of good fortune, adventure and abundance.

★ Jade, on a spiritual level, has an affinity with the Heart chakra. It harmonises relationships, and encourages compassion and the establishment of strong bonds.

★ Emerald is reputedly a stone of constancy in love, and is said to have been brought to Earth from the planet Venus. Because it is green, it also holds deep associations with the Heart chakra.

★ Rhodochrosite can be used to attract one's soul mate. This stone, as with all the pink stones, can be used as an effective love magnet. It encourages you to appreciate yourself by teaching you that you are worthy of love, wholeness and happiness - and so opening you up to receive.

★ Malachite, Citrine, Rhodonite, Moonstone, Morganite, Beryl, Ruby, Mangano Calcite, Garnet, Red and Pink Tourmaline, Tugtupite, Rutilated Quartz, Lodestone, Peridot and Lapis Lazuli are also known for their love properties, and can be used or worn to invite romance into your life, or to bring and retain enduring love.

★ Clear Quartz can be used with any of these listed crystals to amplify their metaphysical properties.

★ Shells: Although shells are not technically a crystal, but rather a natural elemental material, they are associated with love and are sacred to Aphrodite, the Greek love goddess, and are often used in magic talismans to attract romance.

★ ESSENTIAL OILS ★

The following essential oils are known for their aphrodisiac or love-attracting properties also, and can be worn as perfumes on the skin, used in an oil burner or vaporiser, dispersed in a bath, used in spell-casting and wishing rituals, sprinkled on your pillow to imbue your dreams with inspired romantic notions, or in any other creative ways you can think of! **

★ Essential oils, flowers and herbs which contain natural pheromones or like substances, or increase pheromone levels in the body, are: Lavender, Frankincense, Jasmine, Nutmeg, Ylang Ylang, Sandalwood, Patchouli and Asian Agarwood (Oud).

★ The prime love oil, which holds Universal appeal, is rose. Reputedly excellent for both the mind and body, roses are the basis of more than 95 per cent of women's fragrances, and the petals have a long tradition of uplifting the spirits and soothing the soul. *Rosa damascena* is believed to be good for attracting love, while *R. centifolia*, the French rose oil base, is regarded as an aphrodisiac. Rose is traditionally accepted as the all-encompassing Universal fragrance of love, blessed with a reputation for opening up the hearts of all those who come under its spell.

★ Cedarwood oil has been used since ancient times in incense and perfumes. Its deep, woody scent helps to stimulate the Base chakra, increasing sexual passion and desire. Its sedative qualities aid relaxation and encourage openness. In herbal magic, it is also associated with spells for wealth and abundance.

★ Neroli, Geranium, Almond (as a base), Basil, Thyme, Vetiver, Gardenia, Vanilla, Rose Otto, Apple, Cardamom, Lotus, Orange, Ginger, Bergamot, Rosewood and Clary Sage are also exquisitely seductive and sensual, and can be used in any way you like to bring to you that which your heart desires. These oils, when mixed with your own pheromones and magical intentions, will naturally enhance your point of attraction!

** Always research first and use with caution.

SCORPIO ★ LOVE STYLE

To Scorpio love is an intense journey of explosive passions and profundity. Eroticism, kinky games and tantric practices are likely to be a feature in your love life. Your notorious passion may not always be expressed in the expected ways however, for sexuality to you is mostly about emotions - a symbol, a different way of experiencing and being. Many Scorpios have a deep mystical feeling about romance, sex and other matters of the heart and flesh, and view them as having to do less with the body and much more with the soul. In any case, Plutonian types often have strong and enduring relationships, which may be marked by power plays, secrecy, mysteries, and ultimately, personal transformation. You don't do things by halves in life or love, so partnerships are likely to be all or nothing and extreme. Although essentially mistrustful and suspicious, once you do surrender to another, you are faithful, loyal, deeply caring and emotionally involved. But you are the most complex and enigmatic sign of the zodiac, so may perplex your lover with your secretive demeanour, dark undercurrents and rampant fantasies. Suspicious and obsessive, it is not above you to scan your lovers' phone records or computer history to investigate their movements, for you need to know the why, when, how and where of everything in your union before you can fully trust an-other. Your pressing desire to be the complete master of the love game can also be difficult to understand for more simple, superficial types, and your tendency to control and possess can make your partner want to wriggle free, unless of course they are of such intense stock as you! Whether you are the smouldering breed of Scorpio or the explosive type, one thing is a guarantee in *all* your relationships - they will never be experienced in halves, and they are *always* experienced deeply. No one experiences a relationship with a Scorpio without changing - including the Scorpio herself - truly, madly, deeply.

LUCKY IN LOVE? SCORPIO ★ COMPATIBILITY

* Please note the following is based on your Sun sign alone. For a whole and integrated approach to relationship compatibility, your whole natal chart would need to be taken into consideration. Synastry (*syn*: acting or considered together, united; *astry*: pertaining to the stars) is a branch of astrology which delves into more complex areas, and is based upon the natal charts of the two people concerned, to determine overall compatibility, potential conflicts and suitability based upon celestial influences. For the purposes of length, the below information is simplified and only refers to Sun sign connections.

Scorpio ★ Aries * ♏ ♈

Watch out for the clash of titans here! Being ruled by the same mighty planet Mars (albeit the secondary ruler of Scorpio), you're both such forceful and passionate characters that it can turn into warfare. You may have some memorable fights - and equally memorable 'kiss and make up' moments afterwards! Aries's passion and Fire attracts the more reticent Scorpio, but the Ram's impatience and blunt comments may insult the Scorpio's controlled but deeply sensitive nature. This is an intense combination, with the potential for explosive fireworks, aroused tempers, and a battle of the (very strong) wills. Although Water can put the Fire out, here it may serve to make it simmer, spit and spark in all directions. Scorpio is intensely emotional and naturally possessive, and this doesn't always sit too well with the more independent and less emotional Aries. Scorpio may well feel rejected and be left cold by Aries's apparent disregard for her complex feelings. If Scorpio tries to dominate the indomitable Aries, rebellion will result, and when a serious rift develops in this relationship, Aries can easily separate and cut the losses, while Scorpio may brood, sulk and harbour feelings of revenge or vindictiveness. Scorpio is passionate and controlling, while Aries will not be controlled by another, and invariably needs space. Still, this is a particularly sexy and passionate blend of energies and both signs will relish the emotional intensity it evokes. Fire and Water creates a highly charged association to say the least, but since Mars rules over you both, you will likely share a mutual appreciation of each other's strengths and capabilities. Forthright and naïve Aries will not suspect the devious, secretive ways of the Scorpion, and whether this is a good or a bad thing is up to you to determine. Whether this will be a long-term relationship or not is very much in the balance - if you can find any! Overall, you are both strong-willed, forceful and determined, so if you can channel your combined forces into a common goal, great achievements are possible in this relationship.

Overall compatibility rating ★ 7.5 out of 10
Lucky Romance Tip ★ To attract an Aries, wear the colours red or orange, and use the crystal diamond

Scorpio ★ Taurus ♏ ♉

Being Scorpio's natural opposite, the Bull holds a deep appeal to the Scorpion. Their common sense and physical sensuality turning the Scorpion on, but their stubbornness and lack of passion may equally put the Scorpio off. But generally, opposites attract and Earthy types like Taurus generally appreciate the sensitivity of a Water sign. Just be careful that your mutual passion doesn't turn into a locking-of-the-horns/claws competition. Although Earth is usually compatible with Water, your opposition status could prove difficult. Taurus and Scorpio are drawn to each other and an initially physical attraction may bring you together, but when this initial lust settles down a bit, the pendulum may swing the other way unless you have other strong things in common. Both highly sexed and incredibly sensual, there will inevitably be erotic overtones and emotional power plays. But even though you are compatible and even explosive in the bedroom, Scorpio's intensity and depth may unnerve the much simpler and uncomplicated Taurus. Mutual trust is absolutely essential, as Scorpio is prone to be suspicious and Taurus is prone to be jealous - you are both possessive, and (the wrong type of) sparks could fly if one of you catches the other even looking in someone else's direction. It is important to keep in mind that a raging Bull charges, and an enraged Scorpion stings; and neither experience is pleasant. Such intense feelings can also create a love-hate relationship, and emotions and resentfulness may run deep. The greatest potential threats to your relationship are your making of possessive demands on each other, and your jealousy. Trust may also be an issue; if the Scorpion doesn't trust the Bull, Taurus will be deeply crushed. Therefore, tolerance and understanding of each other's differing - but also complementary - natures must be exercised for this relationship to work successfully.

Overall compatibility rating ★ 7 out of 10
Lucky Romance Tip ★ To attract a Taurus, wear the colours pink or green, and use the crystal rose quartz

Scorpio ★ Gemini ♏ ♊

The Twins may seem a bit flippant and superficial for the much deeper and more serious Scorpion. Gemini may also be a bit flighty when the Scorpio is wanting deep discussions. You tend to misunderstand each other. Moreover, Geminians may find it difficult to realise the depth and power of Scorpio emotions. If Gemini's flirtatious ways provoke them to a jealous fury, the Gemini will be taken aback by the heat of the Scorpionic rage. Gemini will certainly feel Scorpio's sting if they try any mental tricks here. Scorpio's moodiness and intensity may make the Twins feel out of their depth, which creates many challenges. Air and Water don't tend to blend easily, and this is highlighted in this coupling. Scorpio is intensely emotional and naturally possessive, and this doesn't always sit too well with the freedom-loving, flighty and ethereal Gemini. Scorpio may feel rejected and left cold by the Twins' apparent disregard for her complex feelings. If Scorpio tries to dominate or control the impossible-to-pin-down Gemini, the Twins will revolt and promptly skip off to a new venture without looking back. Scorpio is passionate and controlling, while Gemini needs space and freedom to move - both mentally and physically. An attraction between you two is highly likely, as Gemini will be intrigued by the mysterious, brooding Scorpion, and Scorpio in turn will be turned on by the lively, carefree flirt in Gemini. But unless the significant differences in your emotional expression are understood, Scorpio will likely feel that Gemini is too indifferent, inconsistent and restless. Also, Gemini's erratic nature will challenge Scorpio's much more stable, fixed character. If Scorpio seeks to possess and overpower, the Twins will simply wriggle free. Although there are many differences between you, if you can channel your combined forces of intellect and power into a common goal, great achievements are possible in this relationship.

Overall compatibility rating ★ 6.5 out of 10
Lucky Romance Tip ★ To attract a Gemini, wear the colours light blue or yellow, and use the crystal citrine

Scorpio ★ Cancer ♏ ♋

Two Water signs can build a cosy nest. Cancer's emotional tactics are an open book to Scorpio and sometimes Scorpio likes to shock the Crab into noticing them. You are both hidden by nature but usually bring out the best of each other when you do come to the surface to share. You two share the

Watery element, making your relationship comparable to a towering, powerful cascade of passion and love. Scorpio is intensely emotional and naturally possessive, and although her intensity may be a little daunting to the Crab's much more delicate expression, there is much common ground here. Facts, logic and reason will rarely feature in this pairing, as you are both ruled primarily by feelings and the inner depths. When harmony reigns, this is a very constructive duo, but if conflicts arise, emotions can get out of control and clear thinking becomes distorted. This also has the potential to be an extreme and complex match: you will either drown each other or swim along merrily together, keeping each other buoyed in the roughest of oceans. Although the Crab is clingy and possessive, the Scorpio's controlling, powerful nature may overwhelm her at times, but she can just as easily be swept off her feet by the suave and magnetic Scorpion. Whether your relationship survives or not will depend upon other factors of the two people involved, but however it turns out in the end, it will be an affair to remember - Scorpio doesn't do anything by halves and Cancer never forgets. Both of you seek security and faithfulness from your partner, so there will be an unspoken agreement here. Each of you is intuitive and can always sense what is going on, so mutual trust is essential here. Cancer, although delicate, has a way of understanding that Scorpio can sometimes be ruthless and tough. Great heights, depths and achievements are highly possible in this relationship.

Overall compatibility rating ★ 9 out of 10

Lucky Romance Tip ★ To attract a Cancerian, wear the colours silver or white, and use the crystal moonstone

Scorpio ★ Leo * ♏ ♌

When the Lion roars and the Scorpion is poised and ready to sting, you know this may be a challenging match. Yet Scorpio's sincere compliments and smouldering passion bring out Leo's enthusiasm, invoke his loyalty and stoke his Fire. But different in nature with the exception of your Fixed mode, you two are usually at odds with each other. Scorpio's internal feelings and your external actions can easily clash. In addition, the Scorpion's jealousy, intensity and possessiveness can seem all too difficult for the Lion, who does not like to be controlled or bossed around. Frank, extroverted Leo will rarely understand or appreciate Scorpio's secretive, hidden motives and manipulative manoeuvres and cool, defensive character. Scorpio guards her secrets, while heart-on-sleeve Leo lays everything on the table. Further, the what-you-see-is-what-you-get Lion may not understand the Scorpio's complex and deeply emotional nature, and Scorpio will in turn find it difficult to trust Leo with her innermost feelings. But there does exist a strong sexual magnetism between you and this could make for a very passionate, physical relationship. Long-term success will depend on whether or not your egos clash and whether you can practise give and take without one trying to dominate the other. The fact that you are both uncompromising may work for or against you. You are both powerful and magnetic, so if you really put your strong wills and ambitious minds together, great heights are highly possible.

Overall compatibility rating ★ 6.5 out of 10
Lucky Romance Tip ★ To attract a Leo, wear the colours gold or orange, and use the crystal ruby

Scorpio ★ Virgo ♏ ♍

You two have a lot in common; you both like to analyse and dissect. However, if Virgo dares turn their analysis and criticism upon Scorpio, the Scorpio's affections may vanish without trace. Virgo's affinity with this Watery sign attracts her to the Scorpion's mystery and passion, however the Scorpion may prove too intense for the Virgin in the long run, and if she criticises the fiercely self-protective Scorpio's ego one too many times, she may be stung by Scorpio's infamous tail and never fully recover. Your relationship may well take a little while to get off the ground, but a mutual sensuality will ensure it heats up to a smouldering union. There is likely to be lots of probing, analysis, discernment and considerable sexual chemistry if this partnership does take off, but emotionally you are worlds apart. Scorpio needs a good emotional rapport and Virgo thrives on a substantial mental rapport, so your natures may be vastly at odds too. Scorpio's complexity may be too difficult for the straight-laced, down-to-Earth Virgo to fathom, and the Scorpion's dark moods may unnerve the delicate Virgin, whose feelings are usually more straightforward. Scorpio has strong, passionate feelings, burning desires and is often at the mercy of her own depths, whereas Virgo believes in keeping emotions under firm control and discipline. However, Scorpio demands much of self and others so will appreciate the Virgo's conscientious, dedicated reliability, loyalty and consistency. In any case, you will inevitably share many pleasures together if this relationship takes off - but only if Scorpio can rein in her brooding intensity and Virgo can keep her harsh criticism under control.

Overall compatibility rating ★ 7 out of 10
Lucky Romance Tip ★ To attract a Virgo, wear the colours white or yellow, and use the crystal sapphire

Scorpio ★ Libra ♏ ♎

Scorpio can see through the Libran's games and know when they are serious or just flirting. Scorpio enjoys the challenge and the magnetism the Scales so effortlessly provide but will not forgive infidelity or sharing the Scales with anyone else. Even though you two operate on different wavelengths, Libra is drawn to Scorpio's intelligent insights. Libra may even surprise himself by appreciating the brooding seriousness of this passionate sign. This is an intriguing combination and surprisingly it often works. Libra goes to enormous lengths to get along with everyone, whereas Scorpio just exudes a magnetic appeal which attracts many. As the Scales seek balance in all areas of their life, especially relationships, the Scorpio will provide him with this stability, and you will both equally dedicate yourself to making the partnership work if you feel it is worthwhile. However, the long-term prospects may be doubtful - Scorpio's complexity may unsettle the harmony-seeking Scales, who never likes to be tipped too far in any one direction. If this union is to work, Scorpio will need to rein in her excessive need to control and possess, and cultivate greater refinement to suit the Libran. Scorpio thrives on living life to the extreme, and her all-or-nothing attitude may fluster the normally unflappable Libran. However, your elements Air and Water may also combine well, because your rulers, the feminine Venus and the masculine Mars, complement each other to create a very strong physical, emotional and sexual attraction. Gentle Libra may find the severity of Scorpio overwhelming, but if these two can overcome their odds, they will find that the secret to their happiness is in finding something to share which gives pleasure and satisfaction to both. Overall, Libra is tactful enough not to provoke Scorpio's sting, and there will likely be an undeniable mutual attraction between the Scales' charming, natural allure and Scorpio's smouldering, charismatic sex appeal.

Overall compatibility rating ★ 7.5 out of 10
Lucky Romance Tip ★ To attract a Libran, wear the colours pink and blue, and use the crystal opal

Scorpio ★ Scorpio ♏ ♏

What a baffling blend of powerful, enigmatic personalities this is! You are bound to have some contests of will, yet with your natural love and devotion to your loved one, you can make an impressive and dynamic team. This double combination of the emotional element of Water will intensify the already intense passions, complexities and desires of your individual make-ups. You will most likely share a deep connection and understanding with each other, but trust may be an issue and you will become suspicious and defensive if the other is pulling tricks - because although it does take one to know one, sometimes a fellow Scorpio can still strike and then scuttle away before she is detected. For she is crafty, clever, manipulative, and will use all her might and pour all her energies into making this union work if she believes it is worth fighting for. There are no halfway measures with the sign of the Scorpion, and this all-or-nothing drive will be the powerful propeller of your relationship. On the other hand, with some extreme characters, you may detest each other - or share a volatile relationship which hangs by a thread. Violent clashes of wills could occur and neither of you will surrender. Erotica, jealousy and deep soulful yearnings will most probably feature in your time together, but sexual tension and the threat of combustion are an ever-present danger. An intriguing and powerful duo, you will both seek to dominate the world together and remain loyal and dedicated to one another through both heaven and hell. In any case, yours will certainly be an affair to remember. But if this relationship does self-destruct for whatever reason, 'revenge is a dish best served cold' is sure to be the order of the day!

Overall compatibility rating ★ 8 out of 10

Lucky Romance Tip ★ To attract another Scorpio, wear the colours red or burgundy, and use the crystal malachite.

Scorpio ★ Sagittarius * ♏ ♐

This is a dangerous and unpredictable liaison as the Sagittarius is sure to get something he hadn't expected with the Scorpion. In essence, the Archer should watch his tactlessness or it will be revenged. The Scorpio may prove too powerful and intense for the Sagittarius's light-hearted and freedom-seeking nature. The open, direct manner of the Archer can be charming at first, but a big problem if the Archer reveals the Scorpio's deepest secrets to all and sundry, as he is prone to do. Sagittarius needs freedom; the Scorpion needs security. The Sagittarius may become agitated if the Scorpio tries to possess or control him, and the Scorpio will feel slighted by Sagittarius's natural tendency to be insensitive and indifferent to feelings. Scorpio likes to keep her cards close to her chest, while Sagittarius has a need to know everything about everyone and lays it all out stark and bare. With the Archer, what you see is what you get, which is a far cry from the very hidden, inner-dwelling Scorpio. Generally, the Sagittarius's need to be free and explore the world at large will arouse the suspicions of the deeply mistrustful Scorpion, who will wallow and brood - something the Archer will not tolerate. Scorpio demands much of herself and others, but Sagittarius is a natural born rebel who will revolt against any attempts by anyone to pin him down, restrict his movements or question his whereabouts.

However, the Archer's natural exuberance, optimism and enthusiasm can be refreshing for the harping, sceptical Scorpio, but it could have the entirely opposite effect also - Sagittarius natural openness and frankness could either fascinate, intrigue, mystify or enrage the Scorpio. The Archer does not hold grudges, and fails to understand why the Scorpion would feel offended by his flirting and wide and varied social circle, which is open all hours and where everyone is welcome. Sagittarius will also feel unsettled by Scorpio's deep, dark complexities and Scorpio will not understand why Sagittarius can just skip off in the other direction whistling a happy-go-lucky tune like nothing has happened. Overall, this could be a passionate match, but could just as likely frustrate both parties as you are both so different in expression and style.

Overall compatibility rating ★ 7 out of 10
Lucky Romance Tip ★ To attract a Sagittarius, wear the colour deep purple or royal blue, and use the crystal zircon

Scorpio ★ Capricorn ♏ ♑

Both naturally reserved, self-controlled, suspicious and secretive, you will also tend towards being loyal to and protective of each other. However, Scorpio may demand too much of the Goat emotionally and keep her from climbing the mountain as high as she'd like to. But generally, you two make for a compatible pair as you share similar goals - based on respect, power and security among other things. The Goat may seem insensitive to the Scorpion at times, but will certainly respect her privacy and need to be introspective. You are both incisive, clear-sighted and consistent, and you both rely on your wits, instincts and resources to get by in life, no matter whose toes you step on - even each other's. Both intense and driven, but in considerably different ways, you could set fire to the bedroom or create a formidable, unbreakable bond. In any case, you are both unerringly faithful, dedicated, determined, wilful and do not stop until you have reached any goal you set for yourself. Scorpio will admire the Capricorn's abundant drive and Capricorn will appreciate the Scorpio's cool, steady, unwavering influence. When conflicts arise however, you can become bitter enemies, as neither is forgiving or compromising and you are both ruthless and brutal in battle. Neither of you will back down, as this would be a weakness, so any serious rifts will not be easily or quickly resolved. Earth and Water are generally harmonious though, so if you can find mutual characteristics, of which there are many, and capitalise on these, your relationship stands a good chance of being a strong, passionate bond which will weather any storm. Yours has great potential to develop into a strong, resilient and powerful match indeed. Just watch your sarcasm and bite.

Overall compatibility rating ★ 7.5 out of 10
Lucky Romance Tip ★ To attract a Capricorn, wear the colours brown or black, and use the crystal garnet

Scorpio ★ Aquarius ♏ ♒

A wild and difficult combination, yet the energy can also be enjoyable. If you can overcome your differences of style and take it slowly, yours can be an intoxicating match. But generally speaking, Air and Water don't tend to blend easily, and this is highlighted in this coupling. Scorpio is intensely emotional and naturally possessive, and this doesn't always sit too well with the freedom-loving, detached and unemotional Aquarius. Scorpio will feel rejected and left cold by Aquarius's apparent disregard for their complex feelings. If Scorpio tries to dominate the indomitable Aquarius, rebellion will result, and when a serious rift develops in this relationship, Aquarius can easily separate and cut the losses, while Scorpio may brood, sulk and harbour feelings of revenge or vindictiveness. Scorpio is passionate and controlling, while Aquarius is dispassionate and needs space. While the Water Bearer sees love in broader, Universal terms, the Scorpion views love in powerfully personal terms. Unless this significant difference in emotions is understood, Scorpio will feel that Aquarius is too indifferent and impersonal. Also, Aquarius's erratic nature will challenge Scorpio's all-or-nothing, extreme attitudes to life and love. Although there are many differences between you, being Fixed signs, you are both strong-willed and determined, so if you can channel your combined forces into a common goal, great achievements are possible in your partnership.

Overall compatibility rating ★ 6.5 out of 10

Lucky Romance Tip ★ To attract an Aquarian, wear the colours electric blue or turquoise, and use the crystal aquamarine

Scorpio ★ Pisces ♏ ♓

Scorpio feels safe and free to be herself around the Fish. You can create deep empathy and tender passion together, but the Scorpio needs to beware of using force or trying to exert control, for the Fish is a slippery character and will not hesitate to swim away. Water harmonises with Water, and you two have the potential to have an intense and passionate meeting of the hearts. Since your signs are naturally emotional and sensitive, you can usually share these qualities with each other, feeling understood without the need for words. There is a magnetic attraction between the Fish and the Scorpion, and in combination you will generate a deeply romantic and feeling bond. Scorpio has an innate desire to dominate and conquer people or situations, and so needs to have others who will succumb to her will, to which the Piscean will usually oblige. However, being a sign of illusion and deception, Pisces can give the impression of being submissive to disguise an inner truth: that she is actually deviously manoeuvring or manipulating the situation. Scorpio is a dab hand at power plays and complexities however, and will not find this daunting or even off-putting, even when she inevitably finds out (and Scorpio will *always* find out). The compassionate and sympathetic Fish is a great balm and soother for the Scorpion's inner tensions, compelling desires and consuming obsessions, and each will intuitively be able to sense the other's moods, fears, needs and shortcomings. If trouble arises in the relationship, emotions can cloud the issue, and Pisces may be easily hurt by the Scorpio's sharp tongue and even sharper sting. Scorpio will also need to curb the need to control Pisces, as the elusive Fish is easily frightened and apt to slip easily from too tight a grasp, swimming away if she feels restricted. The mysterious, charismatic and magnetic Scorpio will usually reel the slippery Fish back in, though. Both are enigmatic in their own ways and will captivate and enchant each other for the most part. While Pisces is gentle and easy going, Scorpio is much more intense and complex, but if you two can overcome your differences in nature, you have the capacity to swim happily along with the current of life's stream. Your emotional rapport alone suggests deep potential here, and this can take your relationship to whimsically dizzying heights!

Overall compatibility rating ★ 9 out of 10
Lucky Romance Tip ★ To attract a Pisces, wear the colours mauve or sea green, and use the crystal amethyst

* With all Fire and Water combinations (i.e. Scorpio with Aries, Leo or Sagittarius), it is easy to see how and why fire and water are natural enemies. Water can quickly put a fire out, and fire can dry up water. Fire usually works quickly, and water gently. In alchemy and astrology, both are important, and both must be carefully manipulated and controlled to make full effective use of their powerful, albeit vastly differing, natures. Fire can be brought back to a steady heat, whereas the pressure and force of water can

be increased vigorously or to circulate more actively. As warm and watery beings, the human body demonstrates the miracle of fire and water combined. Water connects, flows and lubricates, and brings healing, its passive, gentle nature soothing away the scorching harshness of fire. One ancient text offers a mystical view of how water and fire are intertwined in the body, and suggests that it is through consciously combining these two elements that we can transform our inner state. Fire can initiate and inspire this quest for self-transformation, but once the fire burns down, life can be restored anew by water. Natural enemies? Mostly. Astrological passion? Absolutely!

YOUR TAROT CARDS ★ FOR LUCK, MAGIC, ENERGY, ABUNDANCE, QUESTING & MEANING
DEATH, JUDGEMENT, THE TOWER & THE HIGH PRIESTESS

Tarot and astrology are inextricably linked. All the cards of the Major Arcana, which comprises 22 of the Tarot's 78 cards, are 'ruled by' or connected with either one of the twelve zodiac signs, the planets and luminaries, or one of the four elements.

The 22 Major Arcana cards contain the richest symbolism of all the cards in the Tarot deck, each carrying a myriad of messages for the reader to decipher. The symbolism contained within these images represents the archetypal aspects of your character. It also describes the path your soul takes through each stage of life, revealing clues through which you can explore different parts of yourself. Each of the cards also represents an aspect of Universal human experience and has a name that either directly conveys the meaning of the card, such as Strength or Justice, or depicts individuals that represent these human archetypes, such as the Hermit or the Empress. The illustrations on each card contain one or more figures and tuning into a card's imagery enables you to grasp its meaning intuitively. Consider the demeanour of the characters, whether it is day or night, the background, any symbols, the buildings, the colours, the vegetation, the weather and the season. Every card has its own story to impart, and through entering that story you can gain deeper insights into the full picture of your journey so far, as well as illuminating your path ahead.

I have outlined four cards here for your sign: Death, Judgement, The Tower and The High Priestess, all of which have links to your zodiac sign itself Scorpio, your ruling planet Pluto, your traditional ruling planet Mars, and your element of Water. All four cards will have special meaning for your sign, and can carry powerful messages and lessons for you to reflect upon.

★ DEATH ★
Ruled by Scorpio

Keywords ★ Change, Renewal, Transformation

★ KEY THEMES ★
Endings ★ Transitions ★ New Beginnings ★ Death of That Which Has Outlived its Usefulness ★ Regeneration and Rebirth ★ Severance ★ Change ★ A New Outlook on Life ★ Crossroads ★ Necessary Conclusion ★ Beneficial Turning Point ★ Inevitability ★ Transformation ★ Completion

Meditation ★ "All that has gone before, including my mistakes, is preparation for my new life ahead. And this new life will be the right one for me. Death will show me the way.
I surrender to it and am letting go."

Number ★ 13

Astrological Sign ★ Scorpio

THE MESSAGE ★ The skeletal form of the figure in the Death card is a reminder that death exists within life. In the skeleton, we see that the superficial has been pared away; all the desires of the flesh have been banished. He wishes not to be feared, for he symbolises the ultimate rebirth or regeneration that occurs with any death or ending; when transition occurs, new growth arises. An act of release can make it possible to move forward again. Though death can involve profound change, it can also be seen as a form of purging, of liberation. You must destroy old patterns to reveal a new, uncluttered, rewarding path. Endings are usually painful, but ultimately, your fear of Death must be recognised and faced before it is allowed to interfere further with your enjoyment of life. The Death card signifies the end of a phase or situation. This will be a time for spiritual transformation, a time to move on! Shake off the old and welcome in the new! The Death card signifies relief or sadness, but there is no benefit in remaining in this situation. It is a card pointing to inevitable positive changes, confronting your fears, relationship transitions and spiritual evolution.

THE STORY ★ Here we have two symbols which both have a bad reputation: death and the number 13. On no account should this card be regarded as a portent of literal, physical death. Like all the other Major Arcana cards, it is merely a *symbol* of death - essentially, that of an ending or a change.

THE AWAKENING ★ You are beginning to realise how much you have been weighed down by past mental and emotional baggage. Unhealthy relationships and old habits need to be consciously discarded and this is a painful process, but leaves you feeling free to be more truly and fully yourself. A sense of liberation will swiftly follow and replace any pain - in essence, you will undergo a spiritual rebirth and awakening once you allow for this very necessary release.

SYMBOLISM *★ This card, depicting a skeletal figure, most recognised as the Grim Reaper, who wears an unthreatening grin and who rides a white horse while reaping, with a scythe, a harvest of heads, hands and feet, can represent the sudden collapse of events when least expected. The skeleton can symbolise separation and liberation of the spiritual self from the body and the material plane, while the corpses and other human parts on the ground represent obstacles to attaining this revelation, such as misdirected ambition and egotism. The skeleton is indeed busy with his scythe, clearing a path for you on which he encourages you to walk towards the future, uncluttered by past mistakes. Two human heads are sometimes depicted on the Death card; one wears a crown, the other is a lesser mortal, emphasising that we all, in whatever area of life, experience periods of change that lead to new beginnings. In some decks, Death is depicted wearing a full suit of armour. The skeleton image in most decks, is symbolic of the inner self (the skeleton) is the most durable part of the physical self and it is indeed what holds us up.

The figure of Death is also commonly depicted as a skeleton who is cutting down Kings, bishops, maidens and children - no one is excepted - demonstrating that power, status, beauty and youth don't provide protection against the inevitable change that Death insists upon when usefulness has outworn its welcome. Around his skull, death sometimes wears a white funeral shroud, which was once the swaddling cloth of birth. Therefore, the shroud represents the close connection between birth and death. This need not necessarily be a bad thing, and can indeed signal new growth, or the death and subsequent rebirth that is characteristic of Scorpio, the astrological sign with which this card is linked.

The Death card quite simply symbolises rebirth and transformation - new life emerging from old - and warns you that you need to let go of something. It can be seen as the snake that sheds its skin, or the caterpillar morphing into a butterfly upon coming out of the cocoon. The scythe the skeleton is using to clear the path ahead is symbolic of sweeping away the old in order to make space for the new. The river running through the centre of some cards shows a new beginning for the emotions, and the need to move on and go willingly with the flow of change.

In the Tarot tradition, there is nothing alarming about Death - on the contrary, its message is a positive and optimistic one. Spiritual 'death' and 'rebirth' were essential rites in all the ancient mystery traditions. At this stage of the Tarot journey, the traveller knows that life is eternal, and even physical expiration is not the end of existence but simply the spiritual revelation of our true natures.

Its divinatory meanings are transformation, clearing the old to make way for the new, unexpected changes, loss, alteration, the ending of a familiar situation or friendship, abrupt change of the old self through a symbolic 'death', financial loss, illness, or the beginning of a new era. It could also signify inevitability and the futility of trying to change plans or avoid a situation.

The Death card could frighten those who don't fully understand its meaning. It isn't about physical death, but rather, necessary changes, and endings that lead to beginnings, as can be so clearly seen in the seasons. It tells you that you are at a crossroads in your life. It can mean that a change you are facing is actually a blessing in disguise, a clearing out which will make way for something better, but it can be regarded as harsh fate which does not consider personal feelings; it can be an enforced change, such as the removal of something that should have been given up, for it is no longer serving you. Only rarely will the card signify death in its literal sense; mostly it simply means a major change in life.

Death is change. In shamanistic terms, Death is the period of time when the body is still and without a heartbeat, the door opens, and the soul crosses the threshold between this world and the beyond. In one sense the shaman lies in a trance, as an accident victim might lie in a coma; if the soul does not return to the body, then death is complete. Like the night, Death is dark, quiet, lacking sunlight and the warmth of the life force. But night is paired with day, and the

Sun *will* rise again. From the point of view of the physical body, Death is an ending, signifying that one's time on Earth has expired. But from the soul's viewpoint, physical Death is the beginning of a new journey, an expanded state of being, in the formless realms.

The Death card being connected with Scorpio, its force is also attributed to Pluto, named for the Greek god of the underworld. A planet of regeneration, Pluto changes us from that deepest place inside of us. Through the process of facing death, through meditation or dying, one comes to know the soul more deeply. Scorpio rules mysticism, the occult, death, transformation, the sex organs, the deep unconscious, and the ability to channel healing energies.

In Tarot the Death card's number is thirteen, the magical Lunar number of witchcraft and the ancient religion of the Goddess. A year is composed of thirteen Lunar months. It was patriarchal culture that deleted the thirteenth month, contrived the Solar calendar we use today, and put an aura of bad luck around the number thirteen.

Once the most sacred of numbers, signifying the end and the beginning, the number thirteen has fearful connotations borne out of myth and superstition. This could be linked with the fact that when death comes too soon or unexpectedly, as it does so often in our world, the natural cycle of life seems to have no satisfying or discernible 'ending', it leaves the soul somehow 'unfinished', the task undone, the full life unlived, and we may feel intense fear, guilt, frustration and deep grief at this apparent loss. If we can understand that nothing ever really dies, it only transforms, then our fears may slightly abate or dissolve altogether. And in every process of Death, there is simultaneously a rebirth - the central message being that Life and Death are ever shifting poles of the same phenomenon.

When the snake sheds its skin, it acts as if with instinctual consciousness of the rebirth that is occurring, with a calm acceptance of the process. In contrast to the snake, humans often fear losing the old skin, even when it has begun to constrict our growth. We fear the unknown, and are naturally always more comfortable with the old. If we could just become more like the shedding snake, we would allow our outworn ways to fall away and for our inner, renewed skin to emerge. Similarly, this card is a metaphor for that shedding of our old, worn skin so that we can free our spirit to move on to fresh starts.

The Death card should not fill you with fear or dread, but alert you to the fact that something is approaching its natural ending. This may come with sadness or relief, and very often a mixture of the two. However, you feel, take your time in adjusting to this new change in your life; it's not necessary to rush ahead. Be kind to yourself during this period of transition, and seek the support you need.

So many different situations and symbols are connected with the Death card, and many of them are potentially happy events. For example, marriage is the death of single life, but it can be hoped it is the happy transition to a shared life. There is always a sense of nostalgia about any ending, so other examples could be linked with leaving a job, home, or school - they are all healthy, necessary changes, yet each one evokes the emotions portrayed by Death; that is, they all involve saying goodbye to an old, comfortable way of life.

Ultimately, Death comes to all, bringing with it new life. The emphasis here is on the transformation from one state to another; the end of one phase brings the birth of a new. Quite simply, without Death there is no new life, only stagnation. As the ultimate symbol of transformation, this card shows that, by accepting the loss of old love, old links and old ideas, life opens up to great new gains and possibilities. And once you have mastered the powerful lessons and heeded the profound messages of Death, you will fear it no longer.

Scorpios are recommended to carry one of these cards with them to illumine their paths, magnetise that for which they are asking and assist in their journey to transformation. Go forth and claim the magic which is yours!

★ JUDGEMENT ★
Ruled by Pluto & the Element of Fire

Keywords ★ Evaluation, Opportunities, New Directions

★ KEY THEMES ★
Discernment ★ Karma ★ Reaping What Has Been Sown ★ Evaluation ★ Evolution ★ Review ★ Improvement ★ Revelation ★ Renewal ★ Favourable Assessment of the Facts ★ Objectivity ★ New Directions ★ Transformation ★ Legal Situations Resolved Favourably ★ Academic and

Examination ★ Success ★ Promotion ★ Bonus ★ A Career or Life Change ★ Moving in a Different Direction ★ Rehabilitation ★ Sound Decisions Based on Good Preparation and Evaluations ★ Recovery ★ Promotion ★ Admission of Guilt ★ Good News

Number ★ 20
Astrological Signs ★ Scorpio, Aries, Leo & Sagittarius

THE FOOL'S JOURNEY ★ Archetypically, Judgement means resurrection, the rebirth that comes with spiritual awareness and awakening. Arriving at this step on his journey, the Fool understands the possibilities of transformation that can come with change. The Fool reaches for enlightenment.

THE MESSAGE ★ Sometimes called the Angel, this card has a very simple but profound meaning - a second chance. Judgement portrays an end to suffering and the beginnings of a spiritual resurrection. Through Judgement, you are being offered a dissolution of negative past patterns and a resulting spiritual rebirth, the opportunity to review past events, and to offer forgiveness or make amends. Judgement symbolises a time of judgement, when souls rise from the dead to be judged. This card depicts an angel blowing a trumpet to awaken the dead from their graves, and announcing it is Judgement Day. Bodies emerge from their coffins with arms outstretched, often casting off funeral shrouds as they make ready to embrace the new life that is offered to them by the Angel of Judgement.

There are usually three figures rising from the dead, to represent Mind, Body and Spirit, all of which must be brought forth to be judged. The dead are praying for mercy in the hope that the sins of their lifetimes will be forgiven. They now know that their misdemeanours are being exposed, and they are hoping to be allowed to move onto a higher plane of existence. On a spiritual wavelength, this card implies that one particular phase of your soul's journey is ending, and you will shortly assess what you learned and how you dealt with the passing situation, summing up your performance and its value to you. Judgment is telling you that at this point in your life it is time to assess and evaluate yourself, and perhaps address any underlying issues which up until now may have been ignored. To do this, you need simply to become more self-aware. Judgement emphasises that in undertaking this self-examination, you should be fair on yourself and focus on your positive character traits. It is telling you that once you have done this, like the symbolic people on the card, you will be ripe and ready to move in a new direction and onto a higher, more worthwhile plane of existence! You're either near the end of a project or at a crossroads, but either way, you are on the threshold of making an important change in your life.

THE STORY ★ The Judgement card is the respected mentor, who leads the way to a fresh perspective on life and leaves you feeling elated. Its main divinatory meanings are atonement, judgement, improvement, evaluation and finally, rebirth. In the symbolism of the Tarot, Judgement is not concerned with eternal damnation or heavenly bliss based upon this 'judgement' of your life experience so far, but instead with identifying ourselves the lessons we have learned not only from our archetypal Tarot journey so far, but through our whole life from birth onward. It is not a time for punishment and retribution, but a time of being called to account for past actions and experiences. After facing one's 'moment of truth', one can see oneself with more clarity and acceptance, and is then able to see others in the same way. This acceptance is an understanding of the human condition, human beauty, and embraces imperfections and Divine wisdom alongside each other. Our past, having been reflected upon, ensures that a positive resolution will be reinforced. With atonement and repentance, real advancement can occur. Therefore, Judgement is less about guilt and more about self-knowledge.

SYMBOLISM *★ Judgement brings you a new sense of Self. It renews and restores, and signifies that a rebirth process is taking place within the Self. A wider perspective has become available.

The angel in the card uses a trumpet, as if to call the figures from their sleepy sense of unawareness into full awakening. The cloud symbolises that this is spiritual in nature. The figures gradually rise - they are becoming released from the bonds of the past, and begin to look upwards towards an all-encompassing, broader and joyous perspective.

In some decks, the tombs are floating in a sea or river, which associates it with the notion that a river must be crossed before reaching the Promised Land.

At the point of resurrection, evaluations must be made on each soul's life; therefore, this card portrays the need to reflect on life as it has been lived so far, to decide how one should proceed in the future.

This card's divinatory meanings are atonement, self-assessment, the need to repent or forgive, judgement, improvement, rebirth, rejuvenation, promotion, development, the desire for immortality, and the moment to account for the manner in which we have used our opportunities on our life's journey thus far. The Judgement card may also signify the final settlement of a matter, and a time to pay off old debts in preparation for a fresh beginning. It suggests that that which has been lying dormant will spring to life, as symbolised by the dead rising from their coffins. Judgement also indicates that the rewards for past efforts will soon finally be forthcoming.

The word 'judgement', derived from the Latin *judicem*, means 'to show or to speak what is right'. But in the context of this card, is has another meaning: discernment. As far as Judgement is concerned, discernment takes the form of distinction, recognition and separation, and all that can be accomplished. The people in the card standing beneath the figure, wearing only their nakedness, show themselves as they are, stripped of any artifice. The light within may therefore now shine forth and they no longer have any need to feel ashamed of their nudity, or to be themselves. They can discriminate between what is true or false, just or unjust. The information that has shaped their existence and made them live in hope or in fear no longer comes from external sources, but from an internal wellspring - from *themselves*. This is a revelation. For we are all assailed by outside forces which are often unconnected with our lives, that leave us feeling powerless and depressed. With such hubbub and chaos surrounding us, it is hard to hear our inner voice (depicted as the angel on this card) and see and feel the light of our own wisdom (represented by the rays of the Sun around the angel). If we cannot hear these things, how can we detect, dissect and discern? Indeed, Judgement foretells a revelation, a renewal, an inner vision that is more accurate, more profound, more objective and real. Its presence suggests that we can no longer lie to ourselves or hide the truth from others, bringing a relief, a cure, a reconciliation, a state of trust, a relaxing of tenseness, and total receptivity. It can also reveal a vocation, a promotion, a recognition or a reward that comes about as a result of our newfound inner consultations.

The Judgement card indicates that the time is ripe for a period of self-appraisal, which involves taking an honest look at yourself, your motivations and your actions. This means reviewing your accomplishments so far, neither under- or over-valuing them. It also advises that one should carefully consider how present actions affect others around them.

Ultimately, Judgement suggests that it is time to review, assess, evaluate and make some considered and thoughtful judgements regarding your life, and then make empowered decisions. To put it another way, in the words of Henry David Thoreau: "Go confidently in the direction of your dreams. Live the life you have imagined." It is time to practice discernment and then move in a new direction, from that newfound, redeemed, freed spirit.

★ THE TOWER ★
Ruled by Mars

Keywords ★ Collapse, Upheaval, Rebuilding

★ KEY THEMES ★
Liberation ★ Awakening ★ Unforeseen Calamity ★ Upheaval ★ Crisis ★ Destruction ★ Upset ★ Blessing in Disguise ★ Drastic Change ★ Relief ★ Inevitable Collapse ★ A Significant Life Event ★ Time Running Out ★ Confusion ★ Collapse and Ruin ★ A Chance to Rebuild ★ Shattering ★ Total, Inevitable but Salutary Change ★ Evolution ★ Necessary Crisis or Break ★ Catastrophe ★ Sudden Awareness

Number ★ 16
Astrological Sign ★ Aries & Scorpio

Lightning can strike without warning, and the Tower serves to remind us that sometimes change can come out of the blue. Sometimes it's change for the good, and sometimes it can be more difficult. A wonderful haiku to put the Tower into perspective is: "My barn having burned down, I can now see the Moon."

THE MESSAGE ★ The Tower is representative of destructive and cataclysmic change - an earth-shattering stroke of illumination, a powerful revelation that leads to change, and the end of a structure once thought to be secure or solid. Liberation, upheaval and relief are all connected with this card. The Tower denotes the necessary breaking down of existing forms to make way for new ones; the destruction of the old always precedes the building of the new. This card indicates the needs to find fresh ways to do things, as the old have become rigid and imprisoning. We often live our lives as we have been conditioned to, never examining closely whether our lifestyle really suits us, until this complacency comes crashing down around us and forces us to re-consider and revaluate. The lightning that strikes the Tower on the card represents the new visions and possibilities which await us, and which will soon be brought to our attention through an upheaval or crisis. The change may be something that happens to you, an event or situation that transforms you. You may suddenly just know your marriage is over, your job is ending, the time has come for a move. You may have a sudden lucid understanding of your own destructive behaviours or addictions and the need for an immediate and radical overhaul. These insights may be momentary, like a lightning bolt, but the effects are far-reaching and enduring. If possible, open yourself right up to the power of the Tower card. The time has come to spread your wings!

THE STORY ★ A sturdy tower erected on a hill is struck by lightning and explosively blown apart. The castellated top of the tower is lifted by the blast and fire strikes deep within, flames roar from the narrow windows as two figures fall from their ruined refuge. The security afforded by this strong, old structure, has been reduced to ruin by the forces of natural law. Flames erupt and smoke fills the air, sparks and debris fall on either side; there has been a dramatic reversal of fortune. Future plans have been aborted. The Tower represents the shock that shatters your illusions, removes the rug from beneath your feet, and clears away the refuse. A sudden catastrophe may break down all your previous conceptions about yourself. You feel as if there is no firm foundation upon which to rest your life as the veils of illusion are torn away. This forces you to face painful truths, but also liberates you from the past and provides sudden insights. The Tower tears down your world but in doing so provides a new focus. And once the storm settles, you are free! Lightning has struck, but enlightenment is sure to follow.

SYMBOLISM * ★ The Tower symbolises the rebuilding of life upon firmer foundations after it has broken down or collapsed in some way. The Tower itself is a symbol of imprisonment and limitation; it is narrow and restrictive which, on an inner level, translates to emotional restraint. Through the effects of the Tower, your illusions are shattered and your 'world' falls apart. Yet this creates space for a new, more solid foundation upon which to rebuild.

The lightning that strikes and destroys the tower symbolises the destruction of the structure and foundation upon which the falling figures have built their lives. One figure lies on the ground, while the other tumbles to join him. The lightning bolt can also signify the power of Divine justice and the impetus for change. The golden 'rain' symbolise the regenerative energy that can follow devastation. The message of this card is that, ultimately, sometimes only a shock or catastrophe can provide the wake-up call that is needed to push you from complacency into full awareness about your situation. It also symbolises a sudden flash of insight or 'lightning bolt' inner revelation that can show you a clearer way forward. The Tower is a symbol of safety; too much trust had been placed in its thick walls. It ultimately reflects the fact that nothing can stand against the will of the inevitable or the Divine.

The Tower depicts a solidly built tower that has been struck by a bolt of lightning, causing shock and disaster to its inhabitants, who are falling to the ground. The destruction of the Tower symbolises the sudden ending of something in your life, and the possibility of new and better opportunities. A crown is often shown falling from the top of the Tower, representing the danger of vanity, conceit and pride. Its small windows suggest a self-protective element is present that can lead to a limited outlook on life.

It indicates an important and unexpected change, perhaps even a complete break from what you have built up over a sustained period of time. If you are already cautious in all areas of life, the Tower indicates that you will benefit from any clean sweep you make, allowing for a chance to rebuild once the dust has settled.

Its divinatory meanings are complete and sudden change, breaking down of old beliefs, abandonment of past relationships, severing of a friendship, changing one's opinion, unexpected events, loss of stability, bankruptcy, downfall and loss of security.

If its message is not heeded and acted upon and/or learned from, The Tower will ensure continued oppression, the following of old ways, living in a rut, entrapment in an unhappy situation, and the sustained inability to effect any worthwhile change.

★ THE HIGH PRIESTESS ★
Ruled by the Moon & the Element of Water

Keywords ★ Intuition, Wisdom, Knowledge

★ KEY THEMES ★
Desire for Esoteric Understanding ★ Seeking to Uncover Mysteries and Secrets ★ Mystical Powers ★ Dreams ★ Psychic Abilities ★ Unconscious Mind ★ Reliance on Instincts ★ Patience ★ Guided by Intuition ★ Careful Consideration Before Action ★ Inner Calm ★ Knowledge that is Both Inborn and Acquired Experience ★ Forethought ★ Wisdom ★ Purity of Intent ★ Thoughtful Reflection ★ Secret Knowledge

Number ★ 2
Astrological Signs ★ Cancer, Scorpio, Pisces & Virgo

THE MESSAGE ★ The High Priestess is the Seer who tunes into everything happening anywhere, anytime. She represents dreaming consciousness, latent psychic abilities, and the modes of perception many modern cultures have scorned, to their detriment and suffering. She embodies the highest spiritual values, representing an open door to the sacred realms of mysticism and magic. The High Priestess is telling you to learn from emotional situations. The answers you seek lie in your emotions and feelings, so trust your intuition and the power of your natural psychic abilities. Also, by paying special attention to your dreams and any intuitive messages you receive, you will be accurately guided by them. When she appears in a reading it means your intuition is functioning more strongly than your intellect. A wisdom is activated in you that is older and deeper than your ordinary mode of thinking. She signifies decision-making with an awareness of the hidden and the visible aspects of the situation. Stay open to your emotions and your feelings in order to come into contact with what you already know. Study spiritual topics, and remember that silence is golden.

THE STORY ★ The High Priestess is a private, all-seeing and spiritual woman with hidden depths and a deep compassion for others. Passive and quiet, she represents a vessel of memory and holy female wisdom. Her powers are so great that they are almost beyond actions, her timeless secrets communicated through an inner voice, and only those wise enough to retreat into silence and undertake thoughtful study will know them. The crown the High Priestess wears as headdress, is reminiscent of the waxing and waning Moon and the natural rhythms of the feminine cycle. These crescent horns of fertility connect her to the Lunar cycle - the waxing Moon forms one horn, the waning its opposite. It doesn't seem to be mere coincidence that the Greek word *delphi* is linked to the word 'uterus' and connects the High Priestess (and women) with prophecy, insights, divination and oracles. She effortlessly directs her psychic abilities in harmony with the desires of the Universe that is her child.

THE LESSON ★ The High Priestess imparts a simple yet meaningful message: Look for the answers to questions within your heart. Trust your insights, intuition and gut feelings, and act on your hunches. As she also represents learning, she indicates you should undertake a period of study - either formal, or that which comes about through your experience of life. It can suggest the start of training in the Tarot, clairvoyance, astrology, and other mystical studies which rely on intuitive application or psychic insight. She may also represent unnoticed 'power behind the throne', which indicates hidden influences at work and secrets to be revealed later. Something may not be currently known to you and you are not in possession of all the facts, so she advises that you wait until these are more fully uncovered to you before making any further moves. She could also indicate a female teacher or mentor will enter your life soon, or that you yourself will have some knowledge and wisdom to share with and teach to others. If you are in the process of trying to answer an important question about your life, the High Priestess invites you to relax and listen to your inner voice. Take a deep breath, and imagine an open, illuminated space in the centre of your chest where all wisdom resides, and let the answer come to you.

SYMBOLISM * ★ The High Priestess sits between two pillars representing severity and mercy. Her robes are patterned with pomegranates, suggesting the mystery and richness of life and death. Her robe, her posture, the scroll she holds in her hand, and her crown, symbolise intuition and the ability to listen to, and act upon, inner authority and guidance. Symbolising all that is subtle and 'hidden', she holds the keys to the mysteries of life. She carries the knowledge of occult wisdom, which is accessed through her connection with the deep emotional self, and whereas the Magician in the preceding card manifests his power in more tangible ways and using physical tools, the High Priestess contains the power within *herself*, using her abilities for spiritual growth rather than outward expressions of her forces, and uses only her mind and feelings to achieve this.

The staff she grasps appears to connect both the heavens and the Earth, and symbolises that the High Priestess is the gateway to the conscious mind through the subconscious. She is able to access both spiritual and Earthly mysteries.

The peacock pictured in some cards symbolises the High Priestess's ability to choose to display her beauty, or to keep it hidden from view.

Silent, secretive, clairvoyant and enlightened, the High Priestess can guide us through the dark wood of ignorance, indicating that reason alone cannot guide us. Her task is to show us the way to the inner world of the collective unconscious. She has a book of wisdom on her lap, with its most esoteric secrets hidden under the edge of her cloak; behind her is the veil between the inner and outer worlds, or the spiritual and the material planes. And although we, as travellers on the Tarot journey, may not yet be ready to part this veil, we are being shown it exists. Her overall appearance is a message to go quietly within yourself to become aware of your eternal connection to All That Is, and the strength you gain from this knowledge will bring insight.

Depicted as a regal-looking young lady sitting between two pillars, which represent opposing forces such as life and death, The High Priestess acts between them. She has always had a spiritual meaning, and in older decks was known as the Female Pope or The Papess. She rules the shadowy world of the unconscious mind and imagination, and symbolises the creative process of gestation; indeed, the foetus must remain in the womb until it is ripe to birth itself, and nothing should be done to precipitate this moment. The lady shown on the card often wears virginal white, signifying unfulfilled potential. In some decks she appears holding a pomegranate, the many-seeded fruit of fertility, suggesting promise for the future. The High Priestess is connected with the Crescent Moon, which symbolises a new cycle of creativity, and she has links with Persephone, goddess of the underworld, and the Egyptian Lunar goddess Isis (in some cards the High Priestess is depicted wearing the horned crown of Isis).

This card can be a challenging card to interpret because of its hidden, elusive and shadowy quality. Her links with the underworld and the unconscious can suggest that she doesn't reveal her secrets easily. Despite its lack of apparent clarity, its divinatory meanings can be perceived as wisdom, sound judgement, serenity, common sense, penetration, foresight, objectivity, perception, intuition, self-reliance, emotionlessness, and platonic relationships.

The High Priestess compels you to withdraw from the chaos and noise of daily life and seek counsel from your guides and angels. Some secrets need to be decoded first, in order to be deciphered. In this way, the High Priestess has a lock, but she also provides the key to those who seek it. Meanwhile, know that everything you need to know will be revealed in time; you just need to foster patience and be led by your inner wisdom.

Know that the High Priestess only exists to help you and respond to your every question. While galaxies swirl above you, pose your query without any attachment to the answer you will receive. In time she will take her hands from behind her back, and in them will be the symbol of your answer.

* Please note that the images described are not found in all Tarot decks. The images in different decks can differ considerably.

THE TAROT'S SUIT OF CUPS ★ REPRESENTING THE WATER ELEMENT

The Cups correspond with the Water element and are an especially interesting and meaningful metaphor. Water is life-enhancing and sustaining when it flows freely; but if trapped or contained for too long, it becomes stagnant, blocked and unhealthy. And, like our emotions and feelings, water can change shape to fit any channel or container, as well as being able to transform into other forms, such as ice or steam. The Tarot Cups reveal the flow of our emotions, how turbulent or calm our inner seas are, how we express ourselves, and how this all influences the relationships we have with others. Their narrative tells the tale of our inner life and reveals hidden feelings. The symbol of the Cup resembles a chalice or sacred drinking vessel and brings to mind the holy grail or the cup of life. Consequently, the issues the Cups raise have a spiritual quality.

The Cups are connected with the unconscious, artistic abilities, fantasy, feelings, attachments, intuition, love, pleasure, emotions, harmony, sensitivity, fertility, happiness and unity. The decorative imagery and themes that run through the suit of Cups are fish, mermaids and of course water. The fish is a symbol of creative imagination, and the element of Water represents the feelings and the depths of the unconscious mind. The Cups deal with the emotional level of consciousness and are associated with connections, expressions and relationships. The Cups suit can indicate that we are being ruled by our hearts rather than our heads, our emotions rather than our intellects, and therefore they may reflect instinctive responses and habitual reactions to situations. The Cups are also linked to romanticism, fantasy, imagination and creativity. The Suit of Cups connects us to the wellspring of the spiritual source, helping us to develop our emotions and intuitive faculties, and to understand how we attract particular energies, relationships, experiences and events into our lives. The negative aspect of this suit include being overly emotional, relying too much on one's feelings, becoming disengaged or dispassionate, fantasising, idealising, and holding unrealistic expectations of ourselves or of others. All of these may manifest as repressed emotions, an inability to properly express yourself, or a lack of creativity, self-confidence, faith or self-belief. In a deck of playing cards, the Cups correspond to the suit of Hearts.

THE LUCKY 13 ★ SCORPION TIPS FOR INCREASED MAGIC, LUCK & MAGNETISM

1 ★ Incorporate Scorpion symbols into your daily life to remind yourself of your soul's mission.

2 ★ Use the crystal Malachite in any form in your daily life - wear it, meditate with it, hold it and carry it with you everywhere! Malachite is a stone of alignment and can be used for self-exploration journeys, its protective properties and its ability to absorb pollutants and negative energies. Working with malachite ultimately helps you confront whatever it is that is blocking your spiritual unfolding and wellbeing. It is regarded as "the mirror of the soul" and so some crystal experts may warn against wearing malachite as it may prove too powerful and confronting for some - but never for Scorpio. Essentially, it is a true power crystal, which helps you reclaim your dynamism and potential, helping those who are brave enough to work with it, to step into their true power. As a stone of transformation and change, it will enhance spiritual rebirth and growth, facilitating deep emotional healing, allowing one's deepest self to shift in a new, positive direction. However, you use it, malachite will bring about a shift of energy, enhancing emotions and states of being that will assist in attracting wonderful things to you.

3 ★ Wear or surround yourself with the colours sea green, purple and violet.

4 ★ Learn the way of The Eagle ... Fly, soar, surrender yourself to the ether and feel the vastness of all that is below ... and *within*. Also, the Taurean Bull has much to offer you in terms of living life with more sensual awareness, developing more reverence for simplicity and just *be*ing. Still your mind, surrender your intensity, let go of your raging passions, learn the gentle arts of forgiveness and acceptance, trust more, come up from the depths for air once in a while, graze in the meadows of life and let down your guard.

5 ★ Use your lucky numbers 5 and 9, whenever you are needing an extra stroke of luck.

6 ★ Magnify and celebrate your emotions, feelings, transformative powers, your inherent spirituality, and your intuitively in-touch psyche.

7 ★ Remind yourself of your mission constantly, that is by speaking, breathing and *truly living* your dreams and insights - give them form beyond simply brooding, tossing and turning, or dreaming about them!

8 ★ Focus your energies on exploring your inner depths, and transforming yourself through your higher psychic faculties - which are strongly accessible to the acutely feeling, receptive and sensitive Scorpion mind. Connect with your deep imagination and inborn creativity through any means possible.

9 ★ Use your innate powers of shadow-self-awareness, regeneration and renewal, pure belief and metaphysical attunement to visualise and draw that which you desire towards you. If you can develop simple faith in the positive outcome of events, you can easily use your highly-refined intuition to great creative effect.

10 ★ Tap into and utilise your ability to connect, heal, empathise with, and transform others through sharing your emotions, spirit and soul. But to do that, you'll need to soften your daunting demeanour and trust others enough to let them in! You have too much to give to keep it all to yourself.

11 ★ View your charismatic and magnetic qualities as strengths by which you can call forth the powers of your multi-faceted, gifted, unique self. Be who you *really* are, without reservation or apology, and the rest will fall into place.

12 ★ Become the 'Powerful Illuminator' of others - and yourself - that you were born to be! Focus your energies on exploring and transforming yourself so you can help and guide others to do the same.

13 ★ Once you have mastered your true power and self-reliance, and conquered your inner demons and shadow self, learn to share the resulting abundance, insights and knowledge with others so they too can walk the Higher Path!

HAVE YOU PACKED YOUR MAGICAL BAG FOR THE JOURNEY?

If you wish to increase and draw more luck, love and abundance into your life, a power pack is essential. For Scorpions, I would recommend carrying or wearing the following items on you on your travels. Then just sit back and watch as magic pours into your experiences and realities, both inner and outer!

★ One of each of the following gemstones: Topaz, Malachite, Peridot, Red Coral
★ Tarot cards Death and Judgement (and The Tower and the High Priestess cards too, if you wish)
★ A snake in any form (use your imagination!)
★ Something made of iron
★ A Tau symbol in any form
★ A postcard or image from a watery, cool, rainy or oceanic place (representing your Phlegmatic disposition). Bon Voyage!
★ A postcard from the future to yourself, proclaiming, 'Wish You Were Here!'

A FINAL WORD ★ TAPPING INTO THE MAGIC OF SCORPIO

There is something inherently magical about Scorpio, the passionate one. Blessed with an unmatched intensity, strength of will, determination, and personal magnetism, you truly are the potential Shamanic healers and transformers of the zodiac, affecting everyone around you with your intuitive sense of what is hidden and mysterious.

Nothing is meek about you. The cosmos has endowed you with the precious and important gifts of allure, concentration of purpose, intrigue, complexity, depth, emotionality, resourcefulness, strong personal integrity, loyalty, penetration into others' minds, resilience and an all-or-nothing approach to everyone and everything. Whether you are fully cognisant of it or not, a magical reservoir of energy is available to you to tap into whenever it is needed.

Finally, to attune yourself to luck, harmony and success, Scorpions should wear, eat, inhale, meditate upon, create, design, and dance with any or all of the suggested luck-enhancers for your Sun sign to receive the most beneficial astral vibrations these 'boosters' can offer you. Wearing, decorating and working with the amazing powers of all your lucky guides, animals, crystals, colours, woods, cards, herbs, foods, places, talismans, planetary influences, charms, numbers, and other magical tips contained within the words of this very book, will bring you greater abundance, love, magic, energy, happiness and personal power, and attract all manner of things to you like bees to sweet flowers. This, my Scorpion friends, I promise you - and Aquarians *never* lie.

Good luck on the rest of your amazing life journey, and may the LUCK be with you!

Lani is also available for personal Astrology, Numerology, Aura * & Tarot reading consultations, via post, email, Skype and in-person.
Please email lalana76@bigpond.com for more information.

In-person only

Facebook Page ★ Astrology Magic

Other Books in the **Lucky Astrology** Series

Lucky Astrology ★ Aries
Lucky Astrology ★ Taurus
Lucky Astrology ★ Gemini
Lucky Astrology ★ Cancer
Lucky Astrology ★ Leo
Lucky Astrology★ Virgo
Lucky Astrology ★ Libra
Lucky Astrology ★ Sagittarius
Lucky Astrology ★ Capricorn
Lucky Astrology ★ Aquarius
Lucky Astrology ★ Pisces

Order your copies now, from White Light Publishing House, at www.whitelightpublishingau.com

www.ingramcontent.com/pod-product-compliance
Lightning Source LLC
Chambersburg PA
CBHW071153300426
44113CB00009B/1186